AF539411

Language Arts Curriculum

Language Arts Curriculum

By

Prof. Marlow Ediger

Truman State University
201 W, 22nd, Box 417
North Newton, KS 67117
United States of America

And

Dr. Digumarti Bhaskara Rao

R.V.R. College of Education
D—43 Srinivasa Nagar Colony
Guntur—522006

DISCOVERY PUBLISHING HOUSE
NEW DELHI-110002

Published by:

DISCOVERY PUBLISHING HOUSE PVT. LTD.
4383/4B, Ansari Road, Darya Ganj
New Delhi-110 002 (India)
Phone : +91-11-23279245; 23253475; 43596065
E-mail : discoverybooksindia@gmail.com
discoverypublishinghouse@gmail.com
namitwasan9@gmail.com
web : www.discoverypublishinggroup.com

First Published: **2003**

Reprinted: **2022**

ISBN: 978-81-7141-657-8

Language Arts Curriculum

© **Authors**

All rights reserved. No part of this publication should be reproduced, stored in a retrieval system, or transmitted in any form or by any means: electronic, mechanical, photocopying, recording or otherwise, without the prior written permission of the author and the publisher.

This book has been published in good faith that the material provided by authors is original. Every effort is made to ensure accuracy of material, but the publisher and printer will not be held responsible for any inadvertent error(s). In case of any dispute, all legal matters are to be settled under Delhi jurisdiction only.

Printed at:
Infinity Imaging Systems
Delhi

Preface

Language arts is an important area in the educational enterprise. The pre-service and in-service teachers should be well aware of the various aspects concerned to language arts curriculum.

Language Arts Curriculum has been written for the teachers teaching presently the language arts and for the prospective teachers in pre-service programmes of teacher education.

The pre-service prospective teachers and the in-service professional teachers, after studying this book, may develop right objectives, provide appropriate learning experiences, and adopt relevant evaluation procedures which will meet the individual differences in the class setting.

This book will also help the language specialists, curriculum designers, text book writers and educational planners along with the pre-service and in-service teachers in doing their best in the language arts curriculum, instruction and evaluation.

Dr. Marlow Ediger
Dr. Bhaskara Rao

Contents

	Preface	*v*
1.	Objectives and the Learner	1
2.	Linguistics and the Language Arts Curriculum	14
3.	The Literature Curriculum	32
4.	Speaking and the Pupil	47
5.	Speaking Activities and the Pupil	63
6.	Spelling and the Language Arts	78
7.	Spelling in the Language Arts Curriculum	96
8.	Word Selection in the Spelling Curriculum	110
9.	Vocabulary Development and the Pupil	117
10.	Listening and the Pupil	129
11.	Evaluation of Achievement in Language Arts	144
12.	Reading and the Language Arts	158
13.	Reading and Vocabulary Development	175
14.	Reading and the Structure of the English Language	191
15.	Designing the Reading Curriculum	202
16.	Reading in the Content Areas	212
17.	Making use of Ideas Gleaned from Reading	220

18. Improving Teacher Questions in Reading Instruction 228

19. Testing and Evaluating Student Achievement in Reading 236

20. Handwriting and the Pupil 246

21. Writing in the Language Arts Curriculum 261

22. Writing Achievement in Education 285

23. Reading Poetry in the Language Arts 292

24. Poetry in the School 301

25. Grouping Pupils for Instruction 313

Bibliography 329

Objectives and the Learner

Teachers, principals and supervisors need to determine the kinds of learners being taught in the school/class setting. Are pupils by nature good, bad, or neutral? Concepts held pertaining to each pupil assist in determining objectives, learning activities, and evaluation techniques. An educator can observe teaching-learning situations in any classroom and notice concepts held by the teacher pertaining to any one learner.

The Learner as an Evil Individual

The Puritans established Massachusetts Bay colony in 1630. Seemingly the Puritans had the best established system of education in the New World. They believed that individuals were born evil or sinful. A leading objective for Puritan pupils to achieve was knowledge of God, or eternal life. Achieving this end would assist pupils in moving away from evilness and toward the Good. To achieve desired objectives selected learning activities need to be provided to pupils. Among other activities, Puritan pupils experienced to Horn Book. The Horn Book contained one page attached to what basically looked like a wooden ping-pong paddle. The upper and lower case letters of the alphabet in manuscript style, the Benediction, and the Lord's prayer were contained in the Horn Book.

In 1690 the New England Primer was introduced into Colonial Puritan schools. The New England Primer was more comprehensive in religious and secular content as compared to the Horn Book. Parts contained in the New England Primer were the following:

1. the shorter Westminister Catechism containing a series of questions and answers, which Puritans believed were essential religious beliefs;
2. the names of the books of the Old and New Testaments;
3. the Lord's Prayer and the Apostles' Creed.
4. the illustrated alphabet containing religious and moral admonitions, e.g., a picture of Adam and Eve in the garden of Eden, —pupils memorizing and reading "In Adam's fall, we sinned all". For the letter "d", the picture of a dog biting a thief—pupils ultimately learned to read "a dog will bite a thief at night". These learnings, among others, eventually led pupils in learning to read from the Bible.

In addition to learning about God to help the pupil move away from being an evil individual, Puritan teachers generally utilized physical punishment to admonish learners. Spanking, slapping, kneeling on dried beans, and whipping posts were methods used to motivate pupils. Hopefully, the child would then become a good individual. There are still vestiges in classrooms today where teachers emphasize pupils as being bad human beings. The badness than needs to be driven out of pupils.

Joseph Lancaster in 1805 introduced the Lancastrian Monitorial System of Instruction into the United States. Lancaster believed that any reasonably intelligent person could manage a monitorial school. The head person in a monitorial school called a master teacher might be in charge of 1,000 pupils in one large building with no partitions to divide the diverse levels of achievement into classroom settings. The master teacher before the school day began instructed monitors who in turn would each teach a benchful of pupils. Approximately, ten learners sat on each bench with no backs. Textbooks were not used in the school setting. Rather, large charts along the walls contained that which pupils were to learn. In military precision, a benchful of boys marched in front of a chart; the monitor taught these pupils what was perceived to be relevant content. Sequential groups of boys from other benches would also be taught by their respective monitors form these charts.

The reading curriculum contained highly sequenced levels of achievement.

Class I, pupils memorized the individual letters of the alphabet.

Class II, syllables of two letters were read.

Class III, syllables of three letters were mastered.

Class IV, words and syllables of four letters were memorized.

Class V, pupils learned to read words of five and six letters.

Class VI, pupils read from the Old or New Testament.

Class VII, the reading curriculum consisted of books to assist pupils to improve their minds.

In the Lancastrian Monitorial School, pupils on an individual basis could be promoted to the next higher class level if judged ready to do so by the involved monitor. Inexpensive methods of educating pupils were definitely in evidence in the Monitorial Schools. Pupils wrote on slates using chalk as well as in sand instead of on paper. Charts on walls contained items for pupils to learn rather than the utilization of textbooks. Monitors received a free education from the master teacher but initially received no pay. Later on, Monitorial training schools were organized to educate monitors; some money was then received by monitors for their services.

Joseph Lancaster believed that individuals were born as evil beings. He recommended that embarrassing of pupils for misbehaviour was more humane than using physical punishment. A pupil with an unwashed face would be forced to wash before the entire student body. A pupil could be placed in a basket, suspended from the ceiling, for misbehaviour. Or, several pupils who misbehaved might be yoked together to parade in front of other pupils in the school building. In a large city for its day, there could be as many as one thousand onlookers. Embarrassing pupils, according to Lancaster, was a means of driving evilness out of pupils. It was also a method utilized to motivate pupils to achieve at a higher level.

The Learner as a Neutral Individual

Johann Herbart (1776–1841) believed that individuals were born with a mind like a blank sheet. Thus, no content nor innate ideas were present at birth. Whatever happened in the environment imprinted itself on the mind. Herbart then believed it was entirely up to the teacher to furnish right ideas to pupils., Only in this way could any one person become a good individual.

Johann Herbart is credited by many educators for advocating the use of lesson plans in teaching-learning situations. Selected steps were deemed necessary to be written into each lesson plan. First of all, the step of preparation should be emphasized in the daily lesson plan as well as in teaching. Here the teacher reviews with pupils that which the latter had studied previously. If the step of preparation was not emphasized in the instructional arena, the pupil might not be able to recall what had been acquired yesterday or on prior days of teaching. With the step of preparation, pupils develop clear ideas as to previously developed facts, concepts and generalizations.

The second step of teaching advocated by Herbart was presentation. Here, the teacher presented new learnings to pupils. In the third step of teaching, pupils developed associations. New learnings are related to previously gained content in achieving associations. Pupils can then be assisted in developing generalizations in step four. Ultimately, pupils need to use what has been learned (the step of application).

To develop good individual, Herbart advocated morality ends being the ultimate aim of education. A study of literature and history, in particular, would assist learners to become moral persons. In history and in literature, there are many noble individuals who can provide right standards of living for readers. Pupils may then pattern their own lives after those in history and literature who lived superb lives.

Herbart believed that whatever exists imprints itself on the mind of each person. A cruel teacher then imprints itself in the mind of the perceiver. Discipline of pupils for misbehaviour must not be harsh. Harsh behaviour could become a part of a learner if used as means of disciplining pupils. Rather, a logical approach needs to be utilized. If a pupil wastes time in the class setting, the teacher needs to keep track of the amount of time involved in misbehaviour. The teacher then needs to explain to the involved pupil as to what should be done to compensate for the wasted time. During recess time or after school, the pupil needs to complete school work which could have been finished when the involved pupil was not attending to the task at hand.

The Learner as a Good Individual

Friedrich Froebel (1782–1852) believed that individuals were born as being good, wholesome persons. Inherent in each individual at birth is the concept of goodness. If an individual is born as a good person, creative endeavours are vital. Thus, that which is within an individual must come to the surface in terms of products, processes, and efforts. Dictating to pupils what to learn (objectives) and the means of learning (activities) was definitely not emphasized by Froebel.

Friedrich Froebel had specific materials to used in teaching-learning situations. These included:

1. Gifts, such as physical models of lines, planes, and points. Also included in what was known as gifts were cubes, cylinders, and spheres. The larger cube could be taken apart resulting in numerous smaller cubes. Smaller cylinders could be slid out of the original large cylinder. The form and shape of each gift could not be changed by pupils.
2. A second set of teaching-learning materials developed by Friedrich Froebel was called occupations. The learner makes changes as to the form/shape of occupation materials. Paper-folding and cutting, clay modeling, making dots of diverse colors, and the stringing of beads were learning activities classified as occupations.
3. A third type of experience recommended by Froebel for kindergarten pupils involved their participation in mother play songs. While being in a circle and singing songs, pupils would creatively dramatize that which was sung. Spontaneous, unique behaviour was to be encouraged from learners by the kindergarten teacher.

Which creative products and processes would pupils reveal as a result of participating in the use of gifts and occupations, as well as in mother play songs?

(i) The pupil could add and subract items Friedrich Froebel classified as gifts. Learners might also build model scenes and sites with the utilization of gifts.

(ii) Pupils individually could creativily develop unique model animals, people, and buildings from clay (an occupation).

(iii) Novel designs could be cut from folded paper (an occupation).

(iv) Diverse interpretations could be given to singing experiences classified as mother play song.

Froebel then believed that infants are born as being good individuals. Thus, the goodness existing within pupils should come forth as novel, unique products and processes. The teacher sets the stage for pupil learning; the goodness within pupils must then blossom forth.

Concluding Statements on the Nature of Pupils

Three distinct points of view have been presented pertaining to concepts of the learner. The pupil may be perceived of having been born as a bad human being. The Puritans in Colonial America had definite goals in mind to change individuals from being bad to being good. Among other means, religious instruction and physical punishment were utilized. Vestiges of physical punishment are still in evidence in schools and in society.

Individuals are also perceived as being neutral in their initial orientation. The environment in degrees then makes or breaks the individual. Physical punishment cannot be used to change behaviour since the act or deed imprints itself on the mind of the learner.

A third perception pertaining to human nature is that innate goodness exists at birth. Since the learner was born as a good individual, unique content from within the pupil needs to be expressed. Freedom from restraint is important when perceiving learners as being inherently good.

Objectives in the Language Arts

Teachers, principals, and supervisors must thoughtfully evaluate and ultimately select quality objectives for pupils to achieve. Pupils in the elementary school need to achieve useful, relevant objectives. Objectives pertain to the kinds of pupils that the school is attempting to develop. Learning activities help pupils to achieve the chosen objectives. The activities need to meaningful, interesting, purposeful, and provide for individual differences. Ultimately, evaluation must take place to determine if objectives have been achieved by pupils.

General Objectives

General objectives state the kinds of behaviours that are to be developed within learners over a rather long period of time. General objectives can be divided into the following categories; understandings, skills, and attitudes. Understandings objectives pertain to facts, concepts, generalizations, and main ideas that are to be achieved by pupils. The following understandings objectives, as examples, can be stated for pupils to achieve in the language arts:

To develop within pupils an understanding of

1. the structure of patterns of sentences in the English language;
2. diverse kinds of poetry such as couplets, triplets, limericks, haikus, tankar, and free verse;
3. stress, pitch, and juncture as it pertains to the communication of content;
4. how kernal sentences are transformed into the making of new sentences;
5. diverse word recognition techniques to use in identifying new words;
6. different purposes to use in reading to comprehend content.

Skills pertain to doing or performing in terms of what is stated in the general objective. The following, as examples, may be important skills for learners to achieve:

1. to read content in a meaningful way;
2. to utilize legible handwriting in functional writing situations;
3. to use correct spelling when communicating content in writing;
4. to utilize proper punctuation, capitalization, and usage in functional writing situations;
5. to present ideas effectively in the oral use of language;
6. to read for a variety of purposes in comprehending content;
7. to utilize appropriate word recognition techniques to unlock new words;
8. to comprehend content effectively in situations involving listening;
9. to listen to subject matter for a variety of purposes;
10. to evaluate effectively one's own achievement in the language arts.

Attitudinal objectives are very important for pupils to achieve. Achieving proper attitudes influences the attainment of understandings and skills objectives. Positive attitudes toward learning then assist in attaining understandings and skills objectives. The following, among others, might be important attitudinal objectives for pupils to achieve:

1. appreciating creative efforts on the part of individuals;
2. wanting to understand patterns of sentences in the English language;
3. appreciating how sentences can be transformed from kernal sentences to other kinds and types of sentences;
4. developing an inward desire to write creatively;
5. wanting to listen attentively to the contributions of others;
6. having a desire to write for a variety of purposes;

7. wanting to evaluate one's own achievement in the language arts;
8. appreciating how the English language has developed and changed in time and place;
9. wanting to read selected library books during leisure time;
10. desiring to learn appropriate techniques for identifying and recognizing new words;
11. wanting to read for a variety of purposes;
12. wanting to express content clearly in the use of oral language.

Specific Objectives

Selected teachers, principals, and supervisors may wish to have objectives stated precisely for learners to achieve. How specific objectives should be stated is an issue. Objectives can be written so precisely that little leeway exists for interpretation in terms of what will be taught. Notice the following specific objectives which have no leeway in interpreting what will be taught:

1. The pupil will list in writing the names of at least five parts of speech.
2. The pupil will write a haiku poem.

In the first objective, pupils merely recall names of different parts of speech such as noun, verb, adjective, preposition, interjection, conjunction, adverb and pronoun. There is no leeway as to what will be taught when viewing objective number one. Pupils, of course, should engage in learning that which requires a higher level of thinking than merely recalling content, such as parts of speech in the English language. The second objective requires a higher level of thinking as compared to objective number one. Pupils individually or in a committee may then creatively write a haiku poem. By definition, a haiku should possess five, seven, and five syllables for each sequential line of the poem.

Selected educators have frowned at the thought of having objectives emphasising the recall level of information only, in teaching-learning situations. Thus, educational objectives also need to stress the importance of critical thinking, creative thinking, and problem solving. The following objectives emphasize the importance of higher levels of thinking:

1. The pupil will write a limerick using a title of his/her own choosing.
2. The pupil will select a title and write a tall tale.

Affective objectives are very important to stress in teaching-learning situations. Positive attitudes on the part of learners aid in overall achievement in learning. To guide learners in attaining attitudinal objectives, the following principles of learning must be followed in the school setting:

1. Pupils must be ready to achieve new learnings.
2. Learners should be fascinated with ongoing learning experiences.
3. Learnings need to be sequential from the child's own unique point of view.
4. Pupils should enjoy ongoing learning activities.
5. Each child needs to experience success in learning.
6. Pupils should be guided in diagnosing personal difficulties in learning.
7. Learners need guidance to assess their own progress in learning.

The following are examples of specific affective goals for pupils to achieve:

1. The pupil will voluntarily select and read a library book as well as tell the story sequentially in his/her own words.
2. The pupil will volunteer to participate actively in a discussion pertaining to a library book of his own choosing.
3. The pupil will voluntarily write a poem. (The learner will select the title as well as the kind of poem to write).

It is important for pupils to achieve objectives which emphasize psychomotor domain objectives. Thus, there is a balance between cognitive and attitudinal objectives as well as those requiring physical movement. The following specific objectives may be written for pupils to achieve involving the use of neuromuscular skills:

1. The pupil will pantomime a story or library book of his/her own choosing.
2. The learner will participate in a creative dramatics activity relating directly to subject matter of his/her own choosing.

It is important to emphasize balance between and among objectives that pupils are to achieve. Thus, cognitive, affective and psychomotor objectives need adequate emphasis in the curriculum. This does not mean that an even number of each category of objectives will be emphasized. Based on rational thought in the selecting of objectives, pupils should achieve an adequate number of cognitive, affective, and psychomotor goals.

Criteria for Selecting Objectives

Teachers, supervisors and principals must select significant objectives for pupils to achieve. There must be a rational balance among understandings, skills, and attitudinal objectives. Or, using a different classification scheme, balance in objectives should be in evidence pertaining to cognitive, affective, and psychomotor objectives. Objectives should be emphasized in teaching and learning which pupils can achieve. It is important that adequate data be obtained about learners individually if stated objectives have or have not been achieved. Pupils need to be evaluate on all facets of development. Thus, pupils would be assessed in intellectual, social, physical, and emotional development. There should be a broad base of participation in determining objectives for pupils to achieve. Teachers, principals, supervisors, parents, and children should be actively involved in determining these ends. Questions that may be asked pertaining to determining which objectives pupils are to achieve might include the following:

1. Are these objectives significant for learners to attain?
2. Would pupils be interested in achieving these objectives?

3. Is proper sequence in learning involved when achieving the desired objectives?
4. Would learners be motivated in achieving the desired goals?
5. Is readiness for learning in evidence on the part of the pupils in achieving the desire objectives?
6. Would pupils feel that the stated objectives are relevant?
7. Do the stated objectives emphasize the importance of pupils becoming democratic individuals?

It is important to select carefully those objectives which pupils are to achieve.

REFERENCES

1. Burns, Paul C., and Leo M. Schell, (Eds.). *Elementary School Language Arts, Selected Readings*. New York: Rand McNally and Company, 1973. Part One.
2. Dallmann, Martha. *Teaching the Language Arts in the Elementary School*. Dubuque, Iowa: Wm. C. Brown Company Publishers, 1971. Chapter one.
3. Dewey, John. *Democracy and Education*. New York: The Macmillan Company, 1916.
4. Ediger, Marlow. *Social Studies Curriculum in the Elementary School.* Second Edition. Kirksville, Missouri: Simpson Publishing Company, 1980.
5. Ediger, Marlow and D. Bhaskara Rao (1996), Science Curriculum, New Delhi, India: Discovery Publishing House.
6. Green, Harry A., and Walter T. Petty. *Developing Language Skills in the Elementary Schools*. Boston: Allyn and Bacon, Inc., 1975.
7. Lamb, Prose. *Guiding Children's Language Learning*. Second Edition, Dubuque, Iowa: Wm. C. Brown Company Publishers, 1971. Chapter Two.
8. Moore, W. Edgar, et. al. *Creative and Critical Thinking*. Second edition. Boston: Hughton-Mifflin, 1985.
9. National Society for the Study of Education. *Modern Philosophies and Education*. Chicago: University of Chicago Press, 1955.
10. Nerbovig, Marcella H., and Herbert J. Klausmeier. *Teaching in the Elementary School*. Third Edition. New York: Harper and Row Publishers, 1969. Chapter One.

11. Norton, Donna E. *The Effective Teaching of Language Arts*. Second Edition. Columbus, Ohio: Charles E. Merrill Publishing Company, 1985.

12. Ragan, William B., and Gene D. Shepherd. *Modern Elementary Curriculum*. Fifth Edition. New York; Holt, Rinehart and Winston, 1982.

13. Wright, Betty Atwell, et. al. *Elementary School Curriculum, Better Teaching Now*. New York: The Macmillan Company, 1971.

14. Zintz, Miles V. *The Reading Process*. Second Edition. Dubuque, Iowa: William C. Brown Company, 1975.

Linguistics and the Language Arts Curriculum

The contributions of linguists in the language arts curriculum have been numerous. Through these contributions, a modified curriculum has resulted. Teachers of language arts need to be thoroughly versed in content and methodology recommendations made by linguists. The language arts has changed much due to input from linguists in the curriculum. Petty, Petty, and Becking write the following pertaining to structural grammar, a linguistic means of studying language:

> Structural grammar is the product of linguists' scientific study of the way we speak. Structural grammar does not prescribe what is "correct" but simply reports the language as it exists, including its growth and changes. In structural grammar the ways words are put together into utterances have been categorized, and from this categorization certain principles and patterns of the language system have emerged. One difficulty with this grammar is the problem of determining how people actually do speak, a matter that is basic to the categorization that produces the patterns. Not everyone speaks the same way; that is, there are social and regional differences in usage and pronunciation. Then there is the problem of completeness. How large a sample of language must be examined to determine whether or not all possible patterns and principles of the system have been discovered? Of course, both of these weaknesses are of no greater importance to structural grammar than to any other, except that since the basis of this grammar is its scientific determination, they introduce some limitations to generalizing about the completeness of its patterns as a description of the language system.

Structural Grammar

Selected pupils enter the school setting speaking the English language rather proficiently. They generally have little or no knowledge of sentence patterns and yet effective communication on their developmental level is definitely in evidence. A rich learning environment must continually be provided so that learners may enrich their speaking and listening vocabularies to develop further skills in the oral use of language.

Pupils in the school setting need to understand and appreciate how the English language operates. As learners progress through sequential school years, they should experience continuous success in achieving relevant objectives in the language arts curriculum.

The teacher on the present achievement level of each pupil must provide stimulating learning activities to motivate learners in understanding structure and patterns in the English language. The easiest sentence pattern for most learners to understand generally is the noun-verb or subject-predicate pattern. The teacher can select a subject-predicate sentence pattern from an experience chart developed by pupils with teacher guidance. The teacher may also ask pupils to give a sentence of two words pertaining to a picture on the bulletin board or objects at a learning center. Contributions made by pupils must be respected. As an additional approach to use in having pupils understand sentence patterns, the teacher could write two words on the chalkboard resulting in a subject-predicate sentence.

Tiedt and Tiedt write the following involving pupils studying sentence patterns:

> The sentence merits considerable attention in the study of language and in developing composition skills. It is through study of the sentence that students can be made aware of grammar, for there is little justification in teaching grammar as an isolated subject. Grammar is not just a set of terms and rules to be learned; it is a study of the relationships of words and groups of words in the context of a sentence. These ideas should be taught, therefore, as students learn to write, to manipulate words and phrases, to create interesting, varied sentences. Structural linguistics introduced the concept of the sentence pattern, of which there are many. In

the elementary school, however, we might concentrate on working with five basis patterns. After introducing one pattern—for example, the simplest of all, Noun-Verb—let the students play with the pattern as they modify it in many ways. At any time, of course, they can still identify the basic patterns. Challenge class members to create a long sentence beginning with only two words, perhaps: *Horses run*. Compare the results.

The following illustrates the noun-verb or subject-predicate sentence pattern.

1. Lions roar.
2. Birds fly.
3. Boys walk.
4. Girls swim.
5. Babies cry.

In each of these sentences pupils may provide words which replace the verb or predicate. Learners need to be actively involved in presenting these words. Thus, the teacher might ask, "What else do lions do?" Pupils may respond with the following: "walk," "run," "jump," "eat" and "sleep." Pupils may then be guided to notice that the sentence pattern stays the same; however, other words have been utilized in place of the original verb or predicate.

In sequence, the teacher could have pupils think of words to replace the noun or subject of the sentence. In the sentence "Lions roar," what other animals might take the place of the word "lions,"? Pupils may respond with words such as "tigers," "giraffes," "dogs," and "wildcats,". Pupils must have ample concrete and semi-concrete experiences when participating in ongoing learning activities, such as in viewing models and pictures of animals.

A second sentence pattern, not necessarily in sequence taught to pupils, might pertain to pupils developing understandings of the noun-verb-noun or subject-predicate-direct object pattern.

1. John threw the baseball.
2. Ralph held the bat.
3. Sally met her friends.
4. Nancy bought a doll.

In each of these sentences, pupils may present a word which takes the place of the subject, the predicate, or the direct object. The concepts of "subject," "predicate," and "direct object" may be used by the teacher when referring to specific words in a sentence; however, pupils definitely should not be forced to use these terms when oral or written communication is being utilized. Generally, pupils will attach meaning to and use these concepts of speaking and writing at the appropriate developmental level.

A third sentence pattern to be studied by pupils would pertain to the noun-linking verb-adjective or subject-linking verb-predicate adjective pattern.

1. The house looked beautiful.
2. The vase was decorative.
3. The owl was brown.
4. The candy was delicious.

Each of these sentences has a subject, such as the word "house" in sentence one and "vase" in sentence two. The words "house" and "vase" in sentences one and two are nouns. Why are these words nouns? They can be changed from singular to plural or plural to singular in context. "House" is singular, while "houses" is plural. "Vase" is singular, while "vases" is plural. The word "looked" in sentence one and the word "was" in sentence two are linking verbs. Why are these words verbs? Verbs are words which can be changed from past tense to present tense and present tense to past tense, in context. Thus, the word "looked" pertains to a completed action and indicates past tense; however, the word "look" indicates present tense. The word "was" is in past tense; however, the word "is" is in present tense.

Interesting learning experiences can be provided whereby understandings may be developed by pupils in a meaningful way pertaining to the following concepts: "singular" and "plural," "present tense" and "past tense". For example, the teacher might have one boy walk across the front of the room. Other pupils could give a sentence such as the following pertaining to the dramatization: The boy walks. Next, the teacher may call for a second boy to come to the front of the room and join in the same act. The resulting sentence to describe the dramatization reads as follows: The boys walk. In learning experiences such as these, pupils may realize in a concrete, meaningful way the concepts of "singular" and "plural".

Again, the boy (or boys) could walk across the room and viewers give the following sentence: The boy walks (present tense). Once the act has been completed, the resulting sentence might be the following: The boy walked (past tense). Thus, with a variety of concrete learning experiences, pupils may develop understandings pertaining to "present tense" and "past tense". The sentence patterns used in illustrating concepts pertaining to nouns and verbs pertain to the subject-predicate or noun-verb pattern.

A fourth sentence pattern for pupils to attach meaning is the noun-linking verb-noun or subject-predicate-predicate nominative pattern.

1. John was a coach.
2. Bill is an umpire.
3. The man is a grocer.
4. Sally is a singer.

In each of these sentences, the predicate nominative equals the subject of the sentence joined by a linking verb. In sentence one, John equals coach. In sentence two, Bill equals umpire while man equals grocer in sentence three. Sally equals singer in sentence four. Notice that a linking verb joins the predicative nominative to the subject of the sentence.

A fifth pattern of sentence involves pupils inductively developing understandings of the subject-predicate-indirect object-direct or noun-verb-noun-noun pattern. The following would be examples on this sentence pattern:

1. John gave Jerry a gift.
2. George presented Alice a present.
3. Mark wrote Jim a note.

Pupils at Christmas time and at the time birthdays are celebrated frequently use the subject-predicate-indirect object-direct object sentence pattern. For example, at Christmas time, a child may say the following: "Daddy gave me a bicycle". Or, when a child's birthday is being celebrated, the involved pupil may say, "Mother gave me a basketball".

Sentence patterns that pupils acquire should meet the following criteria:

1. Responses should come from pupils.
2. Learning by discovery is to be encouraged.
3. Pupils need to relate sentence patterns to their own unique background of experiences.
4. Learners must attach meaning to sentence patterns.
5. A variety of methods should be utilized in helping learners attach meaning to diverse patterns of sentences.
6 Learning activities should be interesting to pupils.
7. Provision must be made for individual differences; not all learners in a class achieve at the same level of achievement. In which facets of instruction might a teacher provide for individual differences? Disick writes:

> Briefly, individualized instruction is an approach to teaching and learning that offers choices in four areas: objectives of learning, rate of learning, method (or style) of learning, and content of learning. The extent to which choices are offered determines the degree of individualization in a particular program. If a wide variety of choices exists in all four dimensions, then the program may be considered fully realized. Programs that provide fewer areas open to choice may be called uni- or multidimensional. Within this broad category, the type of individualization carried on may be further specified. Programs featuring selection of course objectives arc known as "independent study"; those emphasizing variations in learning rates are known as "continues progress" or "flexibly paced"; those stressing a variety of learning methods or styles are considered "multimedia", and those offering mainly a choice of content are labeled "mini-courses". Naturally, two or more dimensions may be combined in one program of instruction. One such combination would be continuous progress-multimedia, for example.

Expanding Sentences

Sentences are short, choppy, and lack thorough description if the concept of expansion is not utilized in writing situations. The following structural patterns lack expansion:

1. Boys run. (Sub-predicate or noun-verb pattern.)
2. Abe caught the ball. (Subject-predicate-direct object or noun-verb-noun-pattern).
3. The orange was delicious. (Subject-linking verb-predicate adjective or noun-linking verb-predicate adjective pattern).
4. Curt is an auctioneer. (Subject-linking verb-predicate nominative or noun-linking verb-noun pattern.)
5. Bill gave John a top. (Subject-predicate-indirect object-direct object or noun-verb-noun-noun pattern.)

Each of the above sentences is complete and recommendable is speaking and writing. However, clarity in writing in many situations indicates the need for expanding each of the sentences. In the first sentence above (Boys run), pupils might be asked to tell more about the boys. For example, what kind of boys were these? The following examples are given as possible learner responses:

1. *Tall* boys run.
2. *Small* boys run.
3. *Tall* boys *with blue coats* run.
4. *Small* boys *in the yard* run.

Next, pupils may expand the predicate part of the sentence. For example, how did the boys run?

1. Boys run *slowly*.
2. Boys run *very rapidly*.
3. Boys run *with great speed*.

A further question can be asked of pupils pertaining to where boys run. Pupils may give responses such as the following:

1. Boys run *in the yard*.
2. Boys run *here*.
3. Boys run *around the building*.

In sentences above, pupils might think of their own personal experiences in terms of where they have run. Learners may also think of "when" boys run. Examples include the following:

1. Boys run *today*.
2. Boys run *in the morning*.
3. Boys run *at noon*.

Pupils with teacher guidance should have numerous opportunities to expand sentences using modifiess for the subject and/or predicate parts of sentences:

Learners inductively may also expand sentences through the use of appositives. Compare the first sentence with the second sentence.

1. Mr Jones lives on Line Street.
2. Mr Jones, or teacher, lives on Line Street.

In the first sentence, the subject-predicate pattern is in evidence. "Mr. Jones" is the subject while "lives" is the predicate. The words "on Line Street" involve the use of a preposition phrase used as an adverb. These words tell where Mr. Jones lives. In the second sentence, the words, "our teacher," are another name for Mr. Jones. Thus, an appositive has been added.

Dependent clauses may also be utilized to expand sentences. Notice the following two sentences:

1. John likes to swim.
2. John sleeps much.

These two sentences may be written as one sentence, thus eliminating short, choppy statements in writing:

Although John sleeps much, he likes to swim.

In this sentence the dependent clause is "Although John sleeps much". "John" is the subject and "sleeps" is the predicate.

The dependent clause does not stand by itself but makes sense when it is related to the independent clause. The independent clause is "he likes to swim". The word "he" is the subject and "likes" is the predicate. Thus, sentences can be expanded through the use of dependent clauses. The dependent clauses are italicized in the following sentences.

1. *If Jim can earn enough money,* he will buy a new basketball.
2. The boy *who works in the grocery store* is our neighbour.
3. The dog *that wore a new collar* is my pet.

Pupils, will realize that dependent clauses generally do not make sense by themselves. The dependent clauses add meaning to an independent clause. Pupils should have ample experience in expanding any sentence pattern through the use of dependent clauses.

Pupils also need to have ample experience when readiness for learning is in evidence pertaining to expanding sentences through compounding. Notice the following sentences.

1. Sally sings.
2. Sally dances.

These sentences follow the subject-predicate pattern. Monotonous writing is in evidence if all written work consisted of short sentences. The two sentences may be rewritten by compounding the predicate parts: Sally *sings and dances*. Two sentences may also be rewritten by compounding the subject.

1. Jim played baseball.
2. Owen played baseball.
3. Jim and Owen played baseball.

Sentence numbers one and two above pertain to the subject-predicate-direct object pattern. Sentence number three compounds the subjects of sentences one and two.

Hennings writes the following structural linguistics:

> The historical and comparative linguists by relying on analytical techniques were paving the way for the structural linguists of the twentieth century. Using systematic analysis, these linguists have

been able to explain the structures through which speakers communicate meaning in English. They have described how meaning is communicated through

1. intonation—pitch, stress, juncture, or pause;
2. sentence patterns—the order of words in sentences;
3. function words—words like noun markers, verb markers, phrase markers, clause markers, question markers that communicate relationships among the four major word classes, the nouns, verbs, adjectives, and adverbs;
4. inflectional endings like the *s* through which we form a plural noun and affixes through which we change words from one class to another. For example, *govern* a verb, becomes *government*, a noun, with the addition of the affix *ment* while *courage*, a noun, becomes *courageous*, an adjective, with the addition of the affix *-ous*.

Stress, Pitch, and Juncture

Pupils need to become thoroughly familiar with meanings and applications of the concepts *stress, pitch* and *juncture*.

When words are pronounced within a sentence, differences in stress occur. Study the following sentence: "Hand me the toys".

If the word "hand" is stressed more than the other words in the sentence, this means that the toys should be handed rather than thrown or tossed. Stressing the word "me" more than the other words in the same sentence indicates that the toys should go to the person who is speaking rather than to any other individual. If the word "toys" is stressed more than any other word in the sentence, the emphasis is upon "toys" rather than a book, pamphlet, or other object.

Pupils should practice speaking using the same sentence in meaningful ways and stress a different selected word each time more than any other word in the same sentence. A tape recorder might be utilized in this learning activity. Pupils may also perceive how a specific sentence changes in meaning when a selected word is stressed more than other words within the sentence. Linguists recognize four degrees of stress. Pupils with teacher guidance should practice using different degrees of stress when communicating ideas orally in speaking experiences.

Pupils should also have ample opportunities to practice using pitch in oral communication of ideas. Linguists recognize four degrees of pitch. Selected words in a sentence may be pitched higher or lower and thus change the meaning of a sentence. In some cases, words will be pitched higher at the end of a sentence when questions are asked. However, not all words are pitched higher at the end of a sentence when questions are asked. Consider the following sentences:

1. Did you do any reading today?
2. Bill has moved?

In the second sentence, the ending word is pitched higher as compared to the ending word of the first sentence. Pupils with the use of a cassette recorder should practice oral communication involving interrogative sentences. Learners may notice the degree of pitch of ending words in a sentence. Pupils may also notice how other words are pitched within these sentences as well as in imperative, declarative, and exclamatory types of sentences. Attempts should be made in identifying different degrees of pitch of words within sentences.

Much misinterpretation of sentence meaning occurs when juncture is not utilized properly in speaking and writing. Consider the following incorrectly punctuated sentence. At the picnic jello salad ham sandwiches and milk were served. If the difficult to determine how many different kinds of food were served.

The following might be possibilities depending upon pauses in oral communication or commas in written communication within each sentence:

1. At the picnic jello, salad, ham, sandwiches, and milk were served.
2. At the picnic jello salad, ham, sandwiches, and milk were served.
3. At the picnic jello salad, ham sandwiches, and milk were served.

Pupils should practice reading and speaking different sentences where proper placement of commas (or pausing adequately between words) is important. The meaning of a sentence can certainly change depending upon emphasized pauses within a specific sentence. As a further example, pertaining to juncture, consider the following sentences:

1. Leon, my cousin, works in a factory.
2. Leon, my cousin works in a factory.

In the first sentence, the speaker is stating a fact about Leon. In the second sentence, the speaker is speaking directly to Leon. Using the same words in a sentence, meanings can change depending upon printed commas or orally emphasized pauses within a sentence.

Ragan and Shepherd write the following involving language development:

> Just as the language of a child is developed through experiencing, so is the language arts program. The symbols and patterns of language are abstractions applied to the realities of the objects, events, and values experienced by a culture and an individual. Without these applications, the mastery of the skills and tools of language is somewhat like practicing a violin in a vacuum: even if a skill is mastered in abstract, it is inert and valueless until it is activated in a social experience. For example, the skill of diagramming a sentence (for the elementary child) does not conduct into significant changes in the oral or even written language patterns of the child. On the other hand, learning to perceive differences in sounds and patterns does seem to significantly influence the child's oral and written language. Listening and voicing imitations are concrete experiences; diagramming is an abstract experience.
>
> Instruction in language arts must therefore begin with the social maturation and experiences which are already encoded by the learner. From this beginning, additional social maturation and experiencing must be provided as the foundation for the new symbols and patterns to be learned.

Generating New Sentences

Pupils should have meaningful experiences pertaining to how a declarative sentence, for example, can be changed to other kinds of sentences such as an interrogative sentence. First of all, pupils on the appropriate developmental level need to understand and attach meaning to a kernal sentence. A kernal sentence is simple and declarative. A declarative sentence states a fact. The subject of the kernal sentence is the actor, not the receiver of the action. The following are examples of kernal sentences:

1. John plays baseball.
2. Paul works in a store.
3. Josephine eats in the cafeteria.

In each of the above sentences, a fact is stated. Thus, a declarative sentence is in evidence. Also, in each of the sentences, the subject performs the action. That is, in sentence number one, John does the playing. In sentence two, Paul does the working, while in sentence three Josephine does the eating. Each of these sentences may be transformed or changed to a different kind of sentence other than the declarative sentence. In sentence number one which reads, "John plays baseball," the pitch of the ending word may be raised resulting in an interrogative sentence: "John plays baseball?" A few changes may also be made in the original sentence and results in the question: "Does John play baseball?" To change the original declarative sentence to a negative, the following sentence can result: "John does not play baseball". The original declarative sentence might also be rewritten to state a request: "John please play baseball". A command may result when making the following selected changes: "John play baseball". Imperative sentences result when requests or commands are in evidence. Very few changes need to be made when changing declarative sentences to the following:

1. Sentences which ask questions.
2. Sentences which issue commands or requests.
3. Sentences which show strong feeling.

In the declarative sentence reading, "John plays baseball," the statement can be transformed to read, "John plays baseball!" The latter sentence reveals strong feeling and states a exclamatory sentence. The same words were used for the declarative and exclamatory sentences. The only difference was in the end punctuation marks. Declarative sentences end with periods while exclamatory sentences with exclamation points.

Usage and Communication of Ideas

The words a speaker uses when communicating ideas orally or in writing are a matter of choice. Middle class individuals in society, in most cases, demand that standard English be spoken. However, effective communication also takes place with the use of nonstandard English. Contrast the following pairs of sentences.

1. They have completed their work.

   They done their work.

2. I haven't any money.

   I ain't got no money.

3. I ran in a race.

   I ranned in a race.

4. He is going to town.

   He goin to town.

No doubt, effective communication can take place when using either standard or nonstandard English. In selected environments, nonstandard English is accepted as good and sounds right to its users. In other environments, standard English only, is acceptable. An important item to remember is that the teacher accept all pupils as having much worth if standard or nonstandard English is spoken. Each person is important in a democracy. Respect for other is the heart of democratic thinking. Each pupil must be guided in achieving optimum development.

Teachers in the past felt that pupils using nonstandard English should be corrected on the scene so that standard English alone might be an important end result. Linguists have stated the following for not using this approach:

1. The pupil may come to feel that his/her home environment is inferior since nonstandard English is unacceptable in school.
2. Pupils cannot make rapid changes when switching from nonstandard to standard English in the school and class setting.
3. Negative attitudes are developed toward speaking and writing when teachers criticize the speaking efforts to those who speak nonstandard English.

4. Basically, it does not help most pupils in making desired forced changes to speaking standard English.

Anderson and Lapp write the following on usage in the language arts:

> Correct public usage is concerned with proper form. The agreement of verb and subject in number and tense, the form of the pronoun in various positions in the sentence, and the word order in sentences are some of the situations that present learning problems of proper form. The child who says, "I done my work" is using the wrong verb form. Another who says, "Him and me are friends", is using the wrong form of the pronoun. Children use these forms because they hear them at home, on television and on the playground.
>
> First of all, the teacher will encourage the child to enjoy his private language. He will be accepted, no matter what he says or how he says it. His language is a verbal expression of his thoughts and feelings. If we reject it, we reject him. Furthermore, we reject by implication the family who has taught him to speak and with whom he has strong emotional ties that he needs as he develops as a human being.

Pupils who speak nonstandard English can learn to speak standard English in the following ways:

1. by listening to the teacher who may serve as a model in speaking standard English;
2. by reading library books which utilize standard English in their content;
3. by listening to pupils speak where standard English is used;
4. by listening to tapes and records pertaining to content in relevant units of study where meaningful standard English is used by the speaker;
5. by viewing and listening to content in slides, films, and filmstrips where standard English is used;
6. by listening to presentations by resource personnel who utilize standard English in communicating ideas.

Pupils can learn to speak standard English in school and yet respect, as well as use, nonstandard English in the home environment. Thus, usage in speaking and writing pertains to choices of words and word order that are made in communicating ideas.

Anderson and Lapp write about the following forms that teachers might provide needed assistance to learners involving standard English:

1. A transition from all "baby-talk" and "cute" expressions.
2. The acceptable uses in speech and writing of *I, me, him, her, she, they,* and *them.* (Accepted: It's me.")
3. The appropriate uses of *is, are, was, were* with respect to number and tense.
4. Standard past tenses of common irregular verbs, such as *saw, gave, took, brought, struck.*
5. Elimination of double negative" "We don't have no apples".
6. Elimination of analogical forms: *ain't hisn, hern, ourn, hisself, theirselves,* and so on.
7. Appropriate use of possessive pronouns: *my, mine, his, hers, theirs, ours.*
8. Mastery of the distinction between *its* (possessive pronoun) and *it's* (it is, the contraction). (This applies only to written English.)
9. Elimination of *this here* and *that there.*
10. Approved use of personal pronouns in compound constructions: as subject (Mary and I), as object *(Mary and me),* as object of preposition *(to Mary and me).*
11. Attention to number agreement with the phrases *there is, there are, there was, there were.*
12. Elimination of *he don't, she don't, it don't.*
13. Elimination of *learn* for *teach, leave* for *let.*
14. Avoidance of pleonastic subjects: *my brother he; my mother she; that fellow he.*
15. Sensing the distinction between *good* as adjective as *well* as adverb (for example, "He spoke well").

In Summary

It is important for pupils to ultimately understand patterns of sentences in the English language. These sentence patterns include subject-predicate, subject-predicate-direct object, subject-linking verb-predicate adjective, subject-linking verb-predicate nominative, and subject-predicate-indirect object-direct object pattern. Pupils should also attach meaning to the concept of expanding sentences. Sentences may be expanded through the use of modifiers, appositives, dependent clauses, and compounding. It is important for learners to attach meaning to concepts such as stress, pitch, and juncture. Meanings of sentences change when utilizing these concepts.

Learners should be able to change sentences in functional writing and speaking situations from kernal sentences to those involving the asking of questions, the stating of negatives, and the issuing of commands or requests. Pupils with teacher guidance need to understand the concept of usage as it relates to standard and nonstandard English in oral and written communication of content.

REFERENCES

1. Anderson, Paul S. (Ed.) *Linguistics in the Elementary School Classroom*. New York: The Macmillan Company, 1971. Part One.
2. Anderson, Paul S., et al. (Eds.). *Reading in the Language Arts*. Second Edition. New York: The Macmillan Company, 1968. Chapter Six.
3. Anderson, Paul S., and Diane Lapp. *Language Skills in Elementary Education*. Third Ed. New York: Macmillan Publishing company, Inc., 1979.
4. Beane, James A., et. al. *Curriculum Planning and Development*. Boston: Allyn and Bacon, Inc. 1986.
5. Corcoran, Gertrude. *Language Arts in the Elementary School. A Modern Linguistic Approach*. New York: The Ronald Press Company, 1970.
6. Disick, Renee S. *Individualizing Language Instruction*. New York: Harcourt Brace and Jovanovich, Inc., 1975.
7. Donoghue, Mildred R. *The Child and the English language arts*. Dubuque, Iowa: Wm. C. Brown Company Publishers, 1971. Chapter Nine.

8. Hennings, Dorothy Grant. *Communication in Action*. Chicago: Rand McNally College Publishing Company, 1978.
9. Meras, Edmond A. *A Language Teacher's Guide*. Second Ed. New York: Harper and Row Publishers, 1962. Chapters One, Two, and Three.
10. Newman, Harold (Ed.). *Effective Language Arts Practices in the Elementary School: Selected Readings*. New York: John Wiley and Sons, 1972. Chapter One.
11. Orlich, Donald C. *Teaching Strategies*. Second edition. Lexington, Massachusets, D.C. Heath and Company, 1985.
12. Petty, Walter T. *Issues and Problems in the Elementary Language Arts: a book of readings*. Boston: Allyn and Bacon, Inc., 1968, Part II.
13. Petty, Walter T., et al. *Experiences in Language*. Second Ed. Boston: Allyn and Bacon, Inc., 1976.
14. Ragan, William B., and Gene D. Shepherd. *Modern Elementary Curriculum*. New York: Holt, Rinehart and Winston, 1977.
15. Roberts, Paul. *Modern Grammar*. New York: Harcourt, Brace and World, Inc., 1968. Chapters One and Two.
16. Shuster, Albert H., and Milton E. Ploghoft. *The Emerging Elementary Curriculum Methods and Procedures*. Columbus, Ohio: Charles E. Merrill Publishing Company, 1970. Chapter Seven.
17. Tiedt, Iris M., and Sidney W. Tiedt. *Contemporary English in the Elementary School*. Second Ed. Englewood Cliffs, New Jersey: Prentice Hall, Inc., 1975.

The Literature Curriculum

What can the teacher do to encourage pupils to read library books in the classroom setting? Chambers recommends the following:

> First, and above all, is our attitude about the role of reading—real reading—in the classroom. If we help students understand that the purpose of developmental reading and the acquisition of reading skills is to give them the key to the world of literature and all its wonders, we have moved forward, indeed. The library, or the library corner, should not be a place for free activity alone, or an extracurricular activity. Instead, it should be an interesting place to which children can go often, expecting to find an exciting, changing collection of good books. It should be a .place of adventure and delight where children are encouraged to hunt, browse, and explore. It should be a place where he can choose books that will give him answers or provide delight. Weekly book talks can attest to our attitude about books. By our attention to a good trade book in the book talk, we indicate the worthwhileness of children's literature. Children are affected by our attitudes toward things. That is part of the way they learn. The way we view the role of children's literature as part of their lives does a great deal in teaching them the value of reading that literature.
>
> Special and adequate time for reading is vital in helping children become readers of books. Recreational reading is not to be considered a haphazard, spotty activity, or suitable only for out-of-school reading. We can assign regular times during the school week to trade book reading. Often two regular reading periods can be given to recreational reading, leaving and other three days

of that period to basal devices and skill building. These periods of recreational reading can be part of the class routine—to be expected with the regularity of arithmetic, spelling, and social studies.

Pupils need to experience a quality literature curriculum. Thus, the reading curriculum needs to go beyond goals of having learners identify new words as well as developing skills pertaining to diverse types of comprehension. There are numerous reasons for emphasizing a quality curriculum.

First of all, pupils cannot experience all facets of living directly. They can learn, however, from vicarious experiences, e.g., reading what others have done, achieved, acquired, and experienced. There are, of course, selected experiences that none of us would wish to live through. Thus, a reader can learn much from others' deeds, thoughts, and acts. A reader might then be able to formulate his/her own goals in life more adequately through reading what others have experienced. There are groups in society who wish to censor diverse selections from the literature curriculum. The censored selections appear much more so on the senior high school level than the elementary school level. The literature curriculum, however, must assist pupils to formulate their own goals and purposes in life.

Values can be dictated to pupils by parents, teachers, and others in society. Too frequently, dictation of values to the young has not been effective. Also, the dictated values may not be appropriate in a changing society. Conservative values then might not be applicable in the coming years. There are values, however, that have endured in space and time, such as doing unto others that which we would want done to us. Even then, in changing times and situations, the Golden Rule needs reinterpretations and modified implementations. From a study of literature, pupils can evaluate and adopt selected desired values. Donoghue wrote:

> While the children's first exposure to literature is Mother Goose and other rhymes and stories, children should gradually experience every type and form of literature in a school program that is comprehensive and sequentially plotted throughout the elementary grades. Such a program not only strengthens the developmental reading curriculum but contributes in a significant

way to the attainment of several other objectives of elementary education as listed below:

- The school aims to meet the needs of individual pupils—and literature is widely diversified.
- The school aims to provide a learning program which will utilize the natural interests of its pupils—and literature appeals to all age groups.
- The school aims to provide socially satisfying experiences for its children and to develop in its pupils a wider social understanding—and good stories and pleasing verse are enjoyed more when they are shared with others.
- The school aims to give each child self-insight—and books introduced in childhood can sometimes bring about a profound change in one's outlook on life.
- The school aims to give each pupil a knowledge and appreciation of his cultural heritage—and literature is the means whereby much of that heritage is preserved and perpetuated.
- The school aims to stimulate and foster creative expression—and book experiences are an exciting springboard to art, drama, and other expressionistic activities.

Secondly, reading quality literature can provide relaxation for the reader. Much is spoken and written about means of coping with stress. Individuals in society need to cope with many unwanted situations. The involved person needs to find ways of dealing with stress. Reading can be a good way of restoring equilibrium. One can forget about stressful situations when reading. The reader can become so thoroughly engrossed in reading ideas that little or no time is inherently available for worrying, regretting, or fearing.

The teacher and parents must be actively involved in assisting pupils to become proficient in reading. The teacher alone cannot perform this vital responsibility for the pupil. Parents must also like reading and support a quality reading curriculum in the school/class setting. The pupil must assume major responsibility in wanting to learn to read. Otherwise, how can a pupil learn to read in order to achieve goals pertaining to relaxing the self?

Thirdly, literature for pupils can provide a guidance resource. There are learners who experience grave personal and social problems. Difficulties are involved when identifying problems and attempting to assist pupils in overcoming these difficulties. No doubt, an adequate number of good counselors are lacking in the school setting. Children's literature can provide assistance to pupils in attempting to cope with personal and social problems. What kinds of problems do pupils experience? These might well include poverty, shyness, aggressiveness, hostility, ill health, obesity, excessive tallness or shortness, and loneliness. The teacher needs to guide pupils individually to choose library books which assist in coping with problematic situations.

Fourthly, each pupil may receive assistance from reading literature in becoming knowledgeable about diverse kinds of careers. Too frequently, workers in society have drifted into a job or occupation. The "drifting" into the world of work has made for feelings of dissatisfaction in the occupational/vocational arena. Certainly, a quality career education program can provide pupils with selected understandings, skills, and attitudes needed to be successful ultimately in the world of work. Each person needs to achieve optimally in the career arena. Working at jobs/occupations that are not personally rewarding can make for feelings of futility. Literature on careers written for learners on different achievement levels can provide necessary subject matter for pupils contemplating the world of work.

The centralized/classroom library needs library books and other reading materials on diverse levels of achievement pertaining to many relevant careers. The teacher needs to introduce learners to reading materials on careers. With appropriate readiness experiences, learners can be guided to read content pertaining to the world of work.

Fifthly, skills in reading can be developed when literature is being read by children. Too frequently, basal textbooks are read by learners. Basal materials may not meet the reading needs of selected pupils. Then too, library books generally are chosen by the involved learner; the subject matter in these books is usually not assigned to pupils, unless a specific purpose in involved. Teachers may feel that too many pupils are turned off in reading when basal materials are utilized in the reading curriculum. Library books chosen by the involved pupil may provide the needed spark to encourage reading.

Sixthly, pupils can learn much subject matter related to different curriculum areas when engaged in the reading of library books. There are library books written on diverse levels of achievement pertaining to many nations on the face on the earth. Thus, pupil achievement in diverse social studies units can be aided when selected library books are read. In other curriculum areas—science, mathematics, health, art, music, and physical education—related library books are in evidence which learners may read.

Montebello listed the following criteria for teacher self-evaluation suggestions, as well as pupil evaluation suggestions:

Teacher Self-Evaluation Suggestions

1. Do I have a planned literature program as part of an integrated language arts curriculum?
2. Does my classroom reflect a well-planned, thoughtfully organized body of literature experiences?
3. Do I focus on literature as literature as well as use tradebooks to enhance and enrich studies in other curriculum areas?
4. Is "pleasure" present in my literature program?
5. Is there a balanced program between instruction and the encouragement of individual free reading?
6. Is time for independent reading scheduled and provided?
7. Is time available regularly?
8. Do I guide youngsters into the delights of reading for enjoyment as well as for information?
9. Do I read aloud to the youngsters as a way of introducing them to the best in literature?
10. Does the reading aloud occur in intermediate grades as well as in primary grades?

11. Do I go beyond literature stories in the readers?
12. Are enough tradebooks sufficiently accessible to youngsters in my classroom?
13. Do those tradebooks reflect the diversity of interest, tastes, and abilities present in my classroom?
14. Are my feelings for books reflected in the behaviours I exhibit toward and about books?
15. Am I enthusiastic for and about literature?
16. Do I give literature a respected place in the school program?
17. How many new tradebooks have I read this year?

Pupil Evaluation Suggestions

1. Does he read?
2. Does his attitude reflect a desire to read?
3. Is he "catching" an appreciation for good books?
4. Does he read widely?
5. Does he choose to read for enjoyment?
6. Does he read for personal purposes as well?
7. How much does he read?
8. What does he read?
9. How does he interpret his reading achievement? It is limited to skill development, or does progress in reading include appreciational and recreational reading?
10. When he evaluates his success in reading, does he include personal reading and appreciation as part of achievement?
11. Does he apply what he reads to his life?

Quality Literature in the Curriculum

Most basal reading programs tend to emphasize pupils' mastering diverse word recognition techniques, such as using configuration clues, phonetic analysis, syllabication, structural analysis, context clues, and picture clues. The ultimate goal in word recognition for pupils should be to recognize words immediately as sight words. In addition to word recognition techniques, basal reading approach emphasizes learners achieving comprehension skills such as reading to acquire facts, directions, a sequence of ideas, main ideas, and generalization, as well as reading critically, reading creatively, and reading to solve problems. However, there are additional ingredients that need to become a part of a relevant literature curriculum for children.

Setting of the Story

The language arts teacher needs to guide pupils to understand and attach meaning to the setting of a story or library book. Where did the events take place? Pupils need to understand if events took place in a rural, urban, or suburban area. Also, learners need to attach meaning to which city, state, or nation one or more events took place. Certainly, human behaviour differs when events in literature take place in a rural, as compared to suburban or urban region. Behaviour of human beings, of course, differs much among individuals within a rural, or a suburban, or an urban region.

In dealing with the setting of a story, pupils also need to understand *when* an event (or events) took place. Time is a significant factor to consider when the reader attempts to attach meaning to content in children's literature. Historical fiction, for example, pertains to a study of selected events in the past. Types of transportation, clothing, homes, schools, communication, recreational endeavours, and foods eaten might well depend upon the period of time being studied in history. Thus, a pupil needs to consider time elements, as well as geographical regions when attaching meaning to children's literature.

The specifics or details of the setting may either be suggested or stated directly. The setting of a story might also reveal characterization, as well as sequential ensuing events in the story.

Characterization

In addition to the setting of a story, professional writers of novels also spend considerable time in describing the involved characters. What kind of a person (or persons) are specific individuals within a story? Do the individuals remain stable in terms of traits possessed, or are growth and change inherent? There certainly are numerous character traits that any one individual may possess. A person might then be shy but friendly, intelligent, hard working, and achievement oriented. The same person may also possess traits of being altruistic.

A different person might be aggressive, hostile, irresponsible, and handsome. The person may possess traits of being intelligent but not utilizing talents and abilities possessed. Thus, each learner should be guided to describe character traits of human beings in a story. Inferences must also be developed. Writers, of course, do not always state factually the kinds of characters within a story. To be able to attach meaning to content read, pupils need to understand the concept of *characterization* as it related to actual human beings in a story or novel.

There are diverse means used by authors to describe personality and character of human beings. Thus, a writer may discuss the effects of one character on others. The feelings and thoughts within each character might be described. Also, the physical appearance, deeds, and speech of any character need adequate consideration within a story. Reasons for each character behaving as he/she did should be analyzed by pupils.

Plot in the Literature Curriculum

Language arts teachers need to assist learners, inductively and/or deductively, to discover the plot in a given literary selection. Thus, the pupil is guided to ascertain *what* happened in a story. Too frequently, pupils have completed reading a library book without understanding what truly happened in the selection. Diverse kinds of comprehension skills need to be developed within learners in order to understand the concept of plot. Two previous concepts discussed, related to a quality literature curriculum, involved *setting* and *characterization*. These concepts in any literary selection need understanding so that comprehensive meaning is attached to a sequence of happenings involving *plot*. If pupils do not understand what actually happened in a given selection, they have not understood the plot of a library book or story. Essential ingredients in a quality literature curriculum must be emphasized by the language arts teacher. Thus, the *plot* of a selection needs to be understood by learners; otherwise, comprehension and meaning are being omitted in the ongoing literature curriculum.

A quality literature curriculum involves pupils utilizing diverse word recognition techniques. Also, an adequate number of purposes in comprehension needs emphasis in ongoing lessons and units. In addition to mastering word recognition techniques and developing comprehension proficiency, learners need to attach meaning to literary concepts, such as *setting, characterization,* and *plot*.

Tiedt and Tiedt Wrote:

> Literature has seldom been part of the reading program in the elementary school, for reading has been dominated by the basal reading series. What are the advantages of a literature-reading program over the traditional controlled-vocabulary anthology? The use of literature in a reading program for elementary school students offers quality content to a course of study which has concentrated solely on the teaching of skills. It is a time that we acknowledge the value of provocative material in exciting the student about reading. Until we have this excitement present in the reading lesson, we will not develop a nation of readers.
>
> Many titles from children's literature can be, and are being, used as reading text material. The advantages of *Pippi Longstocking, A Wrinkle in Time,* and *Johnny Tremain* over the familiar basal reader are overwhelming:
>
> 1. Excellent writing-imaginary, use of words, storytelling ability.
> 2. Continuity of a longer story—plot development, characterization.
> 3. Greater interest value—intrigue, atmosphere, entertainment.
> 4. Integration of literature, language, and composition studies.

Point of View

In analyzing subject matter in a quality literature curriculum, pupils also need to be guided to understand who, in particular, is telling the story. Thus, from whose point of view are the events and incidents being told? Pupils need to notice if and when characters in a story actually speak, or is a narrative account being presented? Is the first, second, or third person (noun or pronoun) actually presenting ideas, rather than sequential descriptions being utilized in presenting ideas?

Meaning attached to reading a story, novel, or library book may vary much depending upon *who* is presenting sequential content. Professional writers of novels pay much attention to point of view in developing literary works.

If the author or a character in the story tells sequential content, the story is delimited to the thoughts, experiences, perceptions, and expressions of that person relating ordered events in the literature being read. The narrator is the person telling the story. If the author tells the story, he/she generally remains anonymous and makes few or no references to the personal self. Generally, if a character in the story is narrating content, he/she refers to the self as "I".

Theme in Literature

What is the main idea in the story, library book, or novel? Thus, pupils need to consider the concept of *theme*. *Theme* involves the author's idea or ideas pertaining to situations in life. The writer may directly state the involved theme. The theme might also be implied. Ordinarily, *theme* as a concept does not involve moral standards, or rules to live by. In reading a literary selection, the reader needs to ask what the consumable content says about nature, about people, and about life itself.

Irony of the Situation

Each learner needs readiness experience to achieve objectives in the literature curriculum. Never should teachers emphasize selected goals unless pupils can be successful in achieving the stated objectives. Pupils, as well as the teacher, become frustrated if the former are not ready to attain new ends. Feelings of failure hinder pupils in developing an adequate self-concept. Feelings of adequacy are necessary in order to achieve relevant goals. Thus, pupils need to be ready to understand the concept of *irony of the situation*, or it should not be emphasized in the literature curriculum.

What is *irony of the situation?* Events turn out differently for any one character, as compared to what the involved reader anticipated. Supposing, a character is portrayed as having experienced a noble, undefiled background. As a surprise tactic, the writer reveals, directly or indirectly, that the character was involved in a series of thefts and robberies. Or, a person having grown up in highly unfortunate settings becomes a quality leader in the community. As a further example, a person in combat files numerous successful bombing missions over enemy territory. The same character arrives home safely, only to die in an automobile accident involving travel to a routine destination.

In the concept of *irony* in literature, the author tries to hide his true feelings, pertaining to an incident, event, or deed. The character's deeds may not be consistent with stated beliefs.

Satire in Literature

Selected writers in literature emphasize *satire* as a means of evaluating people and society. The purpose involved in satire is to expose ills, evils, or follies in order to promote an improved society. Humor may be used to expose weaknesses in society. Sometimes, caustic bitterness is also utilized by selected writers of satire.

Supposing that satire is used in literature, the writer may state rational, worthwhile listed goals in a school that learners are to achieve. Students, however, are uninspired and bored in school. The absentee rate is high and tardy students are quite apparent when the school day starts.

As a second example of *satire,* the writer may quote teachers saying to pupils how important it is to read good library books and to read whenever it is possible to do so. In reality the teacher is poorly prepared for each day of teaching and views television, uncritically, each spare moment of time devoted to recreational endeavours. Thus, in actual life the teacher does little or no reading.

Learning Activities in the Literature Curriculum

Which kinds of experiences might learners pursue as a result of their endeavours in reading quality literature?

Pupils individually with teacher guidance may discuss content read. The language arts teacher needs to be knowledgeable about the content of many library books written for children. Thus, the teacher may ask selected questions involving comprehension of content in the chosen book completed by the learner. Questions discussed should stimulate, not minimize, reading of children's literature on the part of the learner.

A pupil may pencil sketch a favorite setting, plot or character contained in a library book. Comprehension may well be revealed by the involved learner in the completed pencil sketch. The drawing must reveal comprehension, and not the work of a professional artist. To be sure, quality art work needs to be emphasized by the individual learner in terms of optimal progress.

A learner may write a letter to the author of the library book read. Hopefully, the pupil will receive an actual response from the writer. The pupil may wish to express appreciation for content contained in the book. Also, the pupil may wish to write specifically what was of interest in the completed library book.

A diorama may be made by a learner containing a three dimensional scene of major generalizations achieved, as a result of reading. The goal of diorama development is to protray scenes and situations as neatly and accurately as possible. Hopefully, the art activity will stimulate pupil interest in reading.

Additional learning activities for pupils involving children's literature include:

1. writing an advertisement to encourage other learners to read the same library book;
2. presenting an advertisement orally indicating the merits of the completed library book;
3. giving a critical analysis indicating strengths and weaknesses of a book read in children's literature;
4. role playing the writer of library book to indicate purposes in its writing;
5. writing a different setting or plot;
6. reading a different book by the same author or a book containing a similar title;

7. writing a play based on the contents of the library book;
8. engaging in a pantomime or in a creative dramatics presentation involving selected content read;
9. developing sequential illustrations pertaining to ideas read;
10. presenting an oral report to the class, following desired standards, involving salient ideas in the completed library book;
11. participating in a seminar involving depth discussion with other learners who have read the same literary work;
12. outlining interesting content from a story or library book;
13. writing a summary containing significant subject matter;
14. developing a bookmark or book jacket for a chosen library book;
15. writing creative content, such as what if the setting of the library book had taken place in *(indicate a geographical region)*, rather than its actual setting. Or, what if the main character had not been a part of the story, how would the ending have differed?

Fisher and Terry summarized research from four studies made in the area of children's literature. They wrote the following implications from the involved studies:

1. A literature based language arts program should begin in kindergarten and continue through the elementary grades.
2. A variety of rich . . . reading materials should be provided for children.
3. It is important that teachers consistently read books aloud to their children. Oral language activities—such as discussions of the story, role playing, or puppetry—should frequently be used as follow-ups to reading aloud.
4. Children should be encouraged and motivated to increase their independent reading.

In Summary

Literature is a significant part of the total school curriculum. Each pupil needs to experience a quality children's literature curriculum. The reading curriculum needs to incorporate pupils developing proficiency in diverse word recognition skills, as well as in a variety of purposes involving comprehension. Also, quality literature needs adequate emphasis. Thus, concepts such as the *setting of the story, characterization, plot, point of view, theme, irony of the situation,* as well as *satire* need to be inherent in literature. Each pupil, however, needs to be ready to understand these concepts prior to their implementation in the literature curriculum. Learners individually need to attach interest, meaning, and purpose in ongoing activities and experiences.

REFERENCES

1. American Library Association. *A Multimedia Approach to Children's Literature*. Chicago: American Library Association. 1972.
2. Anderson, Paul S. *Language in Elementary Education*. Second Edition. New York: Macmillan, 1972.
3. Boyd, Gertrude, *Teaching Communication Skills in the Elementary School*. New York: Van Nostrand Reinhold, 1970.
4. Boyd, Gertrude. *Teaching Poetry in the Elementary Schools*. Columbus, Ohio: Merrill, 1973.
5. Burrows, Alvina T., Diane L. Monson, and Russell G. Stauffer. *New Horizons in the Language Arts*. New York: Harper and Row, 1972.
6. Chambers, Dewey W. *Children's Literature in the Curriculum*. Chicago: Rand McNally and Company, 1971.
7. Cohen, Monroe D., ed. *Literature with Children*. Washington, D.C.: Association for Childhood Education International, 1972.
8. Coody, Betty. *Using Literature with Young Children*. Dubuque, Iowa: William C. Brown, 1973.
9. Corcoran, Gertrude B. *Language Arts in Elementary School: A Modern Linguistic Approach*. New York: Ronald, 1970.
10. Donoghue, Mildred R. *The Child and the English Language Arts*. Second Edition, Dubuque, Iowa: Wm. C. Brown Publishers, 1975.
11. Fisher, Carol J., and C. Ann Terry. *Children's Language and the Language Arts*. Second Edition. New York: McGraw-Hill Book Company, 1982.

12. Greene, Harry A., and Walter T. Petty. *Developing Language Skills in the Elementary Schools*. Fourth Edition. Boston: Allyn and Bacon, 1971.

13. Haviland, Virginia, ed. *Children's Books of International Interest*. Chicago: American Library Association, 1972.

14. Hensing, Esther D., ed. *Good and Inexpensive Books for Children*. Washington, D.C.: Association for Childhood Education International, 1972.

15. Hurlimann, Bettina. *Three Centuries of Children's Books in Europe*. Cleveland: World Publishing, 1968.

16. Johnson, Edna, et al. *Anthology of Children's Literature*. Boston: Houghton Mifflin, 1970.

17. Lamb, Pose, ed., *Literature for Children Series*. Dubuque, Iowa: William C. Brown, 1970.

18. Lonsdale, Bernard J., and Helen K. Mackintosh. *Children Experience Literature*. New York: Random, 1972.

19. Montebello, Mary S. *Literature for Children: Children's Literature in the Curriculum*. Edited by Pose Lamb. Dubuque, Iowa: William C. Brown, 1972.

20. Smith, James A. *Adventures in Communication: Language Arts Methods*. Boston: Allyn and Bacon, 1972.

21. Smith James Steel. *A Critical Approach to Children's Literature*. New York: McGraw, 1967.

22. Sutherland, Zena, and May Hill Arbuthnot. *Children and Books*. Seventh edition. Glenview, Illinois: Scott Foresman and Company, 1986.

23. Tiedt, Tris M., and Sidney W. Tiedt. *Contemporary English in the Elementary School*. Second Edition. Englewood Cliffs, New Jersey: Prentice-Hall, Inc., 1975.

24. Whitehead, Robert. *Children's Literature: Strategies of Teaching*. Englewood Cliffs, N.J.: Prentice Hall, 1968.

Speaking and the Pupil

Speaking activities should be stressed alongwith reading experiences emphasized in teaching-learning situations. A good reader has a wide range of vocabulary terms available prior to the actual reading of subject matter. A child who has a rich speaking vocabulary has an easier time of developing reading skills as compared to the learner that lacks a rich speaking vocabulary. Then too, it is much more comfortable to be able to converse well with others due to having a rich speaking vocabulary. Then too, it is much more comfortable to be able to converse well with others due to having a rich speaking vocabulary as compared to those who cannot converse adequately. Feelings of discomfort tend to arise when one is unable to join into a conversation. One needs friends for support, for entertainment, for enjoyment and for learning. Thus, it behooves the teacher to assist pupils to achieve proficiently in oral communication.

Giving Oral Reports

There are occasions when individuals are asked to give oral reports in different organisations in society. It is important then for learners to develop needed skills in reporting to others in a group setting. Any speaking activity in front of groups should satisfying so that feelings of fright are minimized. People who are afraid to get up in front of groups have experienced the unfortunate in previous settings involving speaking in front of others. The teacher and pupils in the classroom should support each other so that satisfying experiences in oral communication are an end result. Confidence in the self in appearing before groups in different speaking endeavours is salient. Learners should never be minimized for mistakes made in oral communication. Rather support must be provided for pupils to improve oral communication skills with renewed confidence.

A.H. Maslow in his theory of motivation developed a hierarchy of needs levels which indicate the necessity of fulfillment if pupils are to do well in school and later as adults. Maslow's lowest level of needs are physiological. These needs include adequate nutrition, rest, sleep, clothing and shelter. Physiological needs are the lowest level of needs that must be met if learners are to do well in school. If a pupil lacks in any of these categories, he/she cannot attain adequately in the school curriculum. The the human body is like a machine and needs proper care. Perhaps, the human machine needs much more care as compared to a mechanical machine. Quality breakfasts and noon meals served in school assists learners to achieve well. Going up higher on maslow's hierarchy of needs in sequence is safety needs. To do well, all need to feel secure and safe. Weapons brought to school or fights among pupils in the school environment and in society make for a lack of security on the part of pupils. Maslow's physiological and safety needs categories are followed by love and belonging needs. Each person wishes to feel being a part of a group which is satisfying. The child who is an isolate or who is shunned does not feel as if he/she belongs to a group, be it large or small. The teacher here must attempt to guide all pupils to develop feelings of belonging and being accepted by others. Next in sequence, Maslow stressed the importance of learners having esteem needs met. Here, the teacher and learners need to recognize talents possessed by pupils. Individuals like to thought of and remembered for what can be done well. Each person has selected strength which need to be recognized and acknowledged. Too frequently, the talents of individuals are never sought after and praised. Ridiculing or ignoring of others seems to be more the order of the day. Is it not much better to praise that which is worthy and good? Certainly, pupils individually possess abilities that need recognition, be it in knowledge, skills or attitudes. Talents possessed by learners should be identified and used in the classroom setting. Next in Maslow's hierarchy of needs is the desire to understand. Here, facts, concepts, generalizations and main ideas of acquired subject matter become salient. Self-realization is the highest goal in Maslow's theory of motivation. To become what one wishes to become represents self-actualization. That is a complex goal to attain but must be sought as an ongoing objective. No doubt, this objectives is sequential and never attained in toto.

Feelings of self-actualization are salient in any curriculum area. Certainly, learner optimal achievement is necessary in the language arts in order to develop feelings of self-actualization. In the area of speaking and oral communication, it is vital to attain the direction of being the self-fulfilled individual. Gestalt theory must prevail here in that the whole or entire person is involved in learning. Thus, the psychological, the safety or security facets, the belonging individual, the person with adequate esteem or recognition for that which is well done and the self-actualization concepts are vital for any person in the language arts and its sub-division, oral communication.

Carefully chosen objectives learning activities to attain the chosen ends, and appropriate evaluation procedures to ascertain if the objectives have been achieved are necessary to ensure quality in oral communication.

Objectives in Oral Communication

Objectives to emphasize in oral communication need to be carefully selected by those involved in teaching-learning situations, be it the teacher(s), principal, supervisor and other involved persons with professional training. Committees need to be at work in adequate time durations to evaluate and ultimately choose those ends which are worthwhile for learner attainment. Workshops, faculty meetings, study groups, staff development programs, research of the current literature, as well as resource personnel assistance should provide input into selecting objectives in oral communication.

The objectives need to be comprehensive and cover all relevant ends in oral communication. Objectives must be new and attainable by learners. The objectives should be arranged sequentially so that pupils might be successful in goal attainment.

They need to be written precisely enough so that it is possible to appraise if each pupil has achieved the stated goals.

There are oral communication goals which would be recognized as being salient for all pupils to attain. These are the following:

1. Speaking clearly so all can hear content spoken.
2. Speaking at a rate which is comprehendible to others.
3. Speaking with voice inflection, including proper stress, pitch and juncture.
4. Speaking with the intent of involving others in an atmosphere of respect and acceptance.
5. Speaking with purpose involved be it in the making of introductions, the presenting of an oral report, taking part in discussions, participating in creative and formal dramatics, interviewing and using of puppets involving oral communication.
6. Speaking using appropriate gestures, facial expressions, body movements and eye contact.
7. Speaking with the use of agreement between subject and predicate, as well as varied sentence patterns, kinds of sentences such as interrogative, imperative, declarative and exclamatory.
8. Speaking with diverse sentences such as simple, complex, compound complex and compound sentences.
9. Speaking with the use of different reasons for oral communication such as to provide directions clearly to others.
10. Speaking to influence others in the political arena.

Learning Opportunities

A variety of learning opportunities should be provided pupils so that interest is ongoing. Then too, individual differences among learners need to be provided for in order that optimal achievement in speaking can be furthered for each pupil. There are numerous purposes involved in speaking.

1. ***Discussions:*** All individuals tend to be involved in discussions at one time or another. These discussions can be quite formal as well as informal. It behooves the teacher to guide each elementary pupil to achieve proficiency in discussions. In the classroom setting, there is subject matter to discuss after pupils have completed reading a specific selection in diverse academic areas. After taking an excursion related directly to an ongoing unit of study, learners with teacher guidance discuss what has been read. The purpose for the discussion might be to determine what the individual learner has comprehended. The discussion may also zero in on having pupils extend content read in an ongoing unit of study. Discussions need to follow definite criteria so that the teacher may appraise learner attainment in the discussions using these standards. Criteria or standards to follow in discussions should include the following:

   (a) The discussion should be stimulating to generate interest in content presented.

   (b) Each pupil should be encouraged to join the discussion.

   (c) No one should dominate the discussion.

   (d) Learners need to develop feelings of belonging when participating in a committee setting.

   (e) Ideas in the discussion should circulate among all group members rather than between a few members in the group setting.

   (f) Content must be presented clearly to others. Meaning needs to be present in learning.

   (g) Respect and acceptance of the thinking of others is important.

   (h) The teacher is a guide and not a dispenser of information.

   (i) Evaluation of progress in a discussion must always follow specific standards and should be stressed frequently.

(j) Learners must attain and grow in becoming proficient in discussion settings.

Creativity must receive ample emphasis in any discussion. Evaluation sessions should not hinder pupil progress in revealing originality and being a quality member of a discussion group.

Making Introduction

Very frequently two or more people are introduced to each other. How is this to be done so that individuals get to know each other? Then too, introduced persons should be able to follow with conversation that is enriching to all involved. Speaking clearly and pleasantly are two key concepts here. Rudeness and being inconsiderate have no roles to play in the making of introductions. When people are introduced to each other, the names should be correctly pronounced in order that people can call each other by name. The one who does the introducing should know something about all involved in the making of introductions so that conversation many follow in sequence. If one knows something of interest about the other person, this assists in moving forward with the conversation. Each person needs to be treated with respect as a human being having much worth. Minimizing others has no role to play in the making of introductions. Eye contact in making introductions tends to show interest toward others. There are a few cultures where eye contact with those being introduced is not stressed. However, on the whole, quality eye contact with others being introduced indicates respect involving the entire introduction process. Criteria and standards to use in appraising learner progress in the making of introductions are the following:

1. Involved persons should indicate a desire to meet others. Quality introductions made should assist in this area.
2. Self-evaluation by participants is an important ingredient in wishing to make improvements.
3. Proper stress, pitch and juncture with appropriate voice inflection should be an inherent part in the making of introductions.
4. Appropriate volume and speed of oral presentations is salient in introducing one person to the others.

5. Looking at each other in face to face communication is important when making introductions.
6. Full attention must be given to each person when an introduction is being made. Being distracted by factors in the environment hinders in the making of introductions.
7. Clarity in expressions and ideas presented is a must.
8. Individuals making introductions should be interested in people. A people centered approach is recommended when introductions are made.
9. Practice is necessary in learning the art of making introductions.
10. Feedback in making introductions is necessary for improvement to take place.

Extemporaneous Speaking

Extemporaneous speaking has much merit for pupils possessing readiness for this activity. Why? Each person is asked at diverse intervals in life to speak on a topic with little prior notice. Or, one needs to make a decision or choices in the spur of the monument. Little time is available in these situation to plan, ponder and analyze. Thus, one must think rapidly and make the best choices possible.

In extemporaneous thinking, the learner is provided with a topic or title to speak on. He/she needs to prepare a talk within the allotted time limits given, such as five minutes. The topic or title could be familiar to the pupil, or it could also be rather new or novel. The title/topic should not be excessively difficult since the time limit for preparation might be rather short such as the five minute time interval. The presentation is then given to the total class or to a committee. Extemporaneous speaking quality may be evaluated using the following criteria:

1. The speaker is able to think within the prescribed time limits.
2. The speaker is able to present content meaningfully to listeners.

3. The speaker is able to obtain the attention of listeners to secure quality listening.
4. The speaker is poised when presenting content in the ongoing talk.
5. The speaker is using noted when there is a need to do so.
6. The speaker uses eye contact when presenting information.
7. The speaker faces all participants who are listeners.
8. The speaker uses facial expressions and gestures as needed to obtain the attention of listeners.
9. The speaker does not exhibit distracting mannerisms.
10. The speaker invites questions after the extemporaneous speech.

Learners need to be taken where they are presently in achievement in extemporaneous speaking and then work for continuous progress. When appraising learner progress, realistic standards must be used. A pupil cannot attain perfection in all ten standards listed above. They can make progress with diagnosis and remediation when improving performance in extemporaneous speaking.

Creative Dramatics

Pupils need to have the opportunities to participate in creative dramatics as a speaking activity. Creativity indicate novel, unique and original ideas pertaining to words and sentences used as well as in planning and implementing the dramatic activity. Being able to dramatize would indicate the need to have background information in order to role play or act out diverse scenes and situations.

Where might the content come from for the creative dramatics presentation? Basal readers, trade books, history texts and other reading materials contain content which can readily be a part of a creative dramatics presentation. Thus, the teacher should correlate content pupils have read from the basal reader, for example, with the creative dramatics activity. Speaking parts are developed as the need arises in the creative dramatics presentation. These parts are not memorized but thought and thinking is inherent as the creative dramatics activity progresses. Ideas presented relate directly to what has been read, but creativity is needed as the dramatization enfolds. Background scenery may be made by learners with teacher guidance. The scenery made should enhance the creative dramatics activity. Time spent on the scenery should have value in terms of objectives to be attained by learners. Busy work is to be frowned upon. Goal centered experiences are needed in the school curriculum. Time on task is to be emphasized. The background scenery may be appraised in terms of:

1. being neatly made;
2. being directly related to the creative dramatics activity;
3. being accurate and yet novel ideas are to be encouraged;
4. being within the achievement levels of learners;
5. being worthwhile for involved pupils;
6. being purposeful for learners so that reasons are inherent for learning;
7. being able to secure the interests of pupils;
8. being a meaningful learning opportunity for pupils;
9. being of assistance to make the dramatics experience more realistic;
10. being a springboard to further interest in reading.

Formal Dramatizations

Formal dramatizations emphasize that learners write play parts pertaining to what has been read. For example in history, pupils read about events and involved people in these happenings. Thus, a committee of pupils may take what has been read and write play parts should be written. It should not be overwhelming whereby pupils lose interest in the ongoing activity. Play parts should be:

1. Accurately written pertaining to content contained in the history textbook.
2. Correctly written containing agreement of subject and predicate, accurate placement of punctuation marks and

content arranged sequentially. Exceptions would be if the language needed in writing must stress non-standard English to portray the speaking part accurately of the involved culture.

3. Written on the basis of what can reasonably be expected of learners in terms of developmental levels. Excessively high or low levels involving teacher expectations should be avoided when pupils write play parts for formal dramatics activities.
4. Challenging and motivating for pupils to write.
5. Written so that all can be involved in this activity. The best writers alone should not be the sole writers. Each pupil should have contributions to make.
6. Fascinating for learner participation in order that roles may be chosen which harmonize with the learner's optimal chances of achievement.
7. Written so that further interest in literature pertaining to diverse academic areas is an end result.
8. Practiced by involved individuals until they feel comfortable for this presentation in front of different classrooms and smaller groups.
9. Stimulating so that increased effort in reading is in evidence.

Roles for the different parts should be assigned or can be volunteered for. Each person in a specific role reading the assigned play part should use appropriate stress, pitch and juncture. Voice inflection and proper enunciation is important for each participant in formal dramatics. Co-operation is needed in writing the parts as well as in the actual role play experience. The formal dramatization should be presented in front of other learners in the school setting.

Using Puppets

Pupils with teacher leadership may make puppets that relate to content read in reading, literature and the social studies, among other curriculum areas. The completed puppets might then be used to role play a given character or situation. Selected puppets are easy to make such as the sack puppet. Here, the learner may use a large paper sack and cut out eyes, nose and mouth. Ears may be drawn or pasted on to the sack puppet. Other forms of puppets are much more time consuming in their making such as a sock puppet. A sock might be used here to make this kind of puppet. The learner might sew on two buttons for eyes, two pieces of felt for the ears, as well as other needed features. Since a sock puppet takes much more time to make as compared to a sack puppet, the teacher might wish to evaluate the desired time that should go into the making of any form of puppet. If artistic endeavours are strongly emphasized by the teacher, then pupils may make sock puppets. There are numerous art objectives to be attained in the making of sock puppets including sequential progress in eye hand coordination and harmonizing specific features such as ears sewed on to the original shape and size of the sock. The sack puppet can be made more quickly and serves and equally purposeful function in its role play use. There are numerous other kinds of puppets that can be made including stick and paper mache' puppets. Regardless of the kind of puppet made, the puppets should be:

1. made neatly and accurately. Creativity can be emphasized as the need arises and is a salient objective for learner attainment;
2. functional according to their purposeful use;
3. related in their making to goals to be attained in the art curriculum;
4. interesting to make in order to obtain learner interest;
5. developed according to their needs to portray definite roles in the curriculum.

Creative dramatics, formal dramatizations and puppetry have specific goals for learner attainment. These activities are not implemented for the sake of doing so but to achieve educational purposes. What are these purposes?

1. To make inherent subject matter more understandable. A pupil may not understand that which has been read but the involved content becomes clear in creative and formal dramatizations as well as in the use of puppetry. Role play experiences tends to breathe life into an ongoing activity.

2. To diagnose what pupils do not understand from reading and discussion of ideas, facts, conclusions and summaries. The diagnosis may be made by the learner in that he/she realizes that what was previously assumed to be understood is vague and needs additional information. The need for additional information was discovered during the creative or formal dramatization, or in the learning opportunity involving puppets.
3. To achieve interest in learning subject matter. The writer has observed numerous times in classroom how learners have become fascinated in attaining subject matter when role play is being used as a teaching device.
4. To perceive transfer values in learning. There are pupils who perceive that role play experiences can be used in numerous academic areas. What is learned then in role play activities in literature may be used in social studies units of study. An increase in integration of subject matter might then be an end result. The integration of literature and social studies provides situations whereby other academic disciplines might also become a part of the previously two mentioned areas of integrated content.
5. To perceive reasons for using what has been learned. Pupils might not understand reasons for using what has been, learned until the inherent subject matter is emphasized in role play experiences. Thus, subject matter learned is used in creative and formal dramatics as well as in puppetry. Use of acquired knowledge, skills and attitudes must be in evidence or pupils will tend to forget previously attained objectives.

Debate in the Classroom

Too frequently, it is believed that debate is for the university level of education, largely or only. The writer believes that early primary grade pupils should have ample opportunities to experience debate on their understanding levels. Thus these pupils need to experience sequential activities in debate which will assist learners to realized that there are opposing points of view on issues. Sometimes within a teacher lead discussion, pupils tend to vigorously discuss both sides of a coin on an issue. The tremendous interest that pupils have on a specific issue propels learners to put forth much effort into discussing the inherent pros and cons. In a debate there are individuals who take a position as well as those who are opposed to that position taken. To be a good debater requires that individuals have much knowledge pertaining to what is being debated. The knowledge is acquired through reading and research. To be a good debater too, requires a clear speaking voice. One here also needs to be influential in presenting ideas. Background information is of utmost importance. A good debater is able to use acquired knowledge to score a victory over the opposition in the debate. How far the teacher wants to stress the rules of a typical debate in the elementary school years is open to analysis. However, the spirit of a debate can be emphasized in any classroom starting with the kindergarten years. To be sure, early primary grade pupils are young and will lack information, skills and inclinations to debate the way juniors and seniors in high school and beyond can perform. However, young children can be guided to attain well in their consideration of a variety of view points, be it pros or cons.

There are definite criteria which should be stressed for elementary pupils in the debate arena. These are the following:

1. Stay on the topic being debated.
2. Be well informed on content and subject matter pursued.
3. Present ideas with clarity and confidence.
4. Maintain quality eye contact when presenting information.
5. Look for additional content when needed to substantiate ideas presented.
6. Justify content presented if asked to do so.
7. Evaluate content presented by others in terms of accuracy, appropriate logic and thought.
8. Ask questions of a presenter of ideas of vagueness is in evidence.

9. Practice using appropriate stress, pitch and juncture when debating ideas with others. A tape recorder or a video-cassette recorder can provide much feedback to the speaker in terms of using language effectively in a debate as well as non-verbal facets of communication.
10. Put forth much effort in becoming a good debater who can use background information to advantage.

No on pupil can achieve all of the above named standards. Each learner, however, should attain as abilities and interests permit. Continuous progress is important for pupils on an individual basis.

If one the intermediate grade levels, a more formal debate between and among learners is desired, the following guidelines need to be followed:

1. Develop a topic for debate involving pupils with teacher assistance.
2. State the topic in debate from such as—Resolved that welfare recipients should not receive any federal assistance after two years of time.
3. Each side in the debate can then prepare content necessary for a quality debate to ensue. Much research is then needed.
4. Ultimately, the debate can be presented in front of the classroom or a larger audience. Each side has a time limit to present ideas to support a point of view.
5. A time for rebuttal by opponents is then necessary. Thus side A rebuts what Side B has said and vice-versa. Questions can also come from the floor.

The debate should challenge each side to prepare well for the event. A challenging debate can certainly make for much learning and motivation for either side of the debate. The topic chosen for the debate should be of interest to the debaters. If interest is inherent, then effort will go in to studying for the debate. The teacher will need to assist each side to locate and use appropriate reference sources. Listeners to the debate should have excellent questions they wish to ask debate participants following the presentation and rebuttal. These questions could provide a further springboard for participants to find needed answers and enrich personal knowledge of the side taken for the debate.

Leisure Time Communication

Being able to visit with others in a recreational setting is certainly a valuable asset to the participant. One can learn much from others in formal conversation settings. Conversing should be an enjoyable experience. The topics to be discussed are endless. A topic selected should be pleasing and interesting for involved persons. Interest seems to keep a conversation going. An interesting conversationalist has much to offer to others. People seem to follow those who converse effectively. Generally, a good conversationalist has much background information and is able to use ideas in a fascinating manner. These individuals are relaxed when conversing and enjoy the company of people. A good conversationalist then is person centered, rather than having sole interest in objects and things en toto. He/she is able to develop and maintain a quality conversation. These individuals are generally admired by others and tend to be popular. Each people should have ample opportunities to become a person who converses well with others. The teacher should be a model and guide here. Creativity rather than direct standards are needed to be able to converse well with others. Classroom time may be given to assist pupils in the art of conversation. This can be time well spent since conversation is the most frequent kind of speaking activity for learners. The teacher then needs to:

1. assist learners to become relaxed individuals when engaging in conversation;
2. reward pupils with praise for genuine improvement in conversing with others. The praise is given to reward, not retard abilities in oral communication. The focal point is upon helping learners to relax and wishing to engage spontaneously in conversation;
3. work worth pupils so that there is no ridicule of what others are saying. Rather each pupil assists the others to participate actively in conversation;

4. plan a wholesome classroom environment in which there are variety of rich learning activities so that pupils achieve skills to have content to converse about;
5. have materials, objects and re-alia in the classroom whereby pupils can learn from these items in an incidental manner. Learning on one's own certainly should build background information within pupils so that improved conversation is a salient end result;
6. develop positive attitudes of each pupil toward the self and toward others. An adequate self-concept is necessary to be a good conversationalist;
7. achieve within the learner feelings of wanting to converse with others;
8. study each pupil carefully to ascertain what would assist each learner in attaining more effectively in conversation;
9. have pupils achieve positive attitudes toward conversation as a valuable speaking activity;
10. continue to work with all pupils in developing sequential conversation skills.

In Closing

There are numerous speaking activities which learners need to achieve skill in. Life in school and in society demands that individuals be quality communicators. The teacher of language arts then must establish goals of excellence in oral communication. These objectives should stress knowledge, skills and attitudinal ends. A balance among these three kinds of objectives should be an end result. Learning opportunities to attain these objectives should provide for individual differences so each pupil may attain optimally in oral communication. The learning opportunities should be of interest, meaningful purposeful and challenging to the individual learner. The world of work needs individuals who communicate well. Personal enrichment also stresses that each person be able to communicate effectively.

Speaking Activities and the Pupil

Being able to communicate content effectively to others is important. Certainly, individuals are at a disadvantage if they cannot make their needs and thoughts known through the use of oral language. Persons with verbal fluency in oral communication have much going in their favour. Generally, they should achieve at a higher level in obtaining and maintaining a desirable job or position as compared to those who communicate ineffectively. Many misunderstandings occur between and among individuals, groups, and nations due to ineffective means of communication. Positive human relations may come about due to proficiency in expressing ideas orally.

The teacher must think of various approaches and techniques to help pupils individually achieve to their optimum in speaking. Furthermore, the teacher needs to determine the present oral communication achievement level of each learner and guide in the direction of achieving continuous optimal progress. Van Allen writes the following involving oral communication:

> The experience of verbalization as well as the verbalization of experience is essential to the education of most human beings. Both require oral interaction within some kind of a language community. When the close language group of a child changes from the home and neighbourhood to a classroom setting, the need for verbalization increases, but often the opportunity decreases. The traditional school emphasis on the acquisition of the literacy skills of reading and writing has overshadowed the need for the oracy skills of speaking and listening.

Literacy skills and oracy skills enjoy a reciprocal relationship in an educational setting and must be thought of as reinforcing each other. Teachers using a language experience approach do not decide whether reading is more important than speaking or vice versa. They plan for both! They are aware that growth in oral communication is likely to represent growth in reading also.

Using Puppets

Puppets can be used effectively to help pupils progress continuously in speaking. Puppets may be purchased, made by the teacher, or developed by pupils. Depending upon the time available in the classroom setting, pupils with teacher guidance might make sack puppets, stick puppets or sock puppets. Stick puppets and sack puppets basically are relatively easy to make by pupils on any grade level. Pupil, individually or in a committee, may make puppets pertaining to an ongoing unit of study. If pupils, for example, are studying a unit on the farm, a puppet pertaining to a farm animal can be made. Thus, learners creatively may develop speaking parts for farm animals in a group setting. If pupils are pursuing a unit on the factor, puppets can be made pertaining to different workers on an assembly line. Speaking parts also need to be developed for these puppets in order to assist pupils to achieve well in the oral use of language.

In learning activities involving the use of puppets in speaking, the curriculum area of art is stressed. Thus, pupils may be evaluated in developing proficiency in oral communication as well as in revealing creative behaviour in art.

Hennings notes the following kinds of puppets which pupils with teacher guidance may utilize:

- hand-sized paper bags to which features have been added with flo-pens, crayons, construction paper, yarn, or colored pictures clipped for magazines;
- socks, stockings, or white work gloves to which features have been added with buttons, yarn, scraps, or material, twine, glitter, tinsel, felt;
- the hand by marking features directly on the fist or the balls of each finger;

- styrofoam or ping pong balls stuck on the ends of the fingers or on the ends of ice cream bar sticks. Again glitter, tinsel, buttons, and yarn form the features of the stick puppets.

Puppets that a puppeteer holds directly over the face can be made from:

- paper plates with features drawn in with crayon and flo-pen, with eyes cut through the plates;
- full-sized paper bags into which eye, nose, and mouth openings have been cut. A fringe of carpet stapled across the top of the bag simulates curly hair, large eyes with long lashes are drawn around the eye openings, and an outwardly projecting nose is stapled above the nose opening. Puppeteers determine locations for eye and nose openings by slipping on their paper bags. This insures a good fit;
- the leg of an old pantyhose slipped onto a wire coat hanger, the large triangle of which has been pulled downward to form a rectangle. The pantyhose is tied top and bottom, perhaps braided at the top to form a pigtail. Features are added to the stretched hose with construction paper and flo-pen.

Body puppets that completely cover the puppeteer can be made from:

- large-sized cartons from which one of the six sides has been removed and through which a head hole has been cut in the opposite side. Cartons can be painted colorfully;
- people-shaped and -sized cutouts. Youngsters stretch out on a piece of heavy graded cardboard while a friend traces the body outline. The youngsters cut out the outline, color themselves in, and hold their puppets in front of them during sharing time.

Using Dramatizations

Dramatic activities can help pupils progress in the oral use of language. Creative dramatics needs to be emphasized much in teaching-learning situations pertaining to different units of study. In a learning activity involving creative dramatics, pupils spontaneously develop speaking parts as the need arises. If pupils on the first grade level have listened to or have read the story,

"Goldilocks and the Three Bears," they might dramatize this story using spontaneous oral language. Pupils may volunteer to play selected roles in the dramatic activity. At other times, the teacher could appoint individual pupils in playing diverse roles in the dramatization.

Dramatic activities help pupils in attaching meaning to what has been learned. Learnings then become more lifelike and real. Pupils can feel and think like the individual whose role is being played. Teacher-pupil planning may be utilized in evaluating learner achievement in dramatic activities. Evaluation procedures used should not hinder creative endeavours of pupils. Nor, should evaluation destroy pupil enjoyment of creative dramatics.

Formal dramatizations might also be utilized in the elementary school. Play parts may then be written by pupils with teacher guidance. The parts are written prior to their use in formal dramatizations. Following the writing of diverse roles of characters in the play, pupils may then practice reading the parts. The final presentation may be presented to peers and to pupils in other classrooms. Background scenery can be developed as the need arises. If learners desire, they may memorize individual play parts rather than reading it orally. Polished performances of the play are not necessary. The formal dramatization should assist pupils to improve in and enjoy being involved in diverse oral communication experiences.

Using Conversation

It is important that pupils develop needed skills in conversation. Conversation is the most frequently used means of oral communication. Pupils need to become proficient in conversation. Friendships may be developed on the basis on individuals being able to converse well with others. An interesting conversationalist in generally in demand in terms of using one's leisure time well. Rubin writes the following:

> Socialization is a process that prepares an individual to live in society. Human beings are social animals. The better we know one another, the better we are able to get along with one another. It is through social discourse such as conversation that we learn

more about our friends and neighbors and, many times, about ourselves as well. The need to converse with one another is seen daily in any classroom, whether it is a university graduate class or a kindergarten. When an instructor is interrupted during a class period and must stop to talk to a visitor or leave the class for a short while, what happens? Practically anyone can predict the students' behaviour in this situation. They start talking to one another. No prompting is necessary, sometimes to the dismay of the teacher. Children naturally like to talk, to exchange pleasantries, ideas, comments, and so on. The teacher must understand this need in students and provide, not only an environment where students will feel free to engage in spontaneous, informal, and nonstructured talks with one another but also provide time for this to take place.

Since children as well as adults spend most of their time in conversational oral discourse, teachers should help students to be more adept, at this skill. Being a good conversationalist helps individuals to be freer to communicate with others and thus plays a large role in enhancing self-concept.

In being a good conversationalist, pupils must inwardly consider the following criteria:

1. much background information is needed;
2. individuals must be interested in and like other people;
3. an adequate self-concept is necessary in being able to communicate ideas with confidence;
4. thoughts must be communicated on the present understanding level of listeners;
5. proper voice inflection is needed when conversing with others;
6. the skilled use of language is important;
7. a good conversationalist needs to have a large speaking vocabulary;
8. proper sequence of ideas is important;
9. nonverbal communication must be stressed when ideas are communicated orally.

The teacher should have pupils practice conversation skills during the school day. Certainly, this is using time wisely in the elementary school, since conversation may be the most frequently used speaking activity used by individuals. Time should be given by the teacher, if at all possible, to converse with pupils before the school day begins as well as when it ends. Pupils may also practice conversation skills in the school cafeteria during lunch time.

Using Discussions

Participating in discussions is a frequent type of speaking activity for most individuals. In group situations in society, participants engage in discussing problem areas. Possible solutions to identified problems are then discussed. There certainly are many problems that individuals in society may discuss with others. Also, in the classroom setting, pupils with teacher supervision should discuss relevant problems on the appropriate developmental level of participants. What are some possible relevant problems that individuals in society and learners in school might discuss?

1. How can an adequate supply of energy to meet the needs of consumers domestically, be acquired?
2. How might wars be minimized or eliminated in diverse areas of the world?
3. How may individuals from minority groups get their fair share of the good things in life?
4. How can an equitable system of taxation be developed?
5. How should candidates for public office be selected?
6. How should campaigns for office be financed?
7. What can be done to cut down on crime locally, as well as nationally?
8. Which are the better approaches available to rehabilitate those arrested and convicted of crimes?
9. How can inflation be curbed to a reasonable degree?
10. What can be done to establish full employment?
11. How can welfare recipients best be assisted in society?

Once problems have been identified, solutions need to be discussed. In the school setting, pupils need to pursue research activities on their developmental level. Background information obtained is used in discussion situations. Solutions to problems should be tentative with possible modifications made as evidence indicates.

There are flexible guidelines developed through teacher-pupil planning which might be used in assessing progress in discussions. These guidelines, among others, may include the following:

1. participators in a discussion should not digress from the topic being considered;
2. each member in a committee should participate in the discussion;
3. effective and clear communication of ideas is important if the discussion is to progress;
4. the chairperson and participants in the discussion must respect the thinking of others;
5. ideas that are not clear need to be clarified in the discussion;
6. discussants must have much background information to be a good member of a discussion group;
7. ideas presented should be evaluated critically in an atmosphere of respect;
8. creative ideas need to be encouraged in ongoing discussion groups.

Anderson and Lapp enumerate the following possibilities for discussion in the children's literature curriculum:

1. ***Character:*** What are the clues to characters suggested in the writing? From what is said or the action taken, what influence can be made about the individual? Why does the character act the way he does? What are his values? Did anyone change in the story? Why?
2. ***Setting:*** Can you see where the story is happening? How do those in the story act because of the setting? Is there a basis struggle between the people in the story and the nature of the place where they live?

3. ***Mood—feeling—tone:*** What words are used to tell you how the writer feels? What is the tone of voice of the storyteller? Is it serious? Humorous? Is this a true experience?

4. ***Story Pattern:*** What would you tell if you had only the first paragraph to guide you? Can you tell what happened by reading only the last paragraph? Is there a theme or lesson that the writer is illustrating? Who is telling the story? What difference does it make?

Using Interviews

Many individuals engage in interviewing others in getting needed information, as well as to explore interests in a variety of topics. It is important for pupils to develop relevant understandings, skills, and attitudinal objectives pertaining to interviewing others. Which important flexible criteria may be developed through teacher-pupil planning and used in assessing achievement in conducting interviews?

1. Pupils must have adequate background knowledge on their level of development to conduct an interview.
2. Respect for others is important when conducting an interview. Ideas need to be clearly communicated.
3. Questions must be carefully developed prior to conducting an interview.
4. It may be necessary to record information obtained during the interview.
5. The interviewer must be a good listener to comprehend information.
6. The interview must be initiated as well as culminated in a way satisfying to both the interviewer and the individual being interviewed.
7. Following the interview, data gathered need to be evaluated, summarized and written.

Pupils with teacher guidance may evaluate if these guidelines or standards have been achieved. If they have not been achieved, pupils should be guided in determining reasons. Perhaps, the standards should be modified or revised as the need arises.

Making Introductions

In society, it is important that individuals learn appropriate methods of making introductions. Visitors must be introduced to others so that feelings of belonging and security result. No one desires to be left out of social situations involving conversation or discussions. Pupils need to develop skills to help visitors feel comfortable and wanted in social situations. Creative ways need devising in assisting pupils to achieve relevant objectives pertaining to the making of introductions. The following guidelines, among others, are important to stress in teaching-learning situations involving the making of introductions:

1. Politeness is of utmost importance.
2. A satisfying way should be devised when introducing one person to another individual or group.
3. Names should be pronounced clearly in the making of introductions.
4. Information about each person being introduced should accompany introductions being made.
5. The introducer should guide those being introduced in following the introduction through with satisfying conversation. Introductions made should be followed with conversation.
6. Consideration for others is important in the making of and following through with the introducing process.

Using Oral Reports

Oral reports presented by pupils to the class can do much in helping develop proficiency in speaking. Reports given might relate to ongoing units of study from diverse curriculum areas. Learners should perceive knowledge as being related rather than isolated. For example, if pupils are studying a unit on the changing surface of the earth in science, pupils may volunteer to report on topics such as the following:

1. erosion;
2. volcanoes;
3. folding;

4. faults;
5. magma;
6. lava.

There are many skills that can be developed during the time that reports are being developed. The following skills are important:

1. reading for a variety of purposes;
2. note taking over content read;
3. outlining content in terms of organisation;
4. using various reference sources;
5. utilizing the card catalog;
6. using the mechanics of writing such as correct spelling, capitalization, punctuation, usage, and handwriting;
7. organizing content in the report to present to listeners.

Pupils should be guided in achieving desired standards when giving oral reports. These standards might well include the following:

1. Visual aids are used in presenting the report.
2. Ideas are clearly presented to listeners.
3. Order of ideas presented is appropriate.
4. Main ideas rather than isolated facts are inherent in the report.
5. A pleasant speaking voice is used.
6. Content in the report is adequately researched.
7. Peers are listening carefully to the report.
8. Main ideas presented are supported by facts.

These standards need to be considered in terms of each pupil's present achievement level. Excessively difficult goals definitely should not be the experience of any individual pupil. Nor, should objectives exist for pupils where little or no challenge is presented for learning. Objectives must be adjusted to the present achievement level of each pupil with new learnings being developed in proper sequence from the child's own unique perception. Good attitudes toward learning may then be developed. Positive attitudes toward learning will guide pupils in achieving desired goals in speaking. Attainable goals only, should be stated for each individual pupil. Learning activities can then be selected in guiding pupils to achieve desired objectives.

The pupil need to have ample opportunities to assess personal achievement after having presented an oral report. This must be done in an atmosphere of respecting the self. The pupil can listen to his/her own recorded voice to evaluate sequential progress. Previous recordings might be compared with later recordings. The teacher serves as a guide in helping pupils to achieve well in oral communication.

Using Oral Reading

Pupils should have ample opportunities to develop proficiency in oral reading. Pupils need to develop competency in presenting ideas to others through oral reading. Learners should have ample opportunities to listen individually to recordings of their very own oral reading. Pupils individually may work in the direction of improving oral reading by listening to recordings of earlier attempts in oral reading and marking comparisons with later attempts. In guiding pupils to achieve in oral reading, the following guidelines might well be followed:

1. Learners should practice reading a given selection before it is read orally to others in the class setting.
2. Guidance must be given to pupils in using proper stress, pitch, and juncture in oral reading.
3. Content must be communicated accurately to listeners.
4. Self-evaluation, as well as group evaluation, of achievement in oral reading is important.
5. Each pupil should be evaluated in terms of his own unique present possible achievement.
6. Each pupil needs to be guided to make continuous progress in oral reading.

7. Oral reading should be an enjoyable learning activity for pupils.

It is important for pupils to become proficient in oral reading to be able to communicate ideas effectively to others.

Giving and Following Directions

Very often, individuals are asked by guests to give directions in going from one place to another. Pupils need to develop proficiency in giving directions. They must then become familiar with important local landmarks. Learners should have much practice in directing individuals to specific places and points of interest. The child's home or school can be the reference point from which directions are given initially. Later, other reference points may be utilized so that learners develop flexibility in thinking pertaining to the giving of directions.

Teacher-pupil planning might be used in determining which landmarks would be relevant in a given community. The following, among others, may be important places or areas in a given community:

1. parks and school buildings;
2. selected stores and offices;
3. major highways and streets;
4. museums and libraries;
5. the train depot and airport;
6. important bus stops;
7. selected churches and governmental buildings.

As the need arises, additional landmarks can be identified. The pupil on the appropriate developmental level should practice giving directions to others in the class setting pertaining to going from the local school to an important place in the community. Learners may also give directions to a classmate so that the latter may locate an object in the classroom or on the school ground.

In learning to follow directions, pupils at a learning center in the class setting may pursue the following activities:

1. make a relief map;
2. develop a diorama;
3. work a written exercise;
4. complete a test;
5. make a model plane or car;
6. develop a selected dish of food;
7. learn to play a game;
8. make a simple musical instrument;
9. develop a set of directions for others to locate a specific object;
10. perform a folk dance.

Pupils must learn to give directions clearly and accurately. A learning center pertaining to activities in the giving of directions should prove helpful to pupils. Teacher-pupil planning may be utilized in developing tasks for the learning center.

In Summary

There are numerous speaking activities in which pupils should become proficient. These include the using of puppets, dramatizations, conversation, discussions, interviews, introductions, oral reports, oral reading, and the giving of directions. Teachers must accept pupils where they are presently in achievement and give guidance in helping learners to make continuous progress in oral communication.

Greene and Petty present the following objectives in oral communication which provide criteria against which learners' progress may be evaluated:

1. To converse with classmates and adults easily and courteously.
2. To participate in discussions, sticking to the point and respecting the opinions of others.
3. To organise information and report it effectively.
4. To plan an interview and carry it through courteously and effectively.

5. To use the telephone competently.
6. To conduct a meeting by means of parliamentary procedures.
7. To give clear directions, explanations, and announcements orally.
8. To tell a story or personal experience effectively and interestingly.
9. To greet others properly in various social situations.
10. To participate in choral speaking.
11. To make use of parliamentary procedures as a member of a group.
12. To take part in a dramatic activity.

REFERENCES

1. Anderson, Paul S. *Linguistics in the Elementary School Classroom*. New York: The Macmillan Company, 1971. Part Two.
2. Anderson, Paul S. and Diana Lapp. *Language Skills in Elementary Education*. Third Edition. New York: The Macmillan Company, 1979.
3. Chenfield, Mimi Brodsky. *Teaching Language Arts Creatively*. New York: Harcourt Brace Jovanovich, Publishers, 1987.
4. Ediger, Marlow. "Teach Them to Communicate," *School and Community* (February, 1971), p. 12.
5. Ediger, Marlow. *The Elementary Curriculum, A Handbook*. Kirksville, Missouri: Simpson Publishing Company, 1988.
6. Greene, Harry A., and Walter T. Petty. *Developing Language Skills in the Elementary Schools*. Boston: Allyn and Bacon, Inc., 1975.
7. Hennings, Dorothy Grant. *Communication in Action*. Chicago: Rand McNally College Publishing Company, 1978.
8. Lorber, Michael A., and Walter D. Pierce. *Objectives, Methods, and Evaluation for Secondary Teaching*. Second Edition. Englewood Cliffs, New Jersey: Prentice-Hall, Inc. 1983.
9. Petty, Walter T. (Ed.). *Issues and Problems in the Elementary Language Arts*. Boston: Allyn and Bacon, Inc., 1968. Chapter Six.
10. Roberts, Paul. *Modern Grammar*. New York: Harcourt, Brace and World, Inc., 1968. Chapter Six.

11. Rubin, Dorothy. *Teaching Elementary Language Arts* New York: Holt Rinehart and Winston, 1980.

12. Tidyman, Willard F., and Marguerite Butterfield. *Teaching the Language Arts*. Second Edition. New York: McGraw-Hill Book Company, Inc., 1959. Chapters Three and Twelve.

13. Tiedt, Iris M., and Sidney W. Tiedt. *Contemporary English in the Elementary School*. Englewood Cliffs: Prentice-Hall, Inc., 1975.

14. Trauger, Wilmer K. *Language Arts in Elementary Schools*. New York: McGraw-Hill Book Company, 1963. Chapter Three.

15. Van Allen, Roach. *Language Experiences in Communication*. New York: Houghton-Mifflin Company, 1976.

6

Spelling and the Language Arts

Pupils need to become good spellers to communicate effectively with others. Spelling is a tool to use to make known personal needs as well as to communicate feelings and appreciations. Correct spelling of words will always be necessary, even with the mass amount of technology available to many in society. Why? A person does not always have a computer at a specific place to process words. If the word processor is available, individuals still need to spell words reasonably close in accuracy for the spell checkers program to work and be effective. Thus, if a word is misspelled greatly, spell checkers will not list the needed correct spelling of the word on the monitor. Then too, sometimes it is more convenient to use long hand in writing rather than starting a computer up and using the attached printer. A personal message written in long hand may convey information to the reader better as compared to a printed document. How then might pupils be assisted to become proficient spellers?

Guidelines for Teaching Spelling

We would like to state selected guidelines which good teachers have used successfully in the teaching of spelling. First, pupils should understand the meaning of words to be mastered before studying their spelling. Meaning theory suggest that if pupils understand context, they will learn more effectively and depth learning may then be in evidence. Teachers need to take time for pupils to give definitions and/or be able to use a word contextually within a sentence. Some words are difficult to define and should then be used by the learner in a meaningful sentence. If a word can be defined and a pupil is ready to explain the meaning, he/she should do so. We believe that being able to use a word in a sentence and with a clear meaning, the learner is then ready to study the correct spelling of that word. We hope that words mastered in spelling will also be retained in memory for reading content as well as for writing in different academic areas. It is good if a pupil makes use of spelling words in many ways such as in reading those same words in literature, social studies, science and mathematics content. If pupils do not identify words correctly or a halting procedure is used in reading, the chances are comprehension will suffer in the process.

Second, the teacher needs to provide a variety of learning opportunities to assist pupils in learning to spell words correctly. Do I approve of the use of spelling textbooks in guiding pupils in learning to spell? It is not the textbook that is good or bad, but it depends upon how they are used by pupils and the teacher. There can be selected fascinating activities for learners within the confines of a spelling textbook that has been carefully chosen. Thus, here are activities that truly benefit and make spelling enjoyable. For example, in one lesson in a spelling textbook, there are the usual list of words for pupils to master. How are they to achieve this task? One approach in the text is to have pupils fill in blank spaces in sentences given, whereby the words for the fill in, come from that list. Pupils can be very attentive in doing this when application is made of the new words to be mastered in spelling. Seemingly, many pupils are interested in this activity even though it does occur generally in each weekly lesson. We think that the activity has variation each week due to changing words that are used to fill in the blank spaces within sentences. The teacher should always observe pupils to notice if boredom sets in and, if it does, to switch to a different experience. The teacher cannot do a prefect job of varying activities when boredom sets in, but he/she can do the best possible to keep pupils on task. With twenty to thirty pupils in a classroom, it is difficult to provide for individual needs of all pupils. Additional tasks in a textbook to be used to help pupils learn to spell words correctly are cross word puzzles that use words from the weekly list in the spelling text. Friendly and business letters are to be written using selected words from the spelling list. The teacher needs to be creative in text use in teaching spelling by thinking of and implementing other learning opportunities than those indicated in the weekly lesson.

Third, we believe that pupils should develop a definite methodology in learning to spell words. A good speller, no doubt, has a workable method of learning to spell words correctly. Those who do not spell words correctly, in many cases, may need a new methodology in mastering the correct spelling of words. We like the method that many pupils have used correctly in learning to spell. Thus, the pupil needs to look at the new word carefully. It is doubtful that a teaching strategy will work if the pupil here does not look at the word carefully if pupils are truly focusing upon a word to acquire in correct spelling. Next, the pupil should pronounce the word correctly. Spelling errors are made due to inaccurate pronunciation of words. Hopefully, the pupil will listen to all the sounds with that word being studied for mastery in spelling. Involved sounds need to be associated with the correct graphemes or symbols. The learner then should practice writing the word once. The written word may then be checked with the correct spelling. Too frequently, pupils are asked to write a word five or ten times immediately; the word written might be misspelled then ten times. Better it is, to write the word once and check accuracy of spelling. Once the word is spelled correctly, the pupil may wish to write it several times in a contextual situation.

Fourth, pupils need to perceive reasons for learning to spell a given set of words, be if from the text book or from other sources. Purpose is vital for success in learning to spell words correctly. The teacher may say why it is important to learn to spell words correctly in a specific lesson. A deductive approach is then in evidence. Inductive procedures may also be used such as a teacher asking questions of learners so that the latter understands the merit of learning to spell a given number of words correctly. Extrinsic rewards are used by some teachers to motivate pupils to study and master the new set of words in spelling. Thus, a teacher may say how many words need to be spelled correctly by Friday to receive a prize. These prizes are generally visible to pupils. Learners then know what to do to receive the award. We recommend that if extrinsic awards are given for learning, pupils should, as soon as possible, feel a desire from within to learn to spell words correctly as an intrinsic motivational device. The extrinsic rewards should be removed as soon as possible and not become a crutch or lever used to spell words correctly.

Fifth, pupils should learn to spell words correctly in a contextual situation. The new words are then used in functional situations. Words and their correct spelling are meaningful within a practical endeavour. We recommend that pupils determine useful ways to spell words correctly within contextual situations. The learner may then use the new words when writing an invitation, for his/her birthday party. Further uses include writing business and friendly letters, content in greeting cards, prose and poetry, narrative and expository accounts, short stories, announcements and thank you notices, among other functional writing activities.

How many words should a pupil learn to spell correctly per week? This depends upon the present achievement level of the involved learner. To be sure, too many words may be required for a pupil to master in spelling. The opposite extreme would be too few words are learned to spell words correctly in a given time interval. The teacher needs to observe each pupil and notice what a reasonable number of words might be. There is nothing sacred about mastering twenty spelling words per week in the third grade, for example. It is important always to challenge pupils to do their very best in all curriculum areas.

Sixth, the spelling curriculum should be as individualized as possible. To some educators this means that each pupil should have a unique set of words to master in spelling. These words may come from those the learner misspelled from diverse writing activities the preceding week. The number of words in this list must be adjusted to fit the abilities of the individual learner so that too many or too few words are not required for mastery within a designated time. This seems to work fairly well in the spelling curriculum provided that learners do not refuse to use words in writing unless they are spelled correctly. The reason for doing this pertains to keeping the number reasonable of those words misspelled and needing to be studied for mastery. Another approach that might be used pertains to adjusting the number of words from the spelling textbook that need to be spelled correctly per week. Pupil A then may find it easy to learn to spell all words correctly plus a bonus list of words per week. Pupil B might be able to spell ten of the twenty words correctly per week. Once Pupil B has experienced success, he/she might become motivated to increase the number of words spelled correctly per week. We have noticed that pupils who are successful do volunteer to do more work then formerly and go beyond minimal levels. It takes time and effort for the teacher to make these adjustments for individual pupils. But with good teaching, teachers attempt to provide for individual differences among learners in the classroom. Even though the spelling curriculum in individualized, there may be pupils who wish to work collaboratively. Learning styles differ from one pupil to another such as wanting to work intrapersonally or by the self as contrasted with interpersonal or committee work. Here, pupils should have a voice in how they wish to study and learn, individually or in a group, to achieve more optimally in spelling.

Seventh, we recommend that creatively be stressed in pupils learning to spell words. So often, spelling is taught as role learning and memorization. Rather, the pupil should have ample opportunities to spell words correctly within creative poetry and prose written or within plays and stories written. Here, we recommend that pupils evaluate correct spelling of words after the creative product has been completed, not during the writing endeavour. Pupils may wish to assist each other when correct spelling of words is emphasized at the end of the creative writing experience.

Eighth, we recommend strongly to provide incentives for pupils to volunteer to learn to spell more words correctly, than those assigned or even going beyond the bonus words. It is surprising what pupils will do to put forth effort when the sky becomes the limit. Intrinsic motivation certainly can come into being when pupils feel rewarded and successful in learning. The teaching of spelling is not known to be the most stimulating curriculum area, but the teacher can work in the direction of it becoming motivating and challenging.

Which Words Should Pupils Master in Spelling?

This question has been debated for a long time. There are teachers who assume that the spelling text alone contains salient words for pupils to master in spelling. The text has had a long history of use in teaching and learning situations. We have looked at spelling texts that came out in the early 1930s. These books had lists of words only for pupils to memorize in spelling per week. There were no suggested learning activities. The teacher each week needed to work out all learning activities that would assist pupils in learning to spell each word correctly. Presently, there are teachers who believe that no spelling texts be used and believe better teaching is an end result. A well chosen textbook should definitely not hinder good teaching. Ingenious teachers can stimulate pupils to learn with interesting activities that capture pupil attention. No textbook needs to be followed religiously in terms of the recommendations in the manual. The good teacher chooses from among the different activities stressed in the manual section. Additional learning opportunities are brought into the teaching and learning situation that provide for individual differences among pupils. No writer of quality materials would suggest following the manual 100 per cent. Writer realize that the teacher is the one to implement the teaching suggestions and must vary the kinds of learning opportunities provided for pupils so that securing the attention of pupils is there and pupils are actively engaged in learning. No using a basal textbook, in and of itself does not make for good teaching. The teacher is there to study and implement teaching strategies that assist pupils to attain relevant objectives in the spelling curriculum.

If the teacher uses words for each pupil that the latter missed in everyday functional writing, the teacher still needs to have quality approaches in teaching so that individual pupils learn and achieve. Pupils need to be motivated when attempting to master the spelling words missed in daily writing. The number per week to be mastered needs to be adjusted to what a child can achieve in a reasonable manner. Certainly, a pupil may experience failure if too many words need mastering or become bored if too little is expected in a given time interval.

There have been successful teachers whom we have observed that emphasize spelling words that have been chosen for pupils to master which are based on research study of pupils' writings were selected by the teacher within a list for mastery learning by local pupils. The Dolch List (1954) has been used in teaching spelling by many teachers, even though it is not a recently developed list. This list has 220 words that Dolch's research found should be learned by pupils as sight words. This might then cut down on the number of errors that pupils make in spelling as well as in word identification in reading. These are the most frequently occurring words in spelling errors in pupils' writing, according to Dolch. We feel the Dolch List still has much merit because these words are commonly used by pupils in everyday writing and reading today. The word list is not divided by grade levels but is contained in one listing. We recommend that teachers study pupils writings to notice which words are used most frequently. Teachers should be involved in doing research and may come up with a revision of the Dolch List. With personal computers in the school and in the home, the statistical procedures, we believe, have been greatly simplified and become user friendly. With personal computers and assistance from educational researchers, teachers now have more opportunities to engage in research and attempt to solve classroom problems than ever before.

There are numerous statements of objectives in spelling that educators have developed over the years. We believe the following are worthy for teachers to emphasize in the curriculum:

1. Assist pupils to master those words which are needed in order to express oneself clearly and accurately in writing.
2. Guide pupils to achieve good study habits which assist the learner to pursue diverse kinds and types of writing experiences. Preservance is a key concept here. Pupils need to establish plans in writing, work toward their achievement and personally monitor progress. We have noticed pupils who attempt to give up too soon on assigned or voluntary written work. Encouragement by peers and the teacher will go a long way in motivating learner achievement. Pupil pride in achievement aids in setting higher goals in spelling within the writing activity.
3. Develop within pupils a set of standards in learning that will help pupils to spell words correctly. These standards involve using phonics to make associations

between symbol and sound where this consistency is in evidence. Pupils also need to learn to spell selected words by sight when the consistency between symbol and sound and sound just is not there. Correct pronunciation of words is important so that spelling errors are not made due to that factor.

4. Help pupils to realize that correct spelling is a social courtesy and incorrect spelling may reflect negatively upon the pupil.

5. Direct quality teaching to have pupils, when ready, learn keyboard skills to use the personal computer to engage in writing. This is necessary for all pupils. Spell checkers can do much to minimize spelling errors when word processing is used. Computers are increasingly becoming user friendly.

6. Provide friendly assistance to pupils who need help in spelling so that success can be stressed as much as possible in the writing curriculum. A good speller in the classroom may also provide this help. If the latter approach is used, change or rotate who gives the assistance. Each pupil also needs to pursue his/her own interests in purposeful learning.

7. Emphasize the interest factor by letting pupils choose the topic to write on, regardless of the purpose involved. Thus, if pupils are to write limericks, the learner may select within that framework the contents of the limerick. Interest goes a long way in providing effort for learning.

8. Let pupils work together in the writing activity involving spelling. Observe theat each is participating actively in the spelling/writing experience.

9. Involve pupils in self-evaluation as well as the teacher participating actively in appraising learner progress. Collaboratively, a learning community may be developed that stresses quality writing in the curriculum.

10. Establish quality sequence in pupil learning to spell words correctly. If pupils are involved in determining which words need to be learned in spelling, a

> psychological spelling curriculum is in evidence. Sequence then resides within the learner, not in other sources. Should the teacher determine sequence in pupil learning to spell words, a logical approach is in evidence since the teacher determines the order of learning activities for pupils (Ediger, 1988).

Pupils should definitely realize that spelling and reading are related, not isolated entities. Being able to spell more words correctly as time goes on should reflect learners' increasing abilities to become better readers. The goals of spelling and reading instruction should develop confidence in the learner to achieve at a higher level commensurate with inherent abilities of the involved pupil (Ediger, 1988).

Cautions in Learning to Spell Words

There are selected cautions that teachers need to be aware of when teaching spelling. Pupils and the teacher should not go overboard on phonics when correct spelling of words is being emphasized. Thus, there are numerous words that lack consistency between symbol and sound such as my, pie, buy, sigh, kite, white and bye. Each of these words contains the long *i* sound and yet that sound is spelled differently from word to word.

Second, pupils need to learn to spell vital words that are truly useful. Too frequently, words listed in a spelling textbook may not be important enough for pupils to learn to spell. We believe the teacher needs to study word lists in spelling texts, if used and ascertain the worth of learning to spell each word. There is so much to learn that it behooves the teacher to choose carefully what pupils are to learn.

Third, if pupils are to learn to spell a given set of words, they should make application of what has been learn. Much forgetting occurs of mastered words in spelling if there are no related practical endeavours, meaning that applying what has been learned is important. We believe much time is wasted in learning if pupils are tested only, on the number of words spelled correctly on Friday and yet the involved pupil perceives no practical application of these kinds of learning activities.

Fourth, too frequently, memorization of correct spelling of words is emphasized and yet meaningful experiences are lacking. Generally, memorization is done for the sake of passing a test and in this case to receive a good grade from the teacher. We would like to see the evaluation process change to where more emphasis is placed upon pupils' making application of words being studied for correct spelling in ongoing lessons and units of study.

Fifth, pupils in many cases lack readiness factors for learning to spell words correctly. What are these readiness factors? Certainly, a pupil should also be able to use the new words being studied contextually in a sentence that makes sense. Pupils individually need to use the proper tools at hand to analyze parts within a word such as grapheme/phoneme relationships. For those irregularly spelled words, a basic sight vocabulary needs to be developed by learners.

Sixth, too often, pupils in a class are taught as if all possess readiness for the same number of words to be mastered in spelling. Pupils are individuals, not a mass of objects. Learners come with feelings, dreams and hopes. They need to be treated as human beings with much worth. Thus, the teacher needs to help each pupil to learn as much as possible. The opportunity for pupil learning is now and we need to take advantage of these opportunities.

Seventh, there is a lack of emphasis upon diagnosis and remediation when teaching spelling. We need to determine why pupils individually are making errors in the incorrect spelling of words. Do pupils go by phonics too much when learning to spell words and yet one or more of these words are not that phonetic in sound/symbol relationships? Is legible handwriting a cause for improper; spelling of words? Pupils need to experience as much success as possible so that motivation is there to learn, grow and achieve.

Technology and Spelling

There definitely is room for technology use in the spelling curriculum. Its use is one way to strengthen teaching and learning in ongoing and units of study. Computer use should be made available to teachers and learners. The software content of the computer should not duplicate with other materials of instruction, but should provide learning activities which also assist pupils to improve in the area of spelling. There are drill and practice exercises which truly help pupils to achieve more optimally. Words here need to be highly useful with strategies of learning that provide for each pupil's ability level. The drill and practice experiences give learners an opportunity to rehearse the correct spelling of words. There are needs for drill and practice so that pupils may practice and retain the correct spelling of words at a more optimal level of achievement. Much of what we remember has been presented to us in different ways using a variety of learning activities. Here software and computer use can provide this variety with innovating ways and procedures displayed on the monitor. Also, there are numerous games that pupils may engage in individually or collaboratively that stress the correct spelling of words, as shown on the monitor. These games may provide wholesome competitive activities between two or three sides. Thus, in rotation, one side may score points for the correct spelling of one or more words whereas the two other sides or single side, in sequence, may come back with spelling other words correctly to score points. The winner has the most words spelled correctly Games in spelling are good for pupils to play competitively, if appropriate attitudes are in evidence.

Tutorial software programs provide new words for pupil mastery, as shown sequentially on the monitor. Diverse learning opportunities are provided so that pupils may master these new words in spelling. Also, there are simulations that attempt to represent life-like situations, where by pupils are to engage in problem solving in virtual reality. The encounters here are quite realistic and provide for situations involving higher levels of cognition such as critical and creative thinking as well as problem solving. At the same time, pupils are engaged in attempting to spell words correctly. Since a more utilitarian situation is involved in simulations, pupils tend to find these activities to be challenging and real.

We find that pupils engaging is using the word processor to write creatively or functionally is one of the better ways to stress correct spelling of words. Here, pupils need to be proficient in spelling during the actual composing situation when using the words processor. It is true that spell checkers does provide much assistance in helping pupils make corrections in spelling. However, the commands provided by the learner in writing content into the computer need to be very close in correct spelling or spell checkers cannot provide the correct spelling on the monitor of the word processor. All pupils, when ready, should master use of the word processor to write prose, poetry, or utilitarian content. Mehlinger (1977) asks the following provocative questions when using computers in the curriculum:

1. How would teachers teach if textbooks were replaced by small-multimedia devices that serve as both computer and communications tool?
2. What would school libraries be like when students have access to the libraries of the word?
3. How would teaching change when students can contact experts who know more about a single topic than the teacher?

These are three excellent questions that need pondering for all educators. We recommend both technology and textbooks, carefully chosen, be used to provide for individual differences among learners. Diverse kinds of materials need to be used in teaching and learning. Individuals possess diverse learning styles and the professional teacher attempts to harmonize instruction with pupil learning styles. Bermman and Tinker (1977) discuss a seminar method of instruction with the use of technology:

Many teachers who experiment with on-line courses report being overwhelmed with enrolments of 10 or 12 students because they set up e-mail conversations with each student. The better model is more than a seminar, in which the teacher determines the topic and activities, encourages substantive interactions among students, monitors and shapes the conversation and promotes and atmosphere in which students respond to one another's work. This model results in more conversation, is far more likely to be constructivist and builds on the rich learning that takes place in groups.

Collaborative endeavours that stress the learning of correct spelling of words within purposeful writing activities certainly do emphasize positive ways in the use of technology. Interactions among learners do tend to make for higher levels of cognitive endeavours within the framework of critical and creative thought as well as problem solving.

Handwriting, Spelling and Print Discourse

Illegible handwriting may be major cause for incorrect spelling of words. Handwriting as a separate subject is receiving much less emphasis than formerly. When attending the elementary school years from 1934 to 1942, handwriting received considerable time for instruction; approximately, fifteen minutes per day was spent in handwriting instruction. We learned to write in the air to form individual letters correctly. The making of ovals so that no line was crossed with another received much emphasis as did push and pull exercises, again with no strokes crossing each other. May be these activities had something to do with a transfer value in becoming better handwriters. We truly doubt if this was the case, however. Probably, more time should have been given to the actual writing of prose and poetry, as well as other forms of print discourse. Thus, use needs to be made of what has been learned in handwriting experiences.

What might the teacher do to assist pupils to improve in handwriting? Here, the teacher needs to give much attention to child growth and development characteristics. A lengthy period of time given to handwriting instruction may not harmonize with psychomotor skills and readiness of the learner. Much tension may be built up by the learner if he/she is required to write extensively. Activities may be changed so this does not occur, such as changing to a reading experience. It is always good procedure in teaching to observe the attention span of pupils to notice when sequential activities need to be changed. We strongly recommend handwriting be taught within an ongoing activity involving purposeful writing. Application might then be made of what is being emphasized in terms of objectives of instruction. Handwriting and content written become one, not separate entities.

The objectives of handwriting need to be chosen carefully so that relevance is in evidence. The making of ovals and push/pull exercises were eliminated from the elementary school curriculum some time ago due to a lack of significance involved. To spend hours and hours on drill pertaining to a set of letters certainly is misusing teaching time. We believe legibility is a key concept to emphasize in the handwriting arena. A pupil does not need to conform specifically to models of upper and lower case letters of the alphabet presented in a handwriting text. The model letters, however, may be used as a guide for pupils to develop legibility in handwriting. If we can read pupil's written products readily, then we are satisfied with the quality of his/her handwriting. If illegible handwriting is in evidence, then objectives of instruction need to be developed and implemented so that the child becomes a writer of legible content.

Pupils should feel successful in ongoing experiences. Thus, a pupil is making progress over his previous work in handwriting. Learners should not be compared with each other in legible handwriting. Why? Pupils individually are at different achievement levels in using neuromuscular skills. Teachers need to develop interest within pupils in achieving at a higher level in handwriting. Three kinds of objectives need to be stressed in handwriting. These are knowledge objectives whereby pupils have the needed content about legible letters, words, phrases, sentences and paragraphs to write in a illegible way; skills objectives whereby learners use what has been learned; and attitudinal objectives in which learners develop positive feelings in wanting to improve over previous levels in handwriting.

More specifically, objectives of instruction in handwriting should achieve the following:

1. how to form letters legibly;
2. how to align letters appropriately;
3. how to space letters and words properly;
4. how to stress proper proportion of letters within words;
5. how to achieve overall legibility in written discourse;

6. how to appraise the self in the quality of handwriting exhibited;
7. how to emphasize neatness in all written products as final copies.

Skills objectives should emphasize the following:

1. form letters and words illegibly;
2. align letters and words properly;
3. appropriate proportion of letters and words;
4. proper spacing of letters and words;
5. self-evaluation in achievement in general as well as specific skills in handwriting;
6. neatness in the handwriting arenas.

Attitudinal objectives for pupils to achieve should place importance on the following:

1. desiring to improve in the area of handwriting;
2. wanting to improve in the area of letter formation;
3. developing positive attitudes toward having proportion;
4. feeling a need to space words and letters properly;
5. voluntarily assessing personal achievement in handwriting;
6. emphasizing neatness in activities involving handwriting;
7. respecting the progress of others in handwriting.

There needs to be proper balance among understandings, skills and attitudinal objective in handwriting. Pupils do need knowledge pertaining to what makes for quality handwriting, but the knowledge needs to be implemented as skills. Hopefully, positive feelings as attitudes within learners will develop as a result.

Quality Handwriting Across the Curriculum

Good handwriting that is legible needs to be stressed throughout the different curriculum areas in the school setting.

Thus in mathematics, written work of pupils becomes difficult to evaluate unless good handwriting is there. Good handwriting needs to infiltrate numerals written as well as story or words problems composed by learners. Reports written such as biographies of famous mathematicians provide more opportunities to have pupils practice proper handwriting skills.

In science, pupils individually or in committees may write up the results of a science experiment, a method of procedure in doing an experiment, a report written on a self selected topic in science, bar or line graphs developed on temperature readings on a daily basis, notes written on content read in science from a well known encyclopaedia, an outline written from a variety of reference sources in science, criteria written on being an effective member of a discussion group in science as well as summaries on main ideas obtained from a video tape.

In social studies, pupils may write business letters to order free and inexpensive materials pertaining to an ongoing unit of study, friendly letters to pen pals, generalizations involving content read from diverse reference sources, relevant facts in reaction to a question raised by pupils in the classroom, as well as announcements to other classes to come to visit the pupil's classroom to observe completed projects related to an ongoing unit of study in social studies. Additional learning opportunities involving handwriting in the social studies include the following:

1. Speaking parts of pupils involving early days of Puritans in the New World.
2. Directions written for making a relief of the continent being studied in the social studies.
3. Standards may be written for evaluating an oral report.
4. An outline might be written to cover content pertaining to conclusions reached on an important selection read from social studies materials.
5. Hypothesis written involving one or more hypotheses written in a problem solving activity.
6. Notes taken on a selection in reading in the social studies.

In the literature curriculum, there are many opportunities for pupils to practice handwriting, including the following:

1. Labeling objects in the classroom in a reading readiness program.
2. Using handwriting texts as the need arises, such as for a model in the writing class.
3. Developing experience charts written by pupils with teacher guidance in a reading readiness curriculum.
4. Writing ideas involving reading for a variety of purposes such as from critical reading, reading to follow directions, factual reading, reading for a sequence of ideas, creative reading, reading for main ideas and reading to develop generalizations.
5. Pupils need ample time to do practice forming letters correctly, writing letters and words with proper alignment, slanting letters correctly, spacing words and letters properly and using proper proportion of letters.
6. Pupils with teacher guidance need adequate time to write news articles. The resulting newsletter could be sent home weekly, bi-weekly, or monthly on important happenings in class.

In the health curriculum, the following writing experiences involve handwriting:

1. Learners may take notes on a talk given by a physician pertaining to improved health practices in everyday living.
2. Main ideas might be written on a set of slides or illustrations presented by a registered nurse on improving healthful living in the community.
3. Each pupil might write a personal experience chart pertaining to content from a filmstrip related to a facet of healthful living.
4. Letters may be written to the city council making recommendations on improving a polluted area.
5. Menus may be written for a week on implementing balanced diets in the school lunch program.

6. Business letters may be written to order free and inexpensive materials relating to an ongoing health unit of instruction.

Conclusion

Handwriting errors certainly may cause spelling errors. The teacher needs to do much diagnosing to ascertain why pupils misspell words in writing. Writing needs to be emphasized in all curriculum areas. Improved communication results when quality spelling and handwriting are involved. Courtesy is also inherent when the learner exhibits the best spelling and handwriting in ongoing contextual writing activities. Purposeful writing experiences propel pupils to put forth effort to attain worthwhile objectives. Quality knowledge, skills and attitudes as three categories of objectives should be achieved by pupils. Pupils need to practice much writing so that increased proficiency is in evidence. The writer has treated spelling and handwriting within the broader perspective of writing. Spelling and handwriting skills can best be developed in context within the writing activity. Successful learners in writing will increase their abilities in spelling and handwriting. Careful selection of objectives, learning opportunities and evaluation procedures need to be in the offing.

REFERENCES

Ediger, Marlow (1998), "Goals of Reading Instruction", *Experiments in Education*, published by the SITU Council of Educational Research (in India), 11-19.

Ediger, Marlow (1988), *Language Arts Curriculum in the Elementary School*, Kirksville, Missouri: Simpson Publishing Company, 73-81.

Dolch, Edward W. (1955), *Methods in Reading*. Champaign, Illinois: Garrard Publishing Company.

Mehlinger, Howard D., "The Next Step", *Electronic School*, A22-A24.

Spelling in the Language Arts Curriculum

Learners in the school setting need to become proficient spellers. Being a good speller assists in communicating written content to readers. Effective written communication is certainly hindered when an increasing number of words is misspelled. Thus, in writing business and friendly letters, plays, poems, stories, announcements, and thank you notes, as well as in filling out job application forms, the writer needs to spell words correctly in order to communicate content effectively to receivers of written products. Writing, which includes spelling, is one of the three r's (reading, writing, and arithmetic) in the curriculum. Society deems it highly significant for all individuals to express themselves well in the area of written expression.

Smith lists the following objectives in the spelling curriculum:

1. To help each child learn to spell correctly those words which he will need in order to express his own ideas in writing.
2. To develop in each child a basic set of principles and concepts that will help him to spell familiar words.
3. To create interesting drill exercises and techniques to help each child fix in his memory images of those spellings which are essential to social courtesy, but which are exceptions to the principles and concepts of ordinary spelling.

4. To install in each child a desire to spell correctly and an attitude that good spelling is a social courtesy in the communication process.
5. To help each child form good study habits in spelling which help him to attack unknown words intelligently. This includes the intelligent use of reference materials.

The Psychology of Learning and Spelling

There are selected guidelines which teachers need to emphasize in the teaching of spelling. These criteria reflect the thinking of educational psychologists pertaining to providing for individual differences among pupils. Which guidelines might be followed by teachers to help each pupil achieve optimally in spelling?

Each pupil should be assisted to perceive interest in learning to spell words. To provide interesting experiences for pupils, the teacher must definitely vary the kinds of spelling activities provided for pupils. Among other activities, pupils may experience spelling activities involving the use of games, puzzles, the basal textbook or multiple series textbooks, films, filmstrips, slides, and transparencies. The language arts teacher needs to capture learner interest if achievement in spelling is to receive optimal development.

Secondly, pupils need to perceive purpose in learning to spell any given set of words. If learners sense purpose in learning, reasons will be accepted intrinsically in mastering the correct spelling of functional words. The teacher needs to guide pupils to accept as worthwhile, effort put forth in iearning to spell words accurately. Correct spelling of words is necessary in order to communicate effectively with others.

Lee and Rubin provide the following purposes in pupils learning to spell a given set of words:

> *Each child needs to learn the words he or she wishes to write at the time that child wants to write them.* Words children need to learn to spell are those they spell incorrectly in their everyday writing. And the only real test of whether children have mastered a word is whether they consistently spell it correctly in their writing.

Spelling programs should be differentiated for children on the basis of need. If children do not misspell words, they do not need to study spelling. If they only occasionally misspell words—and it is impossible to predict which words they will misspell—they need only to learn to spell the words they miss.

It makes no sense for children to learn to spell a word that is not in their speaking or writing vocabulary. There is no point in teaching children to spell words that are unlikely to use in the near future. When a class is discussing crustaceans, the children do not need to learn to spell *crustacean*. The teacher can display the word on a chart or chalkboard for the duration of the project so that children can copy it in their writing. Some children will undoubtedly learn to spell it, but there is no need to burden all of the children with the requirement of learning such terms.

Introducing new words to children as spelling words does not increase their vocabulary significantly. Words that become meaningful are those tied to personal experience—not just experience with the word, but experience with that which the word symbolizes. If children have only looked at pictures and read and talked about crustaceans, most children will forget the word very quickly. They will remember the word and want to use it only if the word has become theirs through experience: finding some crabs, comparing them with lobsters they have seen in the meat market, handling crabs and feeling their firm shells, trying to pull barnacles off the rocks, trying to think of other sea life that belongs in the same category. If children want to write the word *crustacean*, they will learn how to spell it. The words that need to be learned must be related directly to each child's own writing.

Thirdly, learners need to attach meaning to ongoing activities and experiences. Thus, in learning to spell a set of words, pupils must be able to accurately pronounce and read each word. Also, pupils individually need to know vital definitions pertaining to each word being studied in spelling. These words should also be utilized in meaningful sentences by pupils. It is highly significant then for pupils to achieve meaning and understanding in the spelling curriculum. A lack of meaningful learnings hinders pupil achievement in the area of spelling.

Fourthly, individual differences among learners need adequate attention. In any grade level, except perhaps early primary grade pupils, there are highly proficient spellers. Average and slow learners are also in evidence. Thus, it behooves the teacher to guide each pupil to achieve optimally in spelling.

> Within every heterogeneous classroom there are wide variations in the children's physical and emotional health and in their out-of-school experiences. The children are highly individual persons, shaped and influenced by the environment in which they have developed. The teacher's most challenging responsibility is to provide a program that meets children where they are, recognizes their potential, capitalizes upon their strengths, and moves them along at a pace consonant with their ability. She recognized individual variations in—
>
> ability to understand and speak standard English;
>
> ability to observe and listen;
>
> ability to deal with abstraction;
>
> size and appropriateness of vocabulary;
>
> number and accuracy of concepts acquired; and in
>
> desire and ability to verbalize experiences.
>
> Children learn at different rates and consequently require different materials, experiences, and instructional techniques; a single group activity often affects each member differently.

Regardless of the source utilized to select an individual list of spelling words, the number of words to be mastered in spelling by a pupil should harmonize with his/her capability level or levels. A variety of learning activities in spelling should assist pupils to achieve optimally in the language arts curriculum. Pressuring or forcing pupils to achieve at an impossible level defeats tenets of a relevant spelling curriculum for pupils.

Measurably Stated Objectives and the Spelling Curriculum

Words are spelled either correctly or incorrectly. Thus, teachers might wish to emphasize precise objectives in the instructional arena. With the utilization of specific ends, the teacher can gauge the effectiveness of his/her teaching strategies. After instruction, it can be measured if a learner has or has not attained measurable goals.

The following are precise instructional goals in spelling for pupils to achieve:

1. The pupil will spell correctly nine out of ten words from unit ten in the basal textbook.
2. The pupil will volunteer to spell correctly five bonus words.
3. Through teacher-pupil planning of a given set of spelling words, the pupil will spell these words correctly with 90 per cent accuracy.

The above list of spelling goals is an example of sequential ends for pupils to attain. An individualized spelling program might then be emphasized so that each pupil may achieve the stated ends at a unique optimal level of achievement. No two pupils may then be at the same place at the same time in the mastering of words in spelling.

Appropriate learning experiences must be provided by the teacher to assist each pupil to achieve stated ends. If, for example, pupils are to attain the following measurable goal—the pupil will write a business letter making no more than two errors in misspelled words when incorporating twelve words from the new spelling list, the teacher then needs to provide interesting, meaningful, and purposeful experiences to achieve the desired end. Ultimately, the teacher may measure if a pupil has/has not achieved the specific end—writing a business letter containing no more than two spelling errors, involving new words from a specific list. Reasonable spelling goals need to be in evidence for each learner.

Methods in Learning to Spell Words Correctly

Each pupil continually uses a method (or methods) in learning to spell words accurately. If a pupil progresses continually toward optimal achievement in the spelling curriculum, effective methods of studying, no doubt, are being utilized. If an excessive number of words are continually spelled incorrectly, the involved pupil may well need assistance in developing appropriate methodology in learning to spell words correctly. Manuals in basal spelling textbooks suggest methods for pupils to utilize in mastering spelling words. Each learner will need to discover a method or several methods which work. Provisions definitely need to be made for individual differences in the spelling curriculum.

The writer suggests a method for pupils to utilize in spelling words correctly. One criterion in certain, pupils need to look at each work carefully. Pupils, as a whole, will not learn to spell well, if careful observation of each word is not made. An attention span of adequate length is needed in looking at spelling words carefully.

Secondly, each pupil needs to pronounce spelling words correctly. Leeway needs to be made for dialect differences among learners. Regional and local differences exist in word pronounciation. Within that framework, learners need to be guided to identify each word correctly. Linguists have advocated diverse levels of usage in speaking such as words chosen and utilized in presenting a talk to a professional group of educators as compared to utterances utilized in speaking with friends or with preschool pupils. Also, pupils speaking non-standard English may retain respect for their language environment as well as achieve in learning to speak standard English. Standard English seemingly is prized highly in society and provides entrances to jobs, education, and economic opportunities.

As each pupil correctly pronounces a new word, careful attention needs to be given by the involved learner to sound-symbol relationships within the word. Irregularities in these relationships need adequate attention.

Thirdly, pupils need to practice writing the new word without looking at its correct spelling model. Before writing the spelling word again, the learner needs to check if his/her written word was spelled correctly. It pays to check the accuracy of a written word in terms of its correct spelling before using the word in functional writing experiences. Incorrect spelling of words might not become habitual in these situations.

Loban, Ryan, and Squire wrote:

> The difference between good spellers and poor spellers often hinges on an effective method for learning to spell. Good spellers have solved the problem. They have a sequence for studying words they want to learn. Poor spellers merely look at a new word

helplessly, and when they do try, use hit and miss methods that are ineffective and seldom the same from one time to the next.

Why, then, should everyone not adopt the ideal method of learning used by the best spellers? The answer is easy. Good spellers do not all use the same method. However, almost all of them use some method, and by studying their various ways of learning to spell, each pupil can work out an habitual procedure suited to his own individuality. Among the steps used by good spellers, at least ten are often listed: looking at the word, copying the word, visualizing the word, listening to the pronounciation of the word, pronouncing the word, dividing the word into syllables, saying the letters in sequence, writing the word with large muscle movements (in the air or on a chalkboard) to get the feel of the word, analyzing the difficult places in the word, and using the word in a meaningful sentence. In addition, most competent spellers write their words in a careful, neat fashion. Sloppy, careless handwriting often results in a confused image of the word and uncertainly about its spelling.

Fourthly, the teacher needs to provide a variety of activities in writing to assist pupils to spell new words correctly in ongoing experiences and units of study. With continued use of the correct spelling words, learners individually should retain mental images of accurately spelled words.

Cautions in the Teaching of Spelling

There are selected cautions which teachers need to emphasize in the teaching of spelling.

The English language has numerous irregularly spelled word. Thus, a lack of agreement in sound-symbol relationship is in evidence. For example, there are many ways to spell the long i /ī/ sound; among others, notice the following spellings of this sound: *my, pie, sigh, buy, kite, white,* and *bye*. A basic sight vocabulary needs to be developed by pupils pertaining to words which do not follow a rather consistent sound/symbol relationship.

There also are many consistencies between symbols and sounds in the spelling of English words, such as in ban, can, Dan, fan, man, Nan, pan, ran, tan, and van, among many, many others words.

Secondly, pupils need to learn to spell relevant words. Too frequently, learners have been forced to learn to spell unimportant words. Words for pupils to master in spelling should have high utilitarian values. Pupils perceive increased purpose in learning to spell words which can be used in functional situations. What is used in functional situations will not be forgotten as soon as spelling words which have relatively little or no use.

Dolch identified 220 basic sight words for reading mastery in the elementary grades. The sight words should also be relevant for learners in the area of spelling. Frequently used words in writing need to be mastered by pupils to cut down on the number of spelling errors exhibited in completed products. The Dolch words are the following:

a	to	out	could	when	tell	hot
and	two	please	every	who	their	hurt
away	up	pretty	fly		these	if
big	we	ran	from	always	those	keep
blue	where	ride	give	around	upon	kind
can	yellow	saw	going	because	us	laugh
come	you	say	had	been	use	light
down	all	she	has	before	very	long
find	am	so	her	best	wash	much
for	are	soon	him	both	which	myself
funny	at	that	his	buy	why	never
go	ate	there	how	call	wish	only
help	be	they	just	cold	work	own
here	black	this	know	does	would	pick
I	brown	too	let	don't	write	seven
in	but	under	live	fast	your	shall
is	came	want	may	first		show
it	did	was	of	five	about	six

jump	do	well	old	found	better	small
little	eat	went	once	gave	bring	start
look	four	what	open	goes	carry	ten
make	get	white	over	green	clean	today
me	good	will	put	its	cut	together
my	have	with	round	made	done	try
not	he	yes	some	many	draw	warm
one	into		stop	off	drink	
play	like	after	take	or	eight	
red	must	again	thank	pull	fall	
run	new	an	them	read	far	
said	no	any	then	right	full	
see	now	as	think	sing	got	
the	on	ask	walk	sit	grow	
three	our	by	were	sleep	hold	

Thirdly, teachers need to utilize recommended methodology in the teaching of spelling. Readiness factors are very important. Thus, a pupil needs to be able to read a word before mastering its correct spelling. Meaningful learnings also need to be in evidence in that learners need to know a relevant definition or definitions pertaining to words being studied in spelling. Also, pupils need to be able to utilize spelling words correctly within sentences. Meaning theory needs adequate emphasis in teaching-learning situations (Martha).

1. Readiness for an activity implies that the child is sufficiently mature so that under favourable environmental conditions he can learn the skill with success and without undesirable effects upon him in other respects that would counterbalance or outweigh the gain made through acquisition of the skill.
2. Into activities such as "learning to walk," a child cannot be forced. Readiness for walking, like that for many other

activities, is primarily matter of the "unfolding of the design" of the individual. Barring highly unfavourable environmental influences, the child will acquire such a skill in its rudimentary form almost by himself. For the initial acquisition of such skills there is not much that the adult can do the facilitate learning other than provide a background that is not inimical to acquiring them. What is usually referred to as "teaching" is, in such cases, of little or no avail.

3. In the acquisition of many types of skills there is not merely one stage of readiness, namely that for the initial learning of the skill. There also is need for readiness for later stages in learning of the skill. For example, there is not only a necessity for readiness at the beginning stage of reading instruction but also at later stages that include the development of skills such as learning to use the dictionary.
4. Frequently "readiness" for one of the noninitial stages of acquiring a skill is chiefly excellent performance in the preceding stage in the development of the skill. For example, probably the most desirable way of getting ready to learn to arrange words in alphabetical order is to have proficiency in the preceding stage of knowing the letters in alphabetical order.
5. Because frequently the best evidence of "readiness" for one of the noninitial stages of acquiring a skill is excellent performance in the preceding stage, it is important that the teacher should recognize the desires sequence of stages in the development of the skill. This sequence should be in optimum psychological order of learning, not in logical sequence if there is a discrepancy between the two.
6. Frequently all pupils in one classroom are not ready for acquiring a new skill at the same time. Consequently careful diagnosis of the needs and abilities of boys and girls is of paramount importance, and provisions for adapting instruction to individual differences are necessary.

7. Whether or not a child is ready to begin to learn in a given area is dependent to a considerable extent on the methods and materials used in the teaching. Care should, therefore be taken to try to select methods and materials suitable for each child.

Fourthly, selected learners have experienced considerable failure in learning the correct spelling of words. The language arts teacher needs to determine where each learner is achieving presently in spelling. The teacher then needs to provide learning activities which assist each pupil to experience continuous success in spelling.

Too, frequently, pupils have lacked motivation in spelling due to a lack of challenge in learning to spell words. Toward the other end of the continuum, spelling words for pupils to master can be too complex. A learner may then give up in learning to spell words due to complexity of subject matter being emphasized. New spelling words for pupils to master in spelling need to be attainable.

Fifthly, undesirable attitudes toward spelling on the part of pupils are difficult to change. But, language arts teachers must work hard to develop quality feelings within pupils in learning to spell words correctly. Thus, the teacher needs to select important objectives, relevant learning activities to achieve desired ends, and evaluation procedures which are valid and reliable to ascertain learner progress.

Kyte identified 100 vital words for pupil mastery in reading. These words might also be equally significant for learners to master in spelling:

I	go	all	that
a	went	name	girl
the	her	school	out
and	when	are	much
my	for	Santa Claus	party
to	you	said	am
is	has	then	going

we	very	father	sister
in	little	time	man
like	they	snowman	get
it	good	new	were
he	had	toys	made
have	snow	so	birthday
on	at	will	but
was	some	every	pet
me	day	saw	see
play	can	big	boys
with	got	home	not
dog	baby	out	brother
she	him	boy	cat
of	do	nice	them
too	house	up	ball
Christmas	there	fun	Saturday
doll	his	train	put
one	likes	balloon	children

Philosophy of Education and the Teaching of Spelling

There are diverse philosophical schools of thought in teaching learners.

Essentialists believe that a given set of words can be identified which all pupils need to learn to spell. These core words need to be mastered in order that effective communication of written content may eventually be in evidence. Research studies may be made to identify significant words in the spelling curriculum. Carefully designed research studies in spelling may then assist in identifying which words learners need to master sequentially on each grade level in the school setting.

Identified lists of spelling words acquired from educational research need to be available to teachers. The teacher may then pretest pupils to determine which words have already been mastered in spelling. Those words which pupils can spell correctly, of course, need not be studied in ongoing lessons or units.

A variety of methods should be utilized by the teacher in teaching pupils to spell each ensuing word correctly.

Quite different than essentialism as a means of selecting relevant spelling words for pupils to master is experimentalism as a philosophy of education. Correct spelling of words is instrumental to other goals. Thus, within the framework of problem solving experiences, learners need to learn to spell selected words. The spelling words are studied and mastered to use in a functional experience in society. For example, if pupils are to write a thank you note for gifts received, the following spelling words may be useful for the ensuing writing experience; thank you, friend, gift, models, enjoy, wholesome, and entertaining. Words being acquired in spelling pertain to those having utilitarian values in writing the thank you note. Spelling words, according to experimentalists, should not necessarily come for basal textbooks, diverse units of study in the curriculum, and lists based on research results. Only those spelling words useful in a functional writing experience should be mastered. Words deemed useful depend upon the purpose involved in writing engaged in by the individual learner. Useful spelling words in writing a personal friendly letter which will be delivered to an actual receiver will differ from those necessary in a notice of sympathy sent to a person having experienced to unfortunate.

Computer Use and Spelling

Selected software and the computer can assist pupils to achieve well in spelling. Drill and practice programs aid pupils to rehearse correct spellings of words presented previously in ongoing lessons and units. Pupils then need to review the correct spelling of a vital set of words. To develop and retain what has been learned previously, drill and practice software can be relevant and helpful.

Tutorial programs present a new set of words for pupils to master. Essential words must be present in these computerized programs. Tutorials should assist pupils to attain more optimally in spelling. Diagnosis and remediation ingredients are salient in software empahsizing tutorial work for pupils.

Gaming software can be excellent if wholesome attitudes are developed within the framework of competition. Three or four pupils playing a game to see who will be the winner in correctly spelling words in a program might well be highly stimulating. Correctly spelling a more complex word gives a higher score to a pupil as compared to an easier word.

In Summary

Language arts teachers need to be highly knowledgeable about diverse philosophies and methods of teaching spelling. The adopted philosophy/philosophies selected to teach spelling must be followed within the framework of recommended criteria based on the psychology of learning.

Carefully selected objectives need emphasis in the spelling curriculum. Learning experiences to assist learners in achieving the desired ends should be selected on the basis on being interesting, purposeful, as well as meaningful. Thus, provision for each pupil in teaching-learning situations is possible. Learner progress needs continual evaluation to ascertain the amount of growth achieved by each pupil in the spelling curriculum.

REFERENCES

1. Barbe, Walter, et. al. *Spelling: Basic Skills for Effective Communication.* Columbus, Ohio: Zaner-Bloser, Inc., 1982.
2. Dallman, Martha. *Teaching the Language Arts in the Elementary School*, Third Edition. Dubuque, Iowa: Wm. C. Brown Publishers, 1976.
3. Dolch, Edward W. *Methods in Reading*. Champaign, Illinois: Garrard Publishing Company, 1955.
4. Donoghue, Mildred R. *The Child and the English Language Arts.* Dubuque, Iowa: William C. Brown Publishers, 1975.
5. Kyte, George C. "A Core Vocabulary for the Primary Grades," *Elementary School Journal* (November, 1943).
6. Lee, Doris, M., and Joseph B. Rubin. *Children and Language.* Belmont, California: Wadsworth Publishing Company, 1979.
7. Loban, Walter, Margaret Ryan, and James R. Squire. *Teaching Language and Literature*. New York: Harcourt, Brace and World, Inc., 1969.
8. Smith, James. Adventures in *Communication*. Boston, Massachusetts: Allyn and Bacon, Inc., 1972.
9. Stewig, John Warren. *Exploring Language Arts in the Elementary Classroom*. New York: Holt, Rinehart and Winston, 1983.

Word Selection in the Spelling Curriculum

Which spelling words should students master in order to communicate well in writing? This is a question which needs a relevant answer. To be sure, there are a plethora of words for students to learn to spell correctly, but these may not be functional or useful words. There are numerous sources from which spelling words may come for teachers to use and teach and for students to master.

The Basal Spelling Textbook

Basal spelling textbooks have been used over the years as a source of words for students to master. The writers of the text used, selected the words contained therein. The spelling words are listed in terms of what students are to learn per week. Along with the weekly list of words, there are learning opportunities for students for each of the five days of the school week. The following is provided as an example:

1. ***Monday:*** Students with teacher assistance go over the new words by emphasizing correct identification and pronounciation of each (Ediger, 1976, 282-283). Learners are to attach a correct contextual definition of each within a sentence. Meanings of new concepts and vocabulary terms are important. Students then study their correct spelling in different ways. Some write each new word several times to ensure mastery. Others use the words in written sentences. When studying, the correct spelling is frequently checked

against that listed in the basal textbook. The basal also has words to be filled in to sentences, using those from the weekly list.

2. ***Tuesday:*** Students fill in a crossword puzzle contained in the text by using the new words from the spelling list. They also engage in a word search activity contained in the text. The words in the word search activity come from the spelling list for the present week. A trial test is taken to notice which words have been mastered and which are left to learn to spell. Words misspelled are studied for the correct spelling by the learner.

3. ***Wednesday:*** Students are asked to write a story using all or most of the new words in the writing. Correct spelling of each new word is stressed.

4. ***Thursday:*** A second test is given, after students have studied the correct spelling again of the weekly new words. Those students spelling all the words correctly need not be tested on Friday.

5. ***Friday:*** Those students who misspelled words on Thursday are given the final test for the weekly list of words. Diagnosis may occur of misspelled words at any point of the weekly schedule which include handwriting errors.

The teaching model in spelling from a basal text should be examined and assessed by teachers to ascertain if this approach would assist students to become good spellers. There are learning activities in the basal which can serve as a model and be good for teachers to use in any program of spelling instruction. Proper instruction in phonics should be balanced with holism in teaching spelling.

Words Based on Research Studies

There a plethora of research studies which have been made on the most commonly used spelling words in student writings. Researchers here have gone to some pains to identify commonly used spelling words. These can be a source of spelling words for elementary age pupils to master. Dolch (1955) identified through research studies the 220 most commonly used words by pupils in spelling. Even though this list came out in 1955, the author of this article still receives requests from former students for the Dolch list! There are no teaching suggestions provided for having students master the correct spelling of words in the Dolch list. The teacher needs to be creative in guiding students with learning opportunities to spell each word correctly. Also, there are no sequences in terms of order for word mastery. The author here recommended that the teacher use these words for enrichment purposes to challenge those who desired to master additional new words in spelling. An interest center with related tasks may be set up for those who need to be motivated to spell additional words in functional spelling, using the dolch list. Activities in spelling need to be interesting, meaningful, and purposeful. Words being mastered in spelling should be used in functional writing situations. Good study habits need to be developed within students to persevere and accomplish.

Individualized Spelling

There are individual words which students misspell in daily writing. What is misspelled may become a set of spelling words for that child to master. Each misspelled word may be printed on a 3 by 4 inch card. Those words which have been mastered may then be placed in a separate set by the involved learner and then notice that stack of cards grow in number as a motivator. The words misspelled in class work need to be adjusted in terms of what the involved child can reasonably learn to spell correctly within a week or other suitable interval of time. The method to use may be decided by the learner. If necessary, the teacher may assist the student to develop an appropriate methodology in learning to spell these words correctly. Many teachers have found the following method to work well with students in learning to spell words correctly:

(a) the student looks at the word carefully;

(b) he/she needs to pronounce each word correctly and listen to the grapheme/phoneme correspondence of involved letters;

(c) the student should write the word once and then check with the correct spelling;

(d) he/she may write the word within a sentence, checking again to notice the correctness of the spelling (Ediger and Rao, 2000, Chapter Eight);

Individualized spelling may be used along with the enrichment center of important words listed thereon for voluntary student mastery. These words may also become a part of the total spelling program when the basal text is used. The total number of words to be mastered in spelling must harmonize with what is a reasonabl load for mastery learning of a specific student.

Words Taken from Subject Matter Units of Study

Spelling words for students to master may also come from an academic discipline which provides content for an ongoing unit of study. Thus in a social studies unit on the Middle Ages, the student may learn to spell the following words: nobleman, knight, serf, manner, guilds, crop rotation, tournaments, warfare, and plow. Each word needs to be used meaningfully in context when it is being mastered in spelling. Illustrations may be collected or drawn which relate directly to the unit world being mastered in spelling. The spelling curriculum becomes integrated when it cuts across academic lines in search of words for student mastery.

With the strong emphasis being placed upon students learning to read well and on grade level by the end of grade three, it appears to be a good practice to have the teacher take the new words listed in the manual section of the basal reader and have students learn to spell each correctly. These new words then are studied not only from the goal or objective of reading them correctly, but that end is also reinforced with learning to spell each of these words correctly. Certainly, better readers should be in the offing (Ediger, 2001, 79-83).

Making Application of Spelling Words Mastered

Teachers need to guide students to use words mastered in spelling so that their correct spelling is not forgotten. There are then many uses which may be made of the correct spelling of new/old words in context. The following are examples (Ediger, 1977, 25-28.

1. Computerized programmed spelling games played involving individualized/cooperative endeavours.

2. Poetry written using previously learned words in spelling.
3. Crossword puzzles and word searches used in teaching spelling.
4. Games made and used in the spelling curriculum.
5. Labels on charts and graphs containing spelling words mastered.
6. Paragraphs, short stories, and outlines containing spelling words being taught.
7. Summaries and conclusions providing students practice in using spelling words in context.
8. Book reports with current spelling words being taught.
9. Play parts written with new spelling words included.
10. Antonyms or synonyms written from a current list of spelling words from the basal text (Ediger, 2000, 14-21).

Spelling words being studied by students need to be used in order that forgetting the correct spelling is not in vogue. Then too, students perceive the relevance of studying that which has use and is utilitarian.

A Forward Looking Spelling Program

Teachers need to look forward at what might be in a quality spelling program. From what exists to something better needs to be in the offing. What might a futuristic spelling program emphasize for students?

1. It cuts across the different academic disciplines in seeking relevant words for students to master.
2. It begins with where the individual student is presently in spelling achievement and then provides for optimal sequence in learning to spell words.
3. It has a clearly spelled out scope and ordered approach in students learning to spell words correctly.
4. It emphasizes students making application of words spelled correctly.

5. It provides enrichment learnings for students who achieve well and motivates those who need to achieve more optimally in spelling.
6. It helps students to perceive purpose or reasons for learning to spell words correctly.
7. It provides ample opportunities for students to attach meaning and understanding to words being considered for mastery learning.
8. It stresses writing for a variety of reasons using the new words encountered in spelling.
9. It emphasizes reading of subject matter containing the new spelling words.
10. It encourages students individually to compete against themselves, rather then against others (Ediger, 1992, 12-26).

In Closing

The spelling curriculum needs to be kept updated and current so that each student learns to spell relevant words. Relevant words chosen for student mastery should be learned in a variety of ways in providing for individual differences among learners. Students do possess different styles of learning (Searson and Dunn, 2001). They also possess diverse intelligences to show what has been learned and achieved (Gardner, 1993). It behooves the school district to provide the best spelling curriculum possible for each student.

REFERENCES

Dolch, Edward W. (1955), *Methods in Reading*. Champaign, Illinois: Garrard Publishing Company, 373-374.

Ediger, Marlow and D. Bhaskara Rao (2000), *Teaching Reading Successfully*. New Delhi: Discovery Publishing House.

Ediger, Marlow (1974), *"The Pupil, the Teacher, and Handwriting,"* Reading Improvement, 11 (1), 62-64.

Ediger, Marlow (2000), *"Competition Versus Cooperation and Pupil Achievement,"* College Student Journal, 34 (1), 14-21.

Ediger, Marlow (1976), *"Listening and the Child in the Language Arts,"* Lutheran Education, 111 (5), 282-283.

Ediger, Marlow (2001), *"The School Principal; State Standards Versus Creativity,"* Journal of Instructional Psychology, 28 (2), 79-83.

Ediger, Marlow (1977), *"The Child and Writing in the Language Arts,"* Nebraska English Counselor, 22 (2), 25-28.

Ediger, Marlow (1992), "Role of School Administration," Education Magazine, nr. 8, 12-26. Published by the Qatar National Commission for Education—The Middle East.

Garden, Howard (1993), *Multiple Intelligences: Theory Into Practice.* New York: Basic Books.

Searson, Robert, and Rita Dunn (2001), *"The Learning Styles Teaching Model,"* Science and Children, 38 (5), 22-26.

Vocabulary Development and the Pupil

It is of utmost importance to help pupils achieve their optimum in vocabulary development. Reasons for emphasizing a rich listening, speaking, reading, and writing vocabulary on the part of pupils need clarifying. Why should pupils achieve to their optimum in vocabulary development?

1. Ideas and content are expressed more accurately and with greater clarity.
2. Success in many jobs, vocations, and professions in dependent upon proficiency in vocabulary development.
3. Prestige generally is attached to richly developed listening, speaking, reading, and writing vocabularies.
4. Greater enjoyment in reading as a leisure time activity is possible.
5. Problem solving demands optimum achievement in vocabulary development.
6. When conversing and discussing, it is necessary to have proficient command of the English language including the proper meaning and use of words.
7. It is necessary to use words which convey meanings accurately in speaking and writing.
8. Variety in selecting terminology is important in speaking and in writing.

Developing Pupils' Vocabularies

There are numerous learning activities which can be provided for pupils in vocabulary development. These activities must be on the present achievement levels of individual pupils. Interests and needs of pupils must be considered in teaching—learning situations. What are some important learning activities for pupils in vocabulary development?

The teacher should orally read stories and library books to pupils on all grade levels. Pupils will hear new terms and words when listening to diverse stories and poems. Many of the new vocabulary words become meaningful to learners to context. The teacher needs to select subject matter which challenges pupils in wanting to develop their vocabularies more thoroughly.

Pupils learn many new terms by listening to and taking part in discussions. Meanings of new words may be determined in context. Thus, unknown words become meaningful as they relate to other words in the sentence. In discussions, the listening and speaking vocabularies of pupils may be developed more thoroughly.

It is significant for pupils to experience a listening center in the class setting. The listening center should contain tapes and records. Questions on task cards can be utilized periodically at this center to assess pupil achievement in listening. The tasks on these cards need to be open-ended so that much latitude of pupils' responses is possible. Vocabulary development definitely should be emphasized in the chosen tasks.

Pupils should also interact with carefully selected books at a reading center. The center should guide pupils in developing a better reading vocabulary. The library books should pertain to a variety of topics to provide for diverse reading interests of pupils. Also, the books should be on different reading levels to provide for diverse achievement levels among pupils. The learner may then select his/her own library book for reading at an acceptable unique rate of speed.

Lee and Rubin wrote the following involving children's literature in the classroom setting:

> Libraries are a key resource whenever stimulating children's reading is at stake. The room library or reading center should be replenished frequently with books related to major topics of interest to small groups or the whole class. The books should provide a wide range in the maturity of concepts as well as in areas of interest. Teachers need to check frequently to eliminate books that are no longer being used in order to save space for other books of current interest.
>
> Besides published books, the reading center should include books written by the children in the room. Expressive photographs and art work executed by both teachers and students can stimulate the writing of books for use in the classroom. Thus, reading materials created by children can become a valuable part of a library collection. Such materials can provide the art program with a rationale for book illustrating, binding, and production.

In the class setting, the teacher may arrange an audio-visual center. Here, pupils can view filmstrips and slides of their own choosing pertaining to an ongoing unit of study. This experience should aid pupils in attaching meaning to new terms as they view semi-concrete situations in visual presentations. If pupils are studying a unit on Colonial America, they may view and discuss scenes in filmstrips and in slides pertaining to homes, stores, schools, and other facets of living pertaining to that period of time. Improved listening and speaking vocabularies should be an important end result. If pupils see written script on an interesting filmstrip, they may also increase their reading vocabularies.

At a writing center pupils can select, from among many, a picture to write about. The contents of the picture may be discussed in a committee and, no doubt, will aid many pupils in establishing richer listening and speaking vocabularies. When writing about a picture, learners should be guided to improve their writing vocabulary. The written content may be shared with other learners. Hopefully, an increased reading vocabulary will result.

Greene and Petty wrote:

> Writing is a personal act; it is an expression of the self. It is a process that is done for a purpose, which results in a product. It is a process of thought an emotion that requires certain skills and abilities to gain the product and accomplish the purpose. This product has certain qualities and conditions of form that can be

> judged in terms of the purpose. Because writing is personal, the individual determines the purpose and judges the product. As an expression of self, the process changes as the individual changes. As a child's background of experience enlarges, the needs for expression change. As a child grows, the ability to give expression grows—providing the skills necessary for such expression have been learned and the desire to express has not been stifled.

In different grade levels in the elementary school, learners might bring available pictures to school to develop a pictured dictionary. The abstract word can be written in neat manuscript style underneath each illustration. Pupils may discuss content pertaining to each picture. In these learning activities pertaining to developing a pictured dictionary, pupils may develop their listening, speaking, reading, and writing vocabularies.

Pupils with teacher guidance might tell stories pertaining to library books which have been read. Learners may tell stories in small groups. This activity can aid pupils in developing their listening and speaking vocabularies.

At selected intervals, pupils should have opportunities to use a glossary or dictionary to look up meanings of relevant words. This activity should not be carried to an excess since boredom in learning might set in. A variety of learning activities must be provided for pupils in vocabulary achievement.

Anderson and Lapp wrote the following involving initial sequential dictionary skills for learners:

> The first dictionary skill to be taught is the location of a word. Some children may not know the alphabet sequence because it has not been used frequently prior to this time. Check to be sure that the children know the sequence of letters in the alphabet, and then practice until they can find words in the dictionary by their first letters. To avoid the necessity of having some children recite the alphabet before they can locate a word, discuss the relative placement of letters. Have the children discover that when the dictionary is opened in the center we find the words that start with *l* and *m*. If it is opened at the first quarter, we find the words with *d* and *e*, and at the third quarter we find the *r* and *s* words.

Pupils in a small group could take turns orally reading a library book which the learners have not read previously. The library book must be on the reading levels of involved pupils.

Learners are then aided in developing their reading vocabularies as well as their listening vocabularies. In reading orally, pupils need to develop their speaking vocabularies adequately. Each child must have ample opportunity to achieve proficiency in reading orally a given selection. The pupil then should be able also to develop his/her reading and speaking vocabularies more thoroughly. Listeners to the oral presentation might achieve at a higher level in their listening vocabularies. In guiding pupils to read well orally after ample practice, the following criteria need to be followed:

(a) The child should practice using voice inflection properly to convey the author's possible meaning.

(b) Proper attention should be given to punctuation marks so that needed pauses present intended meanings to listeners.

(c) Pupils should practice stressing words accurately so that meaningful reading is in evidence.

(d) Fluency in reading content must be emphasized in oral reading.

(e) Audience contact is important in oral reading since content is being communicated to listeners.

To help pupils write more effectively, an individualized list of spelling words written down for each learner to master in his/her own notebook might aid in learning to spell words correctly. The words a child needs to spell correctly in functional writing situations are then contained in this list. Additional words may be added to the list as needed. When seeing words in print, pupils are guided in developing an improved reading vocabulary. Using these words in writing should assist pupils in achieving at a higher level in developing a quality writing vocabulary.

Hennings wrote the following involving individual differences among learners in spelling:

> In any class, the range of spelling ability is at least equal to the range of reading ability. Some children have a keen sense of sound differences; they can manipulate sound-symbol relationships with ease and can look at groups of related words and identify features common to the group. Others have trouble with sounds, symbols,

> and/or word-building units; they may have trouble with problem solving as well, being able to perceive only the simplest relationships. Schools must structure spelling programs to take into account differences such as these.

A speaking center can house a cassette recorder as well as a record player. Pupils may practice speaking on a variety of topics as well as in diversity of kinds of speeches given. A list might be developed cooperatively by pupils with teacher guidance pertaining to topics as well as kinds of speeches to be given. Reference materials for pupils to gather needed information prior to giving oral presentations should also be located at the center. Library books, encyclopaedias, films, pictures, slides, filmstrips, models, and objects may be used by pupils as reference materials to gather needed information to give an oral presentation. Pupils individually or in groups may record their presentations and listen to feedback. Learners with teacher guidance might then evaluate the quality of the oral presentation.

Standards that may be followed when assessing oral presentations could include the following:

(a) Respect for the contributions of others.

(b) Pupils individually should be evaluated in terms of their own unique past achievement. A child should definitely not be compared with the achievement of other learners.

(c) Proper sequence is important in giving oral reports.

(d) Content in oral presentations should show effort in its presentation.

(e) Ideas must be clearly presented on the understanding levels of listeners.

(f) Organisation of content in the report should meet appropriate standards.

(g) Proper stress, pitch, and juncture is important in presenting content orally.

Loban, *et al.*, wrote concerning the use of oral language:

> Constantly, the teacher of oral communication must be deeply aware of speech as a form of human behaviour—significant behaviour because it reveals the speaker to his public. Instinctively,

we have always known the power of speech to reveal; too infrequently have we considered that silence too can tell things about us. Until recently concern for the fact that our speech might betray us was not thought of as "the desire to project a favourable image," but that is what it is called today. Television has made a vast public conscious of how much more than words even a brief "exposure" may convey. Almost nowhere in the communication context does the wish to protect oneself weigh more heavily than with young people in the classroom. We each have an ideal self-image, inextricably bound to our sense of personal dignity. Even though we may know beyond doubt that our self-image flatters us, one who does not treat that image with respect blocks communication. This is the reason we stress so insistently the need for creating a climate where the student feels secure enough to express himself freely. Many things are necessary in order to help students learn to use oral language with honesty and vigor, but the proper environment is the *sine qua non*.

Further learning activities to aid pupils in vocabulary development include pupils bringing objects for an interest center. For example, pupils in the fall months might bring leaves, insects, empty birds' nests, twigs, and small branches for the center. As the items on this interest center are discussed, pupil will learn new terms in vocabulary development.

An exciting, challenging learning environment should be reality in any class setting. Thus, an aquarium might guide pupils' learning in vocabulary development. Fish in an aquarium can help pupils in developing a richer listening and speaking vocabulary. Pupils may learn the names of different kinds of fish in the aquarium. Learners might also learn vocabulary terms pertaining to different parts of fish. Knowledge about fish food can also be acquired. A terrarium in the class setting may also aid pupils in vocabulary development. Thus, pupils can develop important learnings in vocabulary pertaining to frogs, turtles, and harmless small snakes. Important terms relating to caring for and feeding the amphibians and reptiles may also be inherent in these experiences.

Selected potted plants kept in the classrooms could aid pupils in vocabulary development:

(*a*) Learning the names and functions of different parts of plants.

(*b*) Developing learnings of different types of soil used in potted plants.

(*c*) Understanding photosynthesis as a scientific concept.

(*d*) Experimenting to test variables in ongoing units. The vocabulary terms of "experimental" and "control group" might be emphasized in teaching-learning situations.

(*e*) Taking turns in giving proper care to plants in the classroom. Learning appropriate terminology is a part of the ongoing activity.

Pupils can extend and improve their ability to communicate ideas well through becoming actively involved at a dramatization and puppet center. When utilizing dramatizations, pupils cooperatively may plan a pantomime or engage in creative dramatics. In pantomimes, no spoken words are utilized during the ongoing activity. In ongoing units of study, pupils may pantomime scenes such as the following:

(*a*) Colonizing in the New World.

(*b*) Singing the Declaration of Independence.

(*c*) Participating in the Boston Tea Party.

(*d*) Protesting the Stamp Act.

Each of these pantomimes need to be planned thoroughly in terms of content, sequence of action, roles to be played, and reality of presentation. Much discussion is needed to plan each of the facets of pantomiming. Pupils should be guided in improving their skills to communicate ideas effectively during planning sessions.

In creative dramatics, speaking parts are developed as the need arises. Pre-planning of the dramatization in necessary to some extent such as having adequate content in mind pertaining to what is being dramatized. Thus, depending on the unit being studied, pupils may engage in the following, as examples, involving creative dramatics:

(a) Playing the role of workers on a farm.

(b) Taking care of animals in a zoo.

(c) working on an assembly line.

(d) Being members of the United Nations Security Council.

Learners may engage in research using a variety of reference sources in getting needed information to proceed with creative dramatics experiences. Modification of what has been dramatized can occur after the learning activity has been completed. Questions that pupils with teacher guidance may ask pertaining to the utilization of creative dramatics might be the following:

(a) Did pupils have adequate background information to present content in the form of creative dramatics?

(b) Were the respective roles being played in creative dramatics realistic?

(c) Did pupils enjoy the ongoing activity?

(d) Were learners able to attach meaning to the presentation?

(e) Did the creative dramatization activity provide for individual differences?

(f) Did pupils conscientiously evaluate their own achievement?

(g) Did pupils show feelings of respect toward others?

(h) Did pupils feel that purpose was involved in the ongoing presentation?

Van Allen suggests the following summary of skills and abilities for extending pupils' vocabularies:

Vocabulary Acquisition

— Develops meanings for new words through experiences

— Develops meanings for known words through experiences

— Develops understanding of the emotional connotation of words

— Develops understanding of the aesthetic connotation of words

— Acquires a vocabulary for talking about language

— Reacts with meaning to figurative language such as similes, metaphors, and analogies

— Reacts with meaning to idiomatic expressions

— Acquires new words in line with some systematic plan such as one using personal word cards

Vocabulary Application

— Uses resources in the classroom for specific word classes needed in writing

— Uses a thesaurus to add variety in writing

— Uses a dictionary to verify meanings

— Develops personal resources such as a writing handbook to aid in writing and spelling

— Can write in patterns that require the use of specified form classes. Explains: cinquain and diamante

— Uses inflectional changes according to context. Examples: dog, dogs; leap, leaps, leaped, leaping

— Uses pictures in context with language patterns that use a variety of form-class words

— Uses the same word in a variety of forms. Examples: beauty, beautify, beautiful; love, lovely, lovable, unlovely

— Makes use of descriptive words to clarify and elaborate meaning; words of color, size, shape, texture, sound, taste, smell, feelings, touch, and motion

— Knows and uses more than one name for the same thing. Example: mother, woman, female, girl, wife, aunt

— Knows and uses more than one word for the same action. Examples; run, scamper, hurry, race, trot, flee

In Summary

There are many kinds of learning activities which may be used to help pupils in vocabulary development. Variety in learning activities is important to provide for individual differences. Thus, the following experiences can help pupils achieve to their optimum in vocabulary development:

1. Reading orally to pupils.
2. Having pupils engage in discussions.
3. Participating in ongoing activities at the listening center.
4. Reading library books.
5. Participating at the audio-visual center.
6. Being involved at the writing center.
7. Making pictured dictionaries.
8. Engaging in storytelling.
9. Using dictionaries and the glossary.
10. Taking turns reading orally to small groups.
11. Being involved in individualized spelling.
12. Participating at the speaking center.
13. Discussing objects at the interest center.
14. Viewing an aquarium and a terrarium.
15. Taking care of potted plants in the class setting.
16. Participating at the dramatization and puppet center.

REFERENCES

1. Anderson, Paul S., and Diane Lapp. *Language Skills in Elementary Education*. Third Edition. New York: Macmillan Publishing Company, 1979.
2. Anderson, Verna Dieckman, et al., *Readings in the Language Arts*. Second Edition. New York: The Macmillan Company, 1968. Chapter Ten.
3. Burns, Paul C., and Leo M. Shell (eds.) *Elementary School Language Arts, Selected Readings*. Second Edition. New York: Rand McNally and Company, 1973. Chapter Eleven.
4. Dawson, Mildred A., et al. *Guiding Language Learning*. Second Edition. New York: Harcourt, Brace, and World, Inc., 1963. Chapter Four.
5. Dawson, Mildred A., and Frieda Hayes Dingee. *Children Learn the Language Arts*. Second Edition. Minneapolis: Burgess Publishing Company, 1966. Chapter Four.

6. Greene, Harry A., and Walter T. Petty. *Developing Language Skills in the Elementary School*. Fifth Edition. Boston: Allyn and Bacon, Inc., 1975.

7. Hennings, Dorothy Grant. *Communication in Action*. Chicago, Illinois: Rand McNally and Company, 1978.

8. Lee, Dorris M., and Joseph B. Rubin. *Children and Language*. Belmont, California: Wadworth Publishing Company, 1979.

9. Liebert, Burt. *Linguistics and the New English Teacher*. New York: The Macmillan Company, 1971. Chapter Eight.

10. Loban, Walter, et al. *Teaching Language and Literature*. New York: Harcourt, Brace, and World, 1969.

11. Newman, Harold (Ed.). *Effective Language Arts Practices in the Elementary School: Selected Readings*. New York: John Wiley and Sons, Inc., 1972, Chapter Five.

12. Norton, Donna E. *The Effective Teaching of Language Arts*. Second Edition. Columbus. Ohio: Charles E. Merrill Publishing Company, 1985.

13. Van Allen, Roach. *Language Experiences in Communication*. Boston: Houghton Mifflin Company, 1976.

Listening and the Pupil

Listening carefully to ideas expressed orally by others is important. This is important for a number of reasons. Respect for other individuals and their thinking is then revealed. It is a way or means of developing new learnings. Feelings of belonging may be achieved when interacting with other human beings; listening is important in the process.

There are many situations in life in which careful listening is important. The following, among others, represent some of these situations:

1. Conversing with others.
2. Participating in a discussion.
3. Interviewing visitors and guests.
4. Making introductions.
5. Participating in a dramatization.
6. Answering questions raised by others.
7. Listening to a lecture or explanation.
8. Listening to musical recordings.
9. Responding to sounds in the environment pertaining to one's safety.
10. Reacting proficiently to sounds in the environment requiring selected responses.

Diverse levels of listening are the lot of pupils on an individual basis.

1. Hearing sounds of words but not reacting to the ideas expressed: a mother knows that Daryl is speaking.
2. Intermittent listening—turning the speaker on and off; hearing one idea in a sermon but none of the rest of it.
3. Half listening—following the discussion only well enough to find an opportunity to express your own idea: listening to a conversation to find a place to tell how you handled a child.
4. Listening passively with little observable response: the child knows the teacher is telling him once again how to walk in the hall.
5. Narrow listening in which the main significance or emphasis is lost as the listener selects details that are familiar or agreeable to him: a good Democrat listening to a candidate from another party.
6. Listening and forming associations with related items from one's own experiences: a first-grade child hears the beginning sound of *Sally, says,* and *said,* and relates it to the letter *s*.
7. Listening to a report to get main ideas and supporting details or follow directions: listening to the rules and descriptions of a new spelling game.
8. Listening critically: a listener notices the emotional appeal of words in a radio advertisement.
9. Appreciative and creative listening with genuine mental and emotional response: a child listens to the teacher read *Miracle on Maple Hill* and shares the excitement of sugar making.

Principles of Learning Applied to Listening

The psychology of learning has much to offer in providing guidelines for an appropriate environment facilitating the developing of listening skills. The teacher must follow recommended guidelines pertaining to teaching and learning which aid pupils in developing needed skills in listening.

1. Learning activities should be interesting to encourage improved listening on the part of pupils. Too frequently, experiences in the classroom have been boring and result in poor listening.

Dawson, Zollinger, and Elwell list the following appreciative listening activities, among others, which might well capture learner interests:

> Oral reading will often be the background for responsive listening as the listeners *(i)* sketch an original cartoon of a character or situation portrayed in a story; *(ii)* pantomime, activate puppets, or dramatize spontaneously in response to a story just listened to; *(iii)* individually tell or write an original ending to a high-quality story; and *(iv)* make sound effects with rhythm band instruments as the teacher reads a poem or story portraying different kinds of weather or rates of motion; for instance, as a character stroll, walks briskly, stumbles, lopes, pauses and walks softly, races, and leaps to safety.
>
> Storytelling, too gives opportunity for the children to learn to listen appreciatively and creatively; for instance, they *(i)* tell chain stories in which each participant carries on from where the preceding speaker stopped; *(ii)* witness the first act of a play planned and presented by a committee, then spontaneously make up the next act; *(iii)* listen for leads in prepared stories told by members of a special committee, these leads to suggest spontaneous stories on the part of the listeners; and *(iv)* for advanced pupils, keep notes of the ideas suggested by the poems and stories presented by the teacher or their classmates.
>
> The teacher must know as much as possible about the interests of individual pupils. Learning activities related to unit titles may be based on pupils' interests. Thus, learners having hobbies such as collecting coins, stamps rocks, pennants, and other items, can bring these to school pertaining to a unit on hobbies. As learners tell about their hobbies, skills pertaining to listening are involved. Pupils need to listen carefully to the presentation of others. They also must listen to question of listeners pertaining to specific hobbies being presented.
>
> The teacher then should attempt to select learning activities which stimulate learners in wanting to listen carefully to ideas being presented. Content discussed in films, filmstrips, slides, and other

audio-visual materials on the understanding level of pupils can aid learners to become better listeners. Problem solving activities may guide pupils to improve their listening vocabularies. Ideas are shared when pupils in committees identify problems, obtain needed information, and revise necessary hypotheses. Problem solving activities may generate much interest in learning on the part of pupils.

2. Teacher-pupil planning can aid learners in listening. Teaching very often has amounted to lecturing and explaining. Thus, a one-way street of communication is in evidence. Eventually, pupils may lack purpose in learning since there are few opportunities to ask questions in terms of what is valuable to pupils. Pupils, of course, must perceive reasons for learning. Teacher-pupil planning means that learners participate in actively presenting ideas as well as listening to content. Pupils might then have a voice in determining what is to be learned as well as how the learning is to take place. They may also be involved in assessing their own achievement. Thus, pupils become participants in determining the elementary curriculum. The concerns of pupils should be in evidence in teaching-learning situations in the class setting. If the concerns of pupils become an important part of the elementary curriculum, purpose is then involved in learning.
3. Variety in learning experiences can help to develop needed skills in listening. Sameness in learning experiences generally forces listeners in turning off to ongoing learning activities. If improved listening is to take place within pupils, learning activities must be varied. There are more kinds of experiences that can be provided for pupils than ever before. It behooves the teacher to select those which help pupils to listen more attentively.
4. Pupils must receive direct practice to achieve at an optimum rate in listening. Learnings that pupils have developed pertaining to listening should be applicable and transferable to new situations. The teacher needs to provide experiences for pupils where skills in

listening can be developed. Developed skills must be relevant and useful. Thus, the teacher might have pupils listen to various sounds in the environment when taking an excursion on or near the school grounds. Learners may identify the sounds as to their source or origin. The teacher as well as pupils might record diverse sounds and have learners in the class setting identify their cause or causes. The teacher, also, could have learners put their heads on their desk and not see the source of sounds, while the teacher crumbles paper, pours water into a tumbler, and taps a pencil. Pupils can guess what made each of these sounds to occur. Hopefully, as a result of direct experiences pertaining to the identification of sounds, pupils will transfer learnings to new situations. Improved listening might then occur in the classroom setting.

5. The teacher must provide for individual differences in listening. Each child differs from others in many ways such as in height, weight, energy level, health, capacity, and achievement. The teacher must make definite provisions for individual differences in the class setting. To be sure, selected pupils will be better listeners as compared to others. Two pupils may even be quite similar in capacity and achievement; however, one of these learners will comprehend content better in learning activities involving listening. When differences exist in capacity of two pupils, generally the pupil with the higher capacity should achieve better in listening activities, all things being equal. The ability to comprehend well in learning activities involving listening may well depend upon factors such as the following:

(a) Background information of pupils.

(b) Interest in the topic being presented.

(c) Motivation of pupils in desiring to learn.

(d) Content being presented on the understanding level of pupils.

(e) Sequence of ideas being presented.

(*f*) Methods used in presenting ideas.

(*g*) Enthusiasm of the presenter of content.

(*h*) Impression made by speaker on listeners.

(*i*) Use of appropriate gestures, facial expressions, and body movements of the speaker.

6. The teacher must accept each pupil regardless of race, creed, or socio-economic level. Pupil come to school representing diverse socio-economic levels. The home situation may or may not have the following benefits educationally for pupils:

(*a*) Reading materials for pupils.

(*b*) Discussing content with children in a meaningful way.

(*c*) Having an atmosphere of empathy and respect.

(*d*) Children being involved in the making of decisions.

(*e*) Parents reading to themselves and thus setting a model for pupils.

(*f*) Parents taking pupils to visit places of importance such as museums, circuses, and other points of interest.

(*g*) Appropriate clothing for children.

(*h*) Nutritious meals for members of the family.

(*i*) Concern for health and safety of children.

The home situation must provide what is of benefit to children. However, as is will known and documented, selected pupils lack having needed experiences in the home which make for a sound educational background. Pupils may come to school lacking proper fitting and clean clothing. It may then be difficult for some teachers to accept these individuals as having worth. Each pupil must feel he/she is wanted and valued in the school setting for optimum achievement to take place. A child that feels he/she is not a part of the class will hardly achieve optimal development. All pupils must be accepted by the teacher; each child can then be guided to realize optimal development. This is true of the language arts area of listening as well as other curriculum areas.

7. Pupils should be actively involved in learning for the highest achievement in listening to occur. A passive receiver of information cannot achieve to his/her optimum in listening. Pupils need to have a stimulating environment in order that improved listening habits may result.

The teacher must emphasize proper balance among diverse learning activities to stress pupils growing in listening, speaking, reading, and writing. This definitely means that the listening vocabulary should not be deemphasized. Too frequently, skills objectives in listening have not been stressed adequately in teaching-learning situations. The classroom teacher must stress the importance of having pupils achieve relevant objectives pertaining to listening. If learning centres are used in the classroom setting, the following might serve as a model:

(a) A discussion center. Here, pupils could discuss a selected picture, from among others. The pictures should stimulate curiosity and involve learners in a lively discussion at the learning center. Active participation on the part of pupils is to be desired in learning experiences involving listening. At the discussion center, pupils could also discuss relevant issues in the current affairs program. Issues being discussed should provide for situations in which pupils have an inward desire to listen attentively.

(b) An audio-visual station. Pupils in a committee could view selected filmstrips, films, and s slides pertaining to ongoing units of study. Following the presentation, learners could discuss and present their finding to the total class. In the discussion, learners need to present ideas as well as listen to the thinking of others.

(c) A listening center. Pupils may listen to cassette recordings of their choosing related to specific units being studied presently. A task card could be an inherent part of the center. From the card, pupils individually may select sequential activities to complete. Each pupil might then be assessed in terms of having understood and gained ideas through listening when responding to selected questions on the task card.

(d) Oral reading and storytelling center. Here, pupils in a small group may listen to stories being read orally or to stories being told by learners or by the teacher. Careful listening is important in this teaching-learning situation. Hopefully, the stories read and told make for active involvement in listening.

Chambers and Lowry wrote:

Active listening is specialized listening. It is listening to receive special, important information. This is listening with a definite purpose. The conductor listens actively as he rehearses his orchestra. The physician listens actively through his stethoscope. The athlete listens actively to directions from his coach. Active listening implies readiness, listening for a special purpose. Children listen actively to a spelling list being read by a teacher, since after they hear a word on the list, they are required to write it on paper.

Active listening does not comprise most of the child's listening efforts. Often he does not know how or when to listen actively. He will usually need clues so that he can listen in an active way. A good teacher will provide these clues. She many times will have a device that will bring children's attention to her, so that they will be able to participate in active listening. Such a device as calling for attention and waiting until all eyes are toward her and quite prevails is a common one. Preschool and kindergarten teachers many times will strike a chord on the piano or ring a special bell to bring children to attention so they will listen in an active manner.

It is probably wise also to tell children that they will receive directions or other information that is information to them. It is good to simply tell them that they need to listen carefully! What the teacher is actually doing is structuring their listening. They are told to listen carefully, and why they are to listen carefully. Sometimes it is necessary to present the information and/or directions more than once. After they have been given, many teachers will ask a student to repeat what they have heard, so that additional reinforcement is provided. Active listening is specialized listening. Teachers must realize that some children will not know how to listen in this way and will need help in learning this skill.

Passive listening describes that level of listening that does not require the attention, the concern for detail, or any specific requirements of active listening. This kind of listening is largely an unconscious process and contrasts with active listening, which is largely a conscious process. Passive listening is the kind of listening that one does as he listens to the radio, aware of the sound, but not paying great attention to it. One responds to classroom "hum" in a passive way, aware that it is present, but not consciously concerned with it. The everyday sounds of the world are heard in a passive way. They occur and pass with little attention from the listener. Only when the listener is given a clue that what he is hearing is of importance to him will this unconscious, passive listening become active and conscious.

Most of the youngster's listening (and the adult's, for that matter) is of a passive nature. He is aware of sound activity and accepts it passively. His environment teachers him to be actively aware of certain sounds for his protection or to satisfy needs. Other sounds will go relatively unattended.

Objectives in Listening

Dallmann lists the following do's and don't for teachers in the area of listening:

1. Speak in a pleasant voice, one to which the pupils can enjoy listening.
2. Build upon the listening experiences that the child has had at home and/or in earlier years at school.
3. Remember that listening is more than hearing, and help the boys and girls to recognize the fact that attention to a speaker's words often requires thinking.
4. Encourage the listener not to be so absorbed in his own ideas about a point the speaker has mentioned during the course of his talk that he will not note subsequent points the speaker makes in the rest of his talk.
5. Be a good listener yourself. When a pupil or other person is speaking, show by your behaviour that you are listening to the speaker. Some teachers spend much of the time that they should spend in listening by watching members of the audience. This is bad practice because boys and girls may develop the habit of not listening as they note the teacher's inattentive manner.

6. Guard against giving instructions such as "Let's all pay attention". Rather, indicate for what the pupils should be listening.
7. Avoid the practice, in which some teachers engage, of repeating directions or explanations unnecessarily. Otherwise the pupils may develop poor habits of listening, as they realize the teacher will most likely make his explanation more than once. Or the pupil may be bored by that which the teacher repeats. However, the teacher should be careful that he makes his points clear. At times, for example, after the teacher has given a direction of more than one step, a pupil may be asked to make application of it for demonstration purpose, to insure that the point is made clear to those who are listening.
8. Discourage interruption of the speaker, even if he makes an error in speech or in facts presented or in deductions from facts he presents.
9. Don't encourage fake attention. The teacher might lead a discussion on the fact that merely looking intently at the speaker does not guarantee good listening. He can help the pupils to understand that a person looking intently at the speaker may sometimes feel justified in letting his mind wander rather than concentrating on what the speaker is saying.

Objectives for pupils to achieve in listening must be selected carefully. Only relevant objectives should be stressed in teaching-learning situations. Following the selection of objectives, learning experiences must be selected for pupils. Ultimately, assessment must take place to determine if the objectives have been realized. If objectives have not been achieve, the teacher needs to determine causes. New or modified learning experiences may need to be selected so that pupils can achieve the stated objectives. Or, the original objective(s) may need to be omitted or stated at a less complex achievement level.

The following, among others, may be relevant objectives for pupils to achieve in listening:

1. To recall factual information, main ideas, generalizations, and summary statements.
2. To attach meaning to content presented by others.
3. To utilize learnings obtained within new situations such as in problem-solving activities.
4. To analyze content critically in terms of separating opinion from facts, inaccurate statement from accurate statements, and imaginary situations from situations involving reality.
5. To listen creatively with the intent of achieving new, unique, novel ideas.
6. To listen attentively to ongoing presentations.
7. To listen to ideas of others in an atmosphere of respect.
8. To desire to improve in the area of listening.
9. To diagnose one's own difficulties in listening and working toward remedying these deficiencies.
10. To listen proficiently to diverse types and kinds of oral presentations such as in conversations, discussions, interviews, and in the making of introductions.
11. To develop adequate background information so that goals in listening can be realized to their optimum.
12. To evaluate ideas expressed by others in terms of desirable criteria.

The teacher also needs to have objectives which are relevant to use in teaching-learning situations. Thus, the teacher may emphasize the following objectives involving listening:

1. Presenting content on the understanding level of pupils.
2. Varying the kinds of learning activities to promote optimum pupil achievement in listening.
3. Working in the direction of pupils enjoying ongoing learning activities to increase listening potential.
4. Providing for individual differences among learners in listening.

5. Valuing the worth of each learner so that an adequate self-concept may result.
6. Helping pupils develop respect toward others.
7. Developing a relaxed environment free from threats and tension.

Learning Experiences and Listening

> Imagine you are in a vast convention hall filled with an immense display of the latest, brightest, and best educational materials: film strips, tapes, movies, magazines, workbooks, photographs, craft kits, cutouts, stencils, and textbooks. Except for these items spread in colorful array, the room is empty. Until one human being enters the scene, walks, stops, looks and touches, all the materials are nothing but inert matter, just as the magician's props are nothing but objects until used by the individual who can change them into something wonderful.
>
> Creative teachers can transform ordinary learning into a magical moment. They can translate routine lesson plans into memorable experiences. They can present facts in such original ways that the facts fuse with other, deeper understandings and result in exciting discoveries for the student. (Mimi)

A variety of learning experiences must be provided for pupils so that stated objectives in listening can be achieved.

The teacher may select and read interesting stories and library books to pupils. Periodically, stimulating questions might be asked of pupils pertaining to content read to evaluate achievement in listening. Questions asked should not hinder in developing improved skills in listening.

Pupils in committees may take turns reading selected stories to each other. The content of these stories can be discussed within the committee. The teacher then has opportunities to assess each pupil's achievement in listening.

The teacher, as well as pupils, might engage in the telling of stories. Pictures, objects, and charts may be used in the learning activity. Following the telling of stories, pupils with teacher guidance may discuss major generalizations achieved in the listening activity.

Selected intervals of time may be used to provide direct experiences for pupils in listening. Thus, pupils may tell of sounds heard presently in the class setting. Pupils could bring to class an object that would make a certain sound; listeners not seeing the object may guess the source of the sound. Learners individually might also make selected sounds without the use of objects. Other pupils, having their eyes closed and heads on their desks, may determine the cause of these sounds.

Pupils with teacher guidance may develop appropriate standards pertaining to listening. Periodically, pupils could evaluate their own personal achievement in listening in terms of the agreed upon guidelines.

There are many kinds of learning activities to assist pupils in becoming better listeners. The activities must be interesting, purposeful, meaningful, and provide for individual differences. The following, among others, may provide experiences for pupils requiring skill in the area of listening:

1. Discussing content read from reference sources.
2. Evaluating the results of a science experiment.
3. Planning a mural, frieze, or diorama within a committee.
4. Making and evaluating relief maps, models, and toys relating to an ongoing social studies unit.
5. Working cooperatively in solving a mathematics problem involving a new process.
6. Assessing cooperatively in an atmosphere of respect, written or oral reports presented in reading.
7. Planning well balanced meals in a unit on nutrition in the health curriculum.
8. Assessing achievement in small groups toward achieving objectives in physical education, art, and music, as well as in other curriculum areas in the elementary school.

In Summary

It is important for teachers to follow important principles of learning when guiding pupils toward improved skills in listening. Objectives which pupils are to achieve in listening should be carefully selected and relevant from the learner's own unique perception. Experiences pertaining to listening should assist pupils to achieve desired objectives. How well pupils listen in any given situation may depend upon the following (Smith):

1. The child's maturity level.
2. The child's general ability.
3. The child's interest in the topic at hand.
4. The child's previous experience with the material being presented.
5. The type of material being presented.
6. The listening "climate" created by the teacher.
7. The children's rapport with the teacher or the speaker.
8. The quality of the teaching.
9. The attitude and ability of the teacher (or speaker) to relate to the child.
10. The demands made on the child during the listening period.
11. The child's listening readiness.
12. The child's established listening habits.
13. The child's ability to adjust to any abnormal or unpredicted situation.
14. The physical-emotional tone of the room.
15. The child's acquired listening skills.
16. The adjustment of speed of reception with the speed of delivery.
17. The creative set to listen.
18. The child's general health and the social-emotional climate of his home.

REFERENCES

1. Anderson, Paul S., and Diane Lapp. *Language Skills in Elementary Education*. Third Edition. New York: The Macmillan Company, 1979.

2. Applegate, Mauree. *Easy in English*. Elmsford, New York: Harper and Row, Publishers, 1960. Chapter Four.

3. Chambers, Dewey Woods, and Health Ward Lowry. *The Language Arts*. Dubuque, Iowa: Wm. C. Brown Publishers, 1975.

4. Chenfeld, Mimi Brodsky, *Teaching Language' Arts Creatively*. New York: Harcourt Brace Jovanovich, Inc., 1979.

5. Dallman, Martha. *Teaching the Language Arts in the Elementary School*. Second Edition. Dubuque, Iowa: Wm. C. Brown Company Publishers, 1976. Chapter Four.

6. Dawson, Mildred, Marian Zollinger, and Ardel Elwell. *Guiding Language Learning*. Second Edition. New York: Harcourt, Brace and World, Inc., 1963.

7. Dawson, Mildred A., and Frieda Hayes Dingee. *Children Learn the Language Arts*. Second Edition. Minneapolis: Burgess Publishing Company, 1966. Chapter Five.

8. Ediger, Marlow. "Good Listening Habits a Must," *The Oklahoma Teacher*. (February, 1968), 18-19.

9. Fox, Sharon E., and Virginia Allen. *The Language Arts*. New York: Holt, Rinehart and Winston, 1983.

10. Newman, Harold, *Effective Language Arts Practices in the Elementary School: Selected Readings*. New York: John Wiley and Sons, 1972. Chapter Four.

11. Shane, Harold G., et al. *Improving Language Arts Instruction in the Elementary School*. Columbus: Charles E. Merrill Books, Inc., 1962. Chapter Five.

12. Smith, James. *Adventures in Communication*. Boston, Massachusetts: Allyn and Bacon, Inc., 1972.

13. Strickland, Ruth G. *The Language Arts in the Elementary School*. Second Edition. Boston: D.C. Health and Company, 1957. Chapter Six.

Evaluation of Achievement in Language Arts

The teacher must be an effective evaluator of pupil achievement in the language arts. Thus, the teacher must have ample knowledge of each pupil's growth in achieving desire objectives. The language arts instructor should be able to assess present achievement levels of learners in listening, speaking, reading, and writing. Realistic objectives for learners to achieve may then be stated. Objectives should be attainable for each pupil. A further important task of the language arts teacher is to select those learning activities from which all pupils can benefit to their optimum. Last, but not least of all, the language arts instructor must be able to assess if appropriate appraisal procedures are being utilized:

> There are many ways to assess learner achievement in the different curriculum areas of the elementary school. Not all approaches to evaluating pupil achievement evaluate in the same facets of development. For example, using sociometric devices evaluates learners in social development. It does not assess pupils in general intellectual development. A standardized achievement test evaluates pupils in growth pertaining to different curriculum areas in the elementary school. It would not evaluate personal and social development of pupils. Thus, a variety of evaluation devices must be used to assess learners intellectually, socially emotionally, and physically.

Evaluating Pupils' Products

The teacher of language arts must be highly competent in assessing pupils' products in the language arts. A folder should be kept on each pupil pertaining to written products that have been presently completed as well as those which will be completed later on. The date of completion should be written on each finished product. Comparisons may then be made of earlier work of a child as compared to a presently completed product.

It is important for pupils to engage in an ample number of learning experiences involving creative writing. Comparisons might also be made then of a child's past and present achievement in creative writing. The teacher must answer questions such as the following when assessing an individual child's achievement in creative writing in comparing earlier with present progress:

1. Is the child expressing more of novelty and uniqueness in ideas?
2. Does it appear that the pupil has more confidence than formerly in expressing original ideas?
3. Is the child eager to participate in learning activities involving creative writing.
4. Does the child engage in creative writing during leisure time, inside or outside of the class setting?
5. Does the child have an inward desire in wanting to express ideas creatively?
6. Is the child accepting of creative products of other learners?
7. Does the child have a desire to share creative products with others?
8. Do parents give support in having their child express content in a creative manner?

It is of utmost importance to assess pupil progress in the area of creative writing. Creative thinking is a major goal for elementary school pupils to achieve. Improvements in society come about due to creative endeavours of selected individuals. Thus, teachers, supervisors, and principals must think of important objectives, learning activities, and evaluation procedures in creative writing for pupils.

Tape-recording of each pupil's achievement in oral communication could be dated and stored. Comparisons may then be made of learner achievement in oral communication of earlier with present performance. Pupils individually and with teacher guidance may evaluate their earlier with present achievement in the following speaking activities:

1. Taking part in discussions.
2. Presenting oral reports.
3. Making introductions.
4. Conducting interviews.
5. Reading content orally.
6. Participating in creative dramatizations.

Recording Pupil Achievement

Teachers should record pupil behaviour meaningful patterns. It is easy to forget individual pupil behaviour unless it is recorded at regular intervals. Thus, a behavioral journal ultimately results with representative behaviour recorded of each pupil. The following standards should be followed when writing entries of observed learner behaviour:

1. Random behaviour should be recorded and not unusual deeds and acts unless these are persistent behaviours.
2. Comments written should accurately describe observed behaviour. Loaded or vague words should not be used.
3. Recorded behaviour should only be used to help the teacher do a better job of teaching.

Jarolimek wrote the following involving anecdotal records in recording pupil behaviour:

> An anecdotal record is a description of some incident or situation in the life of the child. A collection of such descriptions of pupil behaviour kept over a period of time, therefore, provides the teacher with a documentary account of changes of behaviour that have occurred or are in progress. It is another way of systematically recording observations. Anecdotal records should indicate the date and time of the incident, the circumstances under which it occurred, and an objective description of the situation. If an interpretation is made of the incident, it should be kept separate from the description of the actual happening. The following are six entries in one teacher's anecdotal record on a child.

Anecdotal Record

Sara Larsen

9/24 Difficulty in getting going in independent choice work; ignored all suggestions of activities . . . "It's boring".

9/26 Found a fiction book related to unit for Sara. Read during work time. Took it home today.

9/27 Finished book . . . took suggestion to make a poster showing main characters.

10/1 Asked for time to show class the poster and to tell about the story.

10/2 Showed work. Talented artist. Received lots of compliments/ support from classmates.

10/3 Sara asked for another book; suggested biography to her, plus suggested she do a map showing the area in which the person lived.

Rating Scales and Checklists

Behaviour of individual pupils is recorded when rating scales and checklists are used. When using a rating scale, the teacher needs to write relevant behaviours pertaining to an ongoing unit of study in the language arts. The following ratings may be used as a basis for evaluation: "Excellent, Very Good, Average, Below Average, and Needs Improvement". Each child should be assessed in terms of his or her present achievement level. One pupil should definitely not be compared against other learners since individuals differ from each other in many ways such as in capacity, motivation, interests, achievement, and energy levels. The following are examples of behaviours pupils individually could be assessed in pertaining to an ongoing unit of study:

Name of pupil ____________________ Date ____________________

---

1. The pupil can write one sentence correctly E VG AVG BA NI for each of five sentence patterns studied.
2. The pupil can expand a kernal sentence utilizing modification.
3. The pupil can change a declarative sentence to an interrogative sentence.

The teacher must remember that when rating scales are utilized to assess learner achievement, subjectivity is involved. For example, not every teacher assesses a pupil in the same way when sentences are written pertaining to different sentence patterns. Also, if rating scales are utilized by a teacher to assess pupils individually at later intervals, the evaluations will differ in terms of perception. The teacher then might not have the same perception when evaluating a pupil from one time to the next. The teacher, of course, does not feel the same way from one evaluation session to a second evaluation session. Teachers do not feel the same way on Tuesday morning as compared to Friday afternoon.

When using checklists, the teacher must list relevant behaviours to evaluate pupils in an ongoing unit of study. The following are examples of behaviours that might be written on a checklist:

Name of pupil ____________________ Date ____________________

---

1. The pupil writes sentences correctly pertaining to the subject-predicate pattern.
2. The pupil expands sentences correctly using appositives.
3. The pupil varies sentence patterns in writing.

The teacher checks behaviours that pupils need more help in. It is difficult for a teacher to realize fully which specific behaviours pupils need more assistance in unless they are recorded. The teacher may then give pupils needed guidance to overcome deficiencies.

Guidelines to follow when developing and using checklist pertain to the following:

1. Relevant behaviours need to be written by the teacher or by pupils with teacher leadership.
2. Behaviours must be written clearly so that agreement exists as to what is being diagnosed.

3. Pupil behaviour must be carefully observed to determine if more appropriate learning activities are needed by pupils to overcome deficiencies.
4. The teacher might not have the same perception from one time to the next in evaluating each pupil in terms of recorded behaviours.

Dellmann lists the following as possible evaluate procedures to check skill in locating information:

1. The boys and girls can answer questions on various parts of a book such as: *(a)* In what part of a book is the index found? *(b)* In what part of a book—the table of contents or the index—are the main entries arranged in alphabetical order?
2. The boys and girls can be timed as they find the beginning page on an entry in the table of contents or as they find the first page on which reference to an entry in the index is given.
3. The boys and girls can tell which word of a series would be the most likely one under which, in the index or encyclopaedia, information to answer a given question would be found.
4. The pupils can be tested on ability to arrange letters and later words in alphabetical order. At first the arrangement of words in alphabetical order might deal only with lists of words in which the first letters are different. Later such lists could include words in which first letters of the words are alike and still later they could also include words in which the first and second, and still later, even subsequent letters are alike. The pupils can rewrite the letters or words in alphabetical order or they can number the words or letters in the right order.
5. The boys and girls can be checked on ability to select the meaning given for a word in a dictionary that fits into the context of the sentence in which the word is used.

Teacher Developed Tests

True-false, multiple-choice, matching, and completion items may not measure achievement as effectively in the language arts as compared to teacher observation of pupil achievement in functional writing situations. However, there are important learnings of pupils that can be measured through the use of teacher developed tests. Consider the following true-false item:

A verb is a word that can be changed from singular to plural in number.

This test item can aid in determining if pupils understand what a verb is. To be sure, pupils can guess the correct response to a true-false item. A true-false test needs to be of adequate length to randomly survey what pupils have learned. However, a true-false test can be too lengthy; thus tiredness and fatigue set in during the testing session. Pupils may then hurry in taking the test rather than concentrating in revealing what is truly known. Guessing in a true-false test can be minimized by using a correction factor, e.g., counting the number of correct responses minus one-shelf times the number of incorrect responses. True-false items should be clearly written so that pupils accurately interpret their content. Test items should be written on the present reading levels of learners. If the content is written at a highly complex level, test results may indicate how well a child reads rather than understandings achieved in a language arts unit.

Pupils have a more difficult time guessing correct answers in a multiple-choice test as compared to responding to true-false items. In multiple-choice items, all responses should be rational. Consider the following multiple-choice item:

Which of the following sentences patterns emphasizes the subject-predicate pattern?

(a) Janice walks to school.

(b) The vase is colorful.

(c) Bill caught the cat.

(d) Jack gave Mike a dog.

Each of the four responses is reasonable in terms of being the correct response. Teachers, in some situations, have written three ridiculous responses together with one correct response in multiple-choice items. No doubt, most pupils then knew the correct response without appropriate learning experiences or study prior to taking the test. Each of the four responses in the multiple-choice test item above is of similar length. If the responses vary much in length, clues may be given to the test taker as to which is the correct response. Each of the responses is correct in terms of stating a complete sentence. Notice the following multiple-choice item which is incorrectly written; pupils could identify the correct response due to speaking or writing in standard English:

Henry Wadsworth Longfellow was a

(a) Engineer on a train in the 1880's.

(b) Famous American poet.

(c) Interested in inventions.

(d) Agricultural and forestry specialist.

In this multiple-choice test item, response "b" only, would be grammatically correct. Each response in a multiple-choice test item should be correct grammatically when it is matched with the stem.

Completion items may guide in evaluating pupil achievement. Relevant learnings should be emphasized in completion tests. The completion items should be written on the reading level of pupils. Adequate information needs to be contained in an item so that meaningful responses on the part of pupils might result. The following completion item lacks content as to its meaning:

__________ and ______________ are __________ in __________.

Thus, the teacher needs to write meaningful test items. Consider the following which gives pupils needed information to successfully complete the required blank:

A ______________ contains two lines of rhymed verse of poetry.

Each blank should be the same length in a completion test so that clues are not given as to correct responses due to length of blanks. The correct answers to the blanks in completion items could be written either to the left or in the right hand margin. This makes for ease in scoring the test. The content of the test should be on the reading level of pupils. The purpose of the test is to assess pupil understandings acquired rather than measure reading achievement.

Matching tests can aid in determining pupil achievement. Items in a matching test should be homogeneous. Homogeneous items involve assessing pupils in content which deals with one topic. Notice the following items in a matching test:

_______	1. free verse	a. shaped like a diamond
_______	2. limerick	b. two lines of rhymed verse
_______	3. quatrain	c. contains five lines in the poem
_______	4. haiku	d. based on the number of syllables per line
_______	5. couplet	e. rhyming is not necessary
_______		f. contains four lines of rhymed verse.

All the items above pertain to the writing of poetry. Validity in testing is important. Thus, pupils are being tested over what they have had opportunity to learn. Learners should not be tested over content that has not been taught. Pupils should do equally well if the same test were taken over again with no opportunity to study inherent related content. The latter generalization is stated to indicate the importance of consistency of results when taking a test; thus, the concept of reliability is important in developing and writing test items.

In writing matching items, the following standards should be followed:

(a) More responses should be written in one column as compared to the second column. The process of elimination then may not be used excessively when pupils respond to the final items in a matching test.

(b) It is important to have responses in one column which are short in length. Pupils might have a difficult time in making needed responses if column one having lengthy sentences is matched with column two also having lengthy sentences.

In the matching test on poetry, pupils are being evaluated in identifying different kinds of poetry. Better it is, to be sure, if pupils can write meaningful poetry which they enjoy and sense purpose in writing.

Using Essay Tests

Pupils can be evaluated in language arts achievement through the use of essay tests. Learners need to have an adequately developed writing vocabulary, however, to reveal desire understandings, skills, and attitudes in an essay test. When essay tests are utilized to evaluate pupil achievement in the language arts, the following criteria should be followed:

1. Approaches in testing as well as types of tests should be varied to provide for individual differences among children.
2. Pupils should sense purpose in the testing situation; that is, learners should desire to find out what they have or have not learned.
3. Testing should be diagnostic in determining specifically where pupils are experiencing difficulty. Learning activities should then be provided to remedy the deficiencies.
4. Teachers should definitely not scold pupils based on perceived low test results.
5. Testing situations should guide learners in developing an inward desire to learn.
6. Interest in learning should not be minimized or destroyed through testing.
7. Test items being responded to should be on the present achievement level of pupils.

In using essay tests to assess pupil achievement, the test items should be clearly written and appropriately delimited. The following essay ifems are too broad and general with many interpretations as to their meaning:

1. Discuss poetry.
2. Write a story.

Essay items can be delimited by writing them in the following manner:

1. Write a haiku poem.
2. Write a setting for a story of your own choosing.

The teacher has a better chance of evaluating pupil achievement in acquired specific learnings if the test items are properly delimited rather then containing ambiguous statements. Essay items can be too delimited whereby strictly factual answers are required, as would be true of the following items:

1. Lists the different parts of speech of the English language.
2. Name five different sentence patterns discussed in class.

Responses in terms of content to essay items should be assessed separately from the mechanics of writing, such as spelling, handwriting, punctuation, and capitalization. The mechanics of writing are always secondary in importance to ideas expressed in writing.

Self Evaluation by the Teacher

The teacher needs to evaluate his own teaching frequently in the language arts curriculum. The teacher must then ask and answer questions such as the following pertaining to teaching the language arts:

1. Do I reward pupils in expressing creative ideas orally and in writing?
2. Are pupils stimulated adequately so that creative behaviour is in evidence?
3. Do pupils enjoy learning experiences involving creative expression?
4. Are a variety of experiences available for pupils to express creative behaviour such as in writing poetry, stories, and participating in dramatizations?
5. Are adequate opportunities available for pupils to make choices and decisions in the school/class setting?

6. Is teacher-pupil planning utilized in determining objectives, learning experiences, and evaluation procedures?
7. Do I encourage pupils to evaluate their own achievement in the language arts?
8. Is a good reading readiness program in evidence for kindergarten and first grade pupils?
9. Are learning experiences adequately individualized in the class setting?
10. Are adequate attempts made to determine present achievement levels of each learner?
11. Are conferences conducted frequently to truly determine each child's interests, needs, and aspirations?
12. Is the reading program organised to provide for diverse interests and goals which learners have?
13. Do pupils engage in realistic and meaningful experiences rather then emphasizing rote learning and memorization?
14. Is adequate emphasis being placed upon pupils being actively involved in ongoing learning activities?
15. Are pupils permitted to make decisions in terms of what is to be studied?
16. Can pupils utilize what has been learned previously?
17. Are pupils developing appropriate skills in working together well with others?

Thus, the teacher of language arts must be a good evaluator of pupil achievement in the language arts. The teacher must also be a good assessor of personal strengths and weaknesses in teaching the language arts. Individual differences among pupils must be provided for in a modern program of language arts in the elementary school.

In Summary

A critical task of the language arts instructor is evaluation. Pupil products in the language arts must be continuously assessed in order that continuous progress might be in evidence. Achievement of pupils must be recorded periodically so that a pattern of behaviour on the part of each child may be observed. Also, the teacher can notice more effectively which pupils need increased guidance and assistance in achieving desired objectives. Teacher made tests might aid in determining learner achievement in the language arts. Based on diagnosis then, the teacher may guide learners to realize desire objectives as a result of teaching and learning. The language arts teacher certainly must continuously evaluate his or her own teaching to provide for pupil optimum achievement.

REFERENCES

1. Anderson, Paul S. *Language Skills in Elementary Education*. Second Edition. New York: The Macmillan Company, 1972. Chapter Nine.
2. Dallman, Martha. *Teaching the Language Arts in the Elementary School*. Third Edition. Dubuque, Iowa: Wm. C. Brown Company Publishers, 1976, pages 252 and 253.
3. Ediger, Marlow. *Relevancy in the Elementary Curriculum*. Kirksville, Missouri: Simpson Publishing Company, 1975, page 193.
4. Ediger, Marlow. *Social Studies Curriculum in the Elementary School*. Kirksville, Missouri: Simpson Publishing Company, 1980, Chapter Eight.
5. Funk, Hal D., and De Wayne Triplett (Eds.). *Language Arts in the Elementary School: Readings*. Philadelphia: J.B. Lippincott Company, 1972. Part VI.
6. Gagne, Robert D. *Principles of Instructional Design*. Third edition. New York: Holt Rinehart and Winston, 1988.
7. Jarolimek, John. *Social Studies in Elementary Education*. Seventh Edition. New York: The Macmillan Company, 1986.
8. Liebert, Burt. *Linguistics and the New English Teacher*. New York: The Macmillan Company, 1971. Chapter Ten.

9. Nerbovig, Marcella H., and Herbert J. Klausmeier. *Teaching in the Elementary School.* Third Edition. New York: Harper and Row, Publishers, 1969. Chapter Seventeen.

10. Schuster, Albert H., and Milton E. Ploghoft. *The Emerging Elementary Curriculum Methods and Procedures.* Columbus: Charles E. Merrill Publishing Company, 1970. Chapter Fourteen.

11. Shepherd, Gene, and William B. Ragan. *Modern Elementary Curriculum.* Sixth Edition. New York: Holt, Rinehart and Winston, 1982.

12. Tiedt, Iris M., and Sidney W. Tiedt. *Contemporary English in the Elementary School.* Englewood Cliffs: Prentice-Hall, Inc., 1975.

Reading and the Language Arts

Each pupil should develop optimum proficiency in reading. Reading can be a very enjoyable leisure activity. Individuals enrich themselves by engaging in reading activities. In society, it is important for individuals to do much reading and thus remain informed about problems and issues on the local, state, national, and international levels. Each person may then have additional alternatives from which decisions can be made. A broad base of background knowledge may assist learners to increase their proficiency to make decisions.

Each pupil differs from other children in the class setting in achievement, capacity, interests, and motivation for reading. Thus, the teacher must make provision for individual differences among learners in the reading curriculum.

Experience Charts and Reading

In a reading readiness program for early primary grade children, experience charts may be developed cooperatively by pupils with teacher guidance. The experience chart approach is sound since it is based upon personal experiences of involved pupils. Thus, pupils experience ideas from excursions, filmstrips, films, pictures, slides or discussions. Following the experience, pupils present content for an experience chart. The teacher in this situation prints the content using neat manuscript letters. Most pupils generally have not developed a writing vocabulary to do the actual writing. After the content has been written in large, highly legible manuscript letters, pupil read what has been written with teacher guidance. The teacher points to words and phrases as they are being read by pupils. Learners then are reading what they have experienced.

The following assumptions support utilizing experience charts:

1. Pupils are actively involved in experiences which provide content for an experience chart.
2. Learners present ideas for the experience chart.
3. Pupils with teacher help read content pertaining to their very own experiences.
4. Learners may notice how ideas are written down utilizing abstract letters and words.
5. The content in the experience chart in familiar to learners since it relates to their own personal lives.
6. The experience chart method may assist pupils to develop interest in reading.
7. Individualization is inherent in using experience charts since each child has unique experiences. Each child may then present content for a group or individual experience chart.

Learning Centers and Reading

A different approach to individualize in reading pertains to the use of learning centers. One of these centers might well be a reading center. Library books should be on diverse reading levels and on various stimulating topics. Ideally each pupil selects an interesting library book to read on the appropriate reading level. Following the reading of a library book, pupil achievement may be evaluated in several ways.

1. Task cards at the learning center could be written with open-ended questions for pupils to respond to.
2. The teacher and pupil might discuss contents of a library book which the latter has completed reading.
3. The child may choose his/her own approach in revealing comprehension pertaining to content in a

library book such as in completing a diorama, a dramatization, a frieze, or a picture.

4. The pupil might share ideas gained from reading a library book within a small group or committee.

Any approach that is used to assess pupil achievement should stimulate learners to do additional reading.

Reading Readiness and Individualized Instruction

There are numerous learning activities which assist pupils in learning to read through a quality reading readiness program. Providing for individual differences is an important concept for teachers to follow when providing learning activities in a reading readiness program.

Background information must be developed within pupils in a quality reading readiness program. Later, pupils will read much content where familiarity with ideas is important. To aid in developing background information, the following learning activities, among others, may be utilized:

1. Discuss pictures with pupils pertaining to ongoing units of study.
2. Show and discuss films, filmstrips, and slides.
3. Have pupils take an excursion and discuss observation made.
4. View and have follow-up activities pertaining to a telecast on educational television.
5. Develop learning centers with appropriate activities to help pupils achieve relevant background information.

For each of the above learning activities, purpose must be developed within pupils prior to participation. The learning activities can provide for individual differences even though learners at selected intervals may be taught in large group instruction. Pupils may then interpret content from audio-visual materials on their own individual present achievement levels. It is best if most of these activities can be used in small group or committee work. Pupils may then have increased opportunities to interact with other learners in discussing acquired facts, concepts, and generalizations. The frequency of interaction in a discussion per pupil in small group work is greater than would be true of larger groups or the class as a whole.

In a quality reading readiness program, it is important for learners to experience hearing likenesses and differences in sounds. Thus, for example, a teacher may ask pupils to present words which have the same beginning sound as does the word "bat". Pupils may also be asked to give words which rhyme with "bat". These activities should aid learners to become increasingly proficient in phonetic analysis. Later, in more formalized programs of reading instruction, the use of phonetic analysis will aid in unlocking new words.

In a reading readiness program pupils begin to make associations between symbol and sound. When pupils are reading from an experience chart with teacher guidance, they may well notice specific letters in words and make the proper associations with sounds.

When selected objects are labeled in a class, pupils ultimately will also make associations between symbols and sounds. If they cannot identify the abstract word, the real object will tell its meaning, such as the labeled abstract word "chair" on a real chair. Pupils learn to identify individual words at different rates of speed. Provision may then be made for individual differences.

Pupils should have ample opportunities to browse through interesting and appealing library books containing quality pictures. Illustrated books have a tendency to provide for individual differences when chosen by pupils. Learners may then interpret illustrations on their own individual achievement level. The teacher also needs to read library books to pupils in a reading readiness program. Thus, pupils may become motivated in wanting to learn to read.

Further learning activities in a reading readiness program might consist of pupils advancing at individual levels of achievement in noticing configuration clues. Experiences in noticing configuration clues must be provided in proper sequence for each learner. Among others, these learning activities may include the following:

1. Pupils make a cross on which word looks different from two other words (man lonely man).
2. Learners place an "X" on which letter appears different from two other letters (h h a).

Gross discriminations need to be made by pupils followed in sequence by those involving finer discriminations. Fine discriminations are involved in which a word or letter looks different in appearance from the remaining words/letters in each of the following sets:

1. house hen house
2. b b 1
3. horse hill hill
4. a a b

Hall, *et al.* write the following involving reading readiness for pupils:

> Observation by sensitive, alert, and formed teachers will be the best source of information about individual children's readiness for a successful start in reading. Teachers who view readiness as an individual matter and as a composite of the many factors discussed previously will be alert to information in all of these areas. Teachers will be assessing readiness while teaching. For example, if children are matching word cards with an experience chart story . . ., their performance will indicate whether they can, in fact, perform the visual discrimination task. Instructional settings will furnish the same information as offered by readiness tests on certain readiness tasks. In addition, the total classroom setting will present opportunities for observation of many factors not represented in the content of the standardized readiness instruments.
>
> As she observes children's responses in the school setting, the teacher evaluates the physical, perceptual, cognitive, linguistic, experiential, and personal adjustment dimensions of readiness. She may notice eagerness or reluctance to participate in discussions and other activities, aggressiveness, gregariousness or shyness, disinterest in or fascination with print and books. Of particular interest to the observant teacher are a child's reactions to activities with print, such as reading names, plans, experience charts, signs, and other printed material in the classroom. As the teacher

conducts the instructional program, she observes alertness in learning as well as knowledge of specific tasks such as matching or naming letters.

Basal Readers and the Pupil

Basal readers are used quite frequently in elementary school classrooms. Teachers need to utilize the manual directly related to the basal reader in a creative manner. Too frequently, the manual is utilized rigidly. Suggestions pertaining to objectives, learning activities, and assessment procedures found in manuals of basal readers should be adopted to individual differences in the class setting. The manual can give teachers many excellent suggestions to use in teaching-learning situations. The following criteria are recommended in helping pupils achieve to their optimum when basal readers are utilized:

1. Basal readers should be on the present achievement level of pupils when learning activities are provided.
2. Prior to reading a given selection, pupils should have adequate readiness activities such as:
   (a) Gaining adequate background information.
   (b) Seeing new words in manuscript print and attaching meaning to these words.
   (c) Establishing purposes for reading. The purposes may pertain to questions which require answers from reading a given selection.
3. Following the reading activity, pupils should have appropriate follow-up activities, such as:
   (a) Discussing purposes or answers to questions after reading a given selection.
   (b) Writing a summary of main ideas read.
   (c) Developing an illustration, frieze, mural, or diorama.
   (d) Reading additional literature related to the content read.
   (e) Selecting stories and books written by the same author.

(f) Reading selected portions oraly.

(g) Writing diverse forms of poetry.

(h) Dramatizing selected selections of the content.

(i) Developing a related bulletin board display.

Basal readers have been misused by classroom teachers. Certainly, teachers must apply relevant principles of learning in teaching-learning situations involving the use of basal readers. These principles would include:

(a) Providing for individual differences.

(b) Attaching meaning to what has been learned.

(c) Stimulating learners in desiring to learn.

(d) Praising pupils for improved performance regardless of past achievement.

(e) Diagnosing pupil difficulties and working toward remediation.

(f) Having learners achieve at their own optimum unique rates of achievement.

(g) Selecting interesting learning activities.

(h) Having pupils sense reasons for participating in ongoing learning activities.

(i) Providing sequential learnings for learners.

(j) Having pupils voice their concerns and interests in selecting reading materials.

(k) Maintaining balance among objectives pertaining to learning word recognition techniques, reading for a variety of purposes, and reading for enjoyment.

There are selected procedures which have been used in situations involving the use of basal readers which definitely cannot be recommended. Among others, these include the following:

1. All pupils in the class being on the same page at the same time in a basal reader.

2. Every learning activity in the manual being utilized in teaching-learning situations for all pupils in the class setting.
3. Pupils rigidly developing learnings pertaining to phonetic analysis and other word recognition techniques when they already are reading proficiently.
4. Teachers emphasizing recall of information largely, when purposes for reading are being pursued on the part of pupils. Higher levels of thinking also need adequate emphasis, e.g., critical thinking, creative thinking, and problem solving.
5. Little emphasis being placed on pupils reading for enjoyment.
6. The same or similar methodology being used rather continuously in teaching reading.
7. Content in basal readers not being correlated or integrated with other curriculum areas in the elementary school.
8. Teachers not diagnosing pupil difficulties in reading adequately and not working toward remediation of problems.
9. Pupils not being taught in terms of using child growth and development characteristics.
10. Recommended principles of learning not being utilized in teaching-learning situations.
11. A lack of teacher knowledge or enthusiasm in teaching reading.

The teacher of reading needs to engage in self-evaluation to determine which trends in a modern reading curriculum should be emphasized in teaching-learning situations in the class setting.

Karlin writes the following pertaining to diverse series of basal readers:

> Although many basal reading systems offer similar materials as the basis of their comprehensive reading programs, the content and the manner of treatment varies from series to series. For example, some first-year programs provide stricter vocabulary control than others by introducing fewer different words and

repeating them more often. There are some basal programs that limit initial vocabulary to words with phonic consistency of the fat-cat or run-jump-bug variety. Some basal reading programs offer initial lessons with a heavy phonics orientation—stress on teaching the sounds of letters. Other introduce children immediately to meaningful sentences through which letter-sound correspondences are taught. Then there are programs that use meaningful ideas with or without the aid of pictures to promote language and reading development. The sequence and pace for introducing word and comprehension skills also vary from series to series. Workbook exercises may precede or follow the reading of selections. Some series have incorporated some features of the so-called linguistic materials by reducing the among of letter-sound variance. While some beginning readers focus on the family, others offer social studies and science materials. And of course, the ways in which the teacher's manuals suggest how the selections should be treated and the skills taught vary from series to series. As children move beyond the word recognition stage and develop some competence, however, differences among the programs to which they are exposed narrow. The content and range of reading skills offered becomes more similar, although the emphasis on different skills varies.

Linguistics and Reading

Selected specialists have emphasized the importance of linguistic approaches in guiding learners to achieve in reading. According to one linguistic school of thought in beginning reading instruction, pupils should learn to read words which have rather thorough consistency between symbol and sound. Pupils may then learn to read sentences in which words follow a specific pattern in pronunciation and spelling. Thus, the teacher might guide pupils in learning to read sentences containing the follow words:

man fan Dan pan tan

ban can Nan ran van

Or, pupils in beginning reading could learn to read words such as the following, within sentences:

bet net pet vet

met let set wet

It is difficult, of course, to write sentences with involved words following a pattern such as in the above named "man" family or "bet" family of words. This approach in teaching of reading has not been well accepted. However, in the curriculum area of spelling, pupils in many units of study, learn to spell words where patterns are important. Thus, pupils are learning the structure of words such as in the following set where the initial consonant can be changed and a new word results: pat, rat, fat, cat, bat, hat, Nat, and sat.

There are advantages that linguistic approaches in the teaching of reading emphasize. These implications may also hold true for spelling. Among others, the advantages include the following:

1. Pupils can be aided in reading instruction by noticing how selected words pattern rather consistently between symbol and sound.
2. Learners develop understanding pertaining to structure of related words following a general or specific pattern.
3. Pupils may learn to identify new words when thinking of related patterns.
4. Learners develop a positive approach in identifying new words when viewing structure or pattern of words.

Disadvantages in using linguistic approaches in the teaching of reading might be the following:

1. Monotonous reading activities may be experienced by pupils, especially in beginning teaching-learning situations.
2. There might be a lack of relationships in terms of how pupils speak using functional sentences as compared to reading content in beginning reading using selected linguistic approaches.
3. Many words are spelled in an irregular manner in the English language and do not pattern well, such as "my," "sigh," "I," "pie," and "lye". These words contain the long "I" sound.

In using linguistic approaches in the teaching of reading, pupils encounter more of irregularly spelled words as they progress through the elementary school years. There also are irregularly spelled words which follow a pattern, such as "blight," "flight," "might," "plight," "sight," and "night".

Tiedt and Tiedt write the following involving linguistic methods of reading instruction:

Linguistic scholars have contributed much to our understanding of the English language and its functioning. Among their contributions have been the following concepts:

1. Language is constantly changing.
2. Change is normal.
3. English sentences follow specific patterns.
4. Word order conveys meaning.
5. There are specific phonemes and graphemes for the English language.
6. The grammar of a language is its structure.
7. Usage is not rigid but relative.

The application of these concepts of language has revolutionized the teaching of language and approaches to composition. It is not surprising that linguists have also attempted to apply linguistic concepts to reading instruction. Thus far, however, the results are disappointing, for the "linguistic" approach, almost solely a phonemic-graphemic presentation, has produced material like this:

had	can	cat	bag
lad	Dan	fat	nag
pad	man	hat	rag
sad	pan	rat	tag

Dan had a bat.

Has Ann a bag?

Ann had a bag.

Nat had a nag.

A fat cat had a rat.

A man had a hat.

Fat had a nap.

The linguist's approach to reading is essentially based on the presentation of words by phonemic and graphemic groups. As in the linguistic approaches to spelling, the child is introduced to a family of words, for example, *look, book, cook, took, hook*. Those advocating this linguistic approach to beginning reading point out that children can learn groups of words rather then single words. While learning *eat*, the child might just as well learn *beat, heat, meat, neat, seat*, and so on.

Specific Objectives and Reading

Selected teachers, supervisors, and administrators advocate the use of specific objectives in the teaching of reading. These objectives are written in a precise manner. It is possible to meaure if pupils have achieved specific objectives after instruction. Through observation, as one method of appraisal, the teacher can evaluate if pupils have or have not achieved the desired ends. Specific objectives must be selected carefully, prior to instruction, by those involved in teaching pupils. Thus, relevancy is an important concept to emphasize in selecting specific objectives for pupils to achieve.

The following are examples of specific objectives which pupils may achieve on their own unique achievement level:

1. The pupil will voluntarily read a library book and be able to answer three out of four questions correctly in evaluating comprehension.
2. The learner will pronounce correctly 95 per cent of words encountered in reading a selection from the basal reader.
3. Reading a story of his/her own choosing, the pupil will state the main idea in the selection.
4. Having identified a problem in any curriculum area, the pupil will select five reference sources to gain a relevant solution.

5. The pupil will present at least three generalizations related to content read from a self-selected library book.
6. The learner will analyze a selection in reading by identifying three opinions given by the writer.
7. After completing the reading assignment, pupils will assess content in terms of presenting two accurate statements and two inaccurate statements.
8. The learner will tell a story pertaining to content read using appropriate sequence of sentences.
9. Following the reading of content in social studies, the pupil will give five facts contained in the selection.
10. Having read content pertaining to five story problems in mathematics, the pupil will tell in his/her own words information needed to provide viable solutions.

It is important for teachers to write significant objectives when specificity is important. Too frequently, specific objectives are written which can be stated quickly and may then represent irrelevant learnings. Each objective in reading must be evaluated thoroughly in terms of acceptable standards.

Determining Reading Levels

One of the most important problems facing teachers of reading is to determine reading levels of individual pupils. Once this has been accomplished, the teacher has a further responsibility in finding materials which are beneficial to each individual. How can the teacher determine present reading levels of each pupil in the class setting?

1. The school may use standardized achievement tests to determine reading levels of pupils. These tests need to be assessed in terms of being valid and reliable. Grade equivalent test results from standardized tests may provide guidance to teachers in determining reading levels of learners on an individual basis.
2. The teacher may mark off approximately 100 running words in a basal textbook, the content of which has not been read previously by pupils.

The learner orally reads the selection to the teacher. Generally, pupils should pronounce 95 to 98 per cent of the words correctly, if the involved book has content on the instructional level of the learner. The teacher also must select with great care four questions covering the selection to be read by pupils. Each pupil basically should be able to answer correctly three out of four questions to asses comprehension in reading.

The figures given pertaining to correct word pronunciation as well as reading comprehension are approximate. If pupils, for example, pronounce 75 per cent of the words correctly in a selection, comprehension will suffer. Thus, the book being considered is not on the instructional level of individual pupils. Or, if a pupil continually pronounces all words correctly without previous practice and continually responds correctly to all relevant questions asked to assess comprehension, the book being considered will generally be too easy for the learner. The textbook might then be considered to be on the recreational level of reading. There is no room for growth in recognizing new words in reading on the part of individual pupils if, without previous practice, the child can pronounce 100 per cent of the words correctly. Thus, in a quality reading program, there is room in each lesson for pupils to learn to identify a few new words as well as be challenged in the area of comprehension.

The teacher then has an important responsibility in determining reading levels of individual pupils. Appropriate materials must be obtained to assist each pupil in achieving optimally in reading.

Heilman, *et al.* wrote the following involving the determination of appropriate reading materials for learners:

> One of the most helpful tools one can use in the classroom to diagnose pupils' reading strength and weaknesses is the informal reading inventory (IRI). Essentially, there are three basic types of IRIs; commercially published, those accompanying basal reader series, and teacher prepared, Regardless of the type of inventory you choose to use, its major purposes are to establish pupils' reading levels and identify their reading strength and weaknesses.
>
> The typical IRI consists of graded word lists, graded reading passages, and comprehension questions.

Graded word lists are lists of ten to twenty words for each grade level represented in the IRI. Most commercially published and basal IRIs have graded word lists for preprimer through sixth grade. A child's performance on the graded word list provides you with information for placement in the graded passages, sight vocabulary, strengths and weaknesses, and strategies used to identify words presented in isolation.

Graded reading passages are series of passages, usually ranging in reading difficulty from preprimer or primer through eighth or ninth grade. A reader's performance on the passage gives you an indication of his reading strategies in using context, attention to meaning, and identification of unknown words, and different levels of reading competence.

Comprehension questions consists of five to ten questions for each graded reading passage. The questions cover several aspects of comprehension, such as vocabulary, main idea, inference, literal, cause and effect, sequence, and so forth. The purposes of the questions are to identify pupils' level of reading comprehension competence and point out comprehension strengths and weaknesses.

Evaluating Reading Achievement

In assessing pupil achievement in reading, teachers need to ask themselves, among others, the following questions:

1. Did I guide each child in learning to read to his or her highest potential?
2. Were reading materials provided for each child's own unique level of achievement?
3. Did pupils engage in more independent reading then formerly?
4. Were pupils guided in developing proficiency in word attack skills so that comprehension of content was at an optimal level?
5. Did it appear that pupils enjoyed learning activities involving reading?
6. Were pupils developing optimal skills in reading for a variety of purposes?
7. Did learners have ample opportunities to assess their own achievement in reading?

8. Were pupils permitted to make an adequate number of choices in terms of selections to be read?
9. Did each child achieve stated objectives in reading instruction?
10. Were attitudinal objectives emphasized adequately as well as skills and understandings objectives in teaching-learning situations?
11. Did pupils develop appropriate appreciations toward quality literature in the reading curriculum?
12. Were pupil difficulties in reading diagnosed adequately?
13. Was remedial reading instruction emphasized adequately for needy learners?
14. Did I attempt to determine reading levels of each pupil?
15. Were appropriate learning activities selected to provide for individual differences?
16. Did I use valid evaluation techniques in assessing learner achievement?
17. If pupils did not achieve desired objectives, did I attempt to determine causes for this happening to remedy identified deficiencies?

In Summary

There are many innovations in the teaching of reading. Teachers, principles, and supervisors must become thoroughly familiar with new methods of teaching. New approaches in teaching reading should be evaluated thoroughly before being introduced in an elementary school. Objectives in reading must be carefully selected for pupils to achieve. Learning activities to achieve desired ends, as well as appraisal procedures to evaluate achievement, need to provide for individual differences among learners.

REFERENCES

1. Anderson, Paul S. *Language Skills in Elementary Education*. Second Edition. New York: The Macmillan Company, 1972. Chapter Five.
2. Anderson, Verna Dieckman, et al. *Readings in the Language Arts*. Second Edition. New York: The Macmillan Company, 1968. Chapter Seven.

3. Duffy, Gerald B., and George B. Sherman. *How to Teach Reading Systematically*. New York: Harper and Row Publishers, 1973.

4. Funk, Hal D., and DeWayne Triplett (Eds.). *Language Arts in the Elementary School: Readings*. New York: J.B. Lippincott Company, 1972, Part Five A.

5. Hall, Mary Ann, et al. *Reading and the Elementary School Child*. Second Edition. New York: D. Van Nostrand Company, 1979.

6. Heilman, Arthur W., et al. *Principles and Practices of Teaching Reading*. Fifth Edition. Columbus, Ohio: Charles E. Merrill Publishing Company, 1981.

7. Hirsch, Katrina de, et al. *Predicting Reading Failure*. New York: Harper and Row, 1966.

8. Karlin, Robert. *Teaching Elementary Reading*. Second Edition. New York: Harcourt Brace Jovanovich, 1975.

9. Kephart, Newell C. *The Slow Learner in the Classroom*. Columbus: Charles E. Merrill, 1960.

10. Lee, Dorris M., and R.V. Allen. *Learning to Read Through Experience*. Second Edition. New York: Appleton-Century-Crofts, 1963.

11. McKim, Margaret G., and Helen Caskey. *Guiding Growth in Reading in the Modern Elementary School*. Second Edition. New York: The Macmillan Company, 1963.

12. Moffet, James, and Betty Jane Wagner. *Student Centered Language Arts and Reading, K-13 • A Handbook for Teachers*. Boston: Houghton Mifflin Company, 1983.

13. Russell, David H. *Children Learn to Read*. New York: Blaisdell Publishing Company, 1961.

14. Spache, George D. *Good Reading for Poor Readers*. Champaign, Illinois: Gerrard Press, 1964.

15. Tiedt, Iris., and Sidney Tiedt. *Contemporary English in the Elementary School*. Second Edition. Englewood Cliffs. New Jersey: Prentice-Hall, Inc., 1975.

Reading and Vocabulary Development

Developing a rich listening, speaking, reading and writing vocabulary is important in all curriculum areas. In the reading curriculum, in particular, a quality vocabulary needs to be achieved by each pupil. One reason that pupils do not read well is that they do not possess a functional vocabulary for reading. Enriching and developing pupil vocabularies should be a major goal in each academic discipline. The following are reasons for teachers guiding leaners to possess a rich vocabulary:

1. Subject matter and ideas are expressed with more clarity and accuracy.
2. Proficiency in the work place might well depend upon individuals having a quality vocabulary.
3. Individuals seemingly have more prestige if their listening, speaking, reading and writing vocabularies and adequately developed.
4. Greater enjoyment of reading is in the offing if a person has a rich functional vocabularies.
5. Vocabulary development is salient in problem solving. A person with a rich vocabulary should have a better opportunity to develop his/her vocabularies.
6. Conversations carried on with other persons require a rich vocabulary. There needs to be an appropriate number of words used that carry intended meanings.

7. Variety in selecting words to convey accurate meanings is necessary in speaking and writing, the outgoes of the language arts.
8. Use of diverse terms and concepts in speaking and writing adds variety to quality communication. Vocabulary development becomes a tool to take in, such as listening and reading, as well as provide communication to others within the framework of speaking and writing.

Very closely related to the background knowledge required for reading a text is vocabulary knowledge. . . . By about the third grade and certainly by the fourth grade, most of the selections of the newer reading programs are drawn from independently published materials, as compared to selections created by a publisher for inclusion in their series. The newer basals are virtually anthologies. Authors of the selections are professional writers using the best words available from the general vocabulary to communicate their ideas. Thus, the kind of vocabulary control found in the older basals is not in evidence in current programs. The sophisticated vocabulary in the selections from the newer basals has both positive and negative potential for students. The negative potential is obvious—too many unfamiliar words will cause comprehension problems. The positive potential is also obvious—children can add words to their store of vocabulary.

Vocabulary development strategies created for each story lesson begin with the identification of a subset of words that developers believe may cause meaning or decoding difficulty. These words are listed in the teacher's manuals. By the third or fourth grade the programs assume competent decoding most of the words noted in the teacher's manuals are of the meaning variety difficulty. These words become "target words" for vocabulary development activities. Traditionally, the development of word meaning is attended to by instructional events that occur prior to reading, during reading and after reading. . . . (Beck 1984).

Developing the Vocabulary of Learners

The reading teacher needs to select quality objectives for pupils to achieve in the areas of vocabulary development. These objectives need to emphasize that is relevant and functional in vocabulary development. Certainly, pupils should be able to use what has been learned. Learning should not be for its own sake but rather be for personal use and application in society. Important vocabulary terms should be acquired by pupils. Adequate time must be given in choosing what pupils need to learn in vocabulary development. This cannot be hurried, because vocabulary development emphasizes that which must be learned in depth, not survey approaches.

Objectives pertaining to vocabulary development need to stress securing the interests of pupils in ongoing lessons and units of study. Ways of developing and maintaining pupil interest in learning must be emphasized in vocabulary studies. If pupils do not reveal interest in learning, they will not achieve as optimally as possible.

There needs to be objectives reflecting pupils working collaboratively. Within the cooperative endeavour, pupils listen to others and use oral communication with opportunities to achieve in vocabulary development. There are definite social goals here in that pupils need to learn to work harmoniously with others. And yet pupils also should be able to work by the self and achieve on an individual basis.

Vocabulary development emphasizes that pupils seek purpose in learning. Purposeful learning in vocabulary development means that pupils perceive reasons for learning. I think that one cannot stress too strongly that vocabulary development for pupils should have as a goal that purpose is involved in learning. Purposeful learnings have as a goal that pupils perceive the values inherent in vocabulary activities. If these values are lacking, the teacher should stress other vocabulary development lessons for learners.

Objectives in vocabulary development need to emphasize the importance of meaningful learnings. If meaning is lacking, the chances are pupils will memorize terms and concepts for testing purposes only or largely. Meaning stresses the importance of pupils understanding that which has been learned. Use cannot be made of a new vocabulary term unless understanding of prerequisites in vocabulary terms in prevalent. With prerequisites, background information is needed to attach meaning to vocabulary terms being studied.

Objectives in vocabulary development for pupils should emphasize pupils experiencing the concept of providing for individual differences. There are pupils who learn more rapidly that others while some pupils take more time to learn the same content/skills as written in the statement of objectives. Each pupil regardless of socio-economic level must be accepted as a human being and taught in a manner which provides for all pupils.

Learning Opportunities to Achieve Objectives

To achieve vital objectives in vocabulary development, the teacher needs to select worthwhile activities for pupils. These activities need to be selected carefully so that each pupil's achievement is as optimal as possible. Pupils should not be labeled as being fast, average, or slow learners. Rather all should be accepted and develop feelings of belonging to the group.

To achieve objectives in vocabulary development. We recommended selected learning opportunities that student teachers and cooperating teachers whom we supervise have used successfully.

Each day the teacher should read aloud to pupils during story time. The book chosen should interest pupils and keep their attention. Voice inflection using proper stress, pitch and juncture should be in the offing when the teacher reads during story time. Words should be pronounced clearly and accurately. The teacher should have good audience contact with listeners. For young children, it is especially good to show the book's illustrations to pupils as the library book is being read. Throughout the story time activity, pupils should understand an increased number of facts, concepts and generalizations. Knowledge received provides background information for more complex ideas that should be forthcoming. Knowledge is sequential and cumulative for learners. A love for learning by pupils might be a further end result when the teacher reads orally to pupils during story time.

A second activity stressed pupils discussing ideas obtained from listening to the library book read or from personal reading pursued. Through discussion participation, pupils should learn effective ways of working within a small or large group setting. Pupils should learn to be polite, accepting and cooperative in the discussion learning activity. Being a good listener, valuing the thinking of others and actively participating in a polite manner should help a discussion to move forward in quality. Thus, the processes of being a member of a discussion group need to be emphasized continuously.

Then too, during the discussion, pupils should achieve quality ideas, facts, concepts and generalizations. Learners need to stay on the topic to achieve subject matter learnings during a discussion. Straying from the topic at hand merely wastes time. Ideas need to circulate within the group so that all have opportunities to participate. Active participation by each pupils should be an objective. Use of language during a discussion helps pupils to achieve more optimally in speaking. This translates content acquired to be used to comprehend subject matter in reading. The content and vocabulary gained by the learner might then provide background information for reading. Generally, what pupils are able to discuss represents meaningful subject matter. The subject matter might then provide the necessary knowledge, prior to reading, which helps pupils to understand increasingly complex vocabulary read.

Third, it is good to have once or more listening centers in the classroom. There are excellent cassette tapes related to an ongoing lesson on unit of study. Information gleaned from listening to a tape may guide pupils to answer related questions contained at the center. The information might well assist pupils to use this as background content to understand better what will be read from a basal or library book.

At the listening center, pupils may choose sequential tapes to listen to, for a variety of purposes. These purposes might well be the following in listening for:

1. Facts, concepts and generalizations.
2. Information to use in problem solving.

3. Critical thinking purposes such as separating facts from opinions accurate from inaccurate information and fantasy from reality.
4. Opportunities to do creative thinking in the reading curriculum such as coming up with novel, unique ideas and originality in thought.
5. Obtaining directions in reaching a certain place.
6. Securing a main idea when relating facts, concepts and generalizations.
7. Obtaining the setting of a story.
8. Securing ideas pertaining to characterization within a writing.
9. Determining the plot of a selection in reading.
10. Understanding the theme of the speaker.

Fifth, the reading teacher needs to have one or more speaking centers in the classroom. Listening (discussed above) and speaking are interrelated. We will mention some activities here that emphasize speaking more than listening.

1. Giving oral reports on library books read, related directly to the ongoing lesson and unit of study being taught. The oral report should follow good sequence in content presented. The ideas need to be presented clearly and at an appropriate rate of speed so that listening comprehension is optimal. The pupil presenting the oral book report needs to have the content well in mind. An outline, in proper form, should be used to convey the contents therein. The presenter of the book report should have good eye contact with the audience. Reading for enjoyment and for solving problems are two purposes in having pupils become proficient in reading.
2. Having pupils video-tape their individual oral book reports given to the class. Here, pupils individually or with a peer may appraise the quality of the oral report given. Standards used to appraise may be the same as under number two above. The contents of the videotape may also evaluate distracting mannerisms of the

speaker such as rubbing the nose excessively. It is good to have the presenter appraise the quality of his/her own oral report in terms of quality standards. Vocabulary terms are developed from the reading of library books as well as from the oral presentations given of library book content.

3. Interacting with audio-visual materials to locate information for problem solving. The AV materials may include video-tape, CD ROMS, films, filmstrips, large illustrations, snapshots enlarged for class viewing with an opaque projector, internet and worldwide web, as well as computer packages. Among others, With pupil interaction with AV materials of instruction, there are many opportunities to gather information for a committee project such as developing a mural. The mural must be planned cooperatively with all participating and no one dominating collaborative endeavours. After the planning, the implementation of the plan comes in sequence. With implementation, each pupil on the committee does his/her fair share of the work. The project represents the best work each pupil can do. Thus, neatness, accuracy and attractiveness become key ingredients when appraising the mural. Art work correlates well with reading. Through art, pupils may reveal what has been learned. Vocabulary development is definitely inherent in planning, implementing and appraising the project.

Sixth, ample emphasis should be placed upon pupils doing much writing with. Writing, pupils read their own written products as well as read those of other learners whose works are posted on the bulletin board. Reading and writing cannot be separated from each other but are complimentary. There are numerous forms of written work that pupils may engage in. Journal entries should be written freely to indicate what had been learned in a given lesson. Diary entries may be written each day and should be dated. These diary entries portray what pupils learned for a day. As pupils write these diary entries, they read written content. In this way pupils also review that which was learned previously from reading and re-reading diary entries covering subject matter learned. Additional written work may include the following:

1. **Logs**—logs summarize what was contained in diary entries for one week. Clarity of ideas and proper sequence is important in writing logs.
2. **Book reports**—these relate to an ongoing lesson or unit of study. Meaningful content in an appropriate order must be inherent in the written work.
3. **Outlines**—here proper style needs to be used such as Roman numerals to indicate main ideas, captain letters in sequence to indicate subordinate ideas and Hindu-Arabic numerals to reveal details. The subordinate ideas relate directly to the main ideas whereas the details tell more about the subordinate content. Outlines are very helpful to use in giving a report on a certain topic to classmates. Thus, the oral report will have improved sequence to ideas presented as well as if the pupil forgets certain ideas, the outline is there to aid memory in oral communication.
4. **Poems**—poetry written in any lesson should relate to an ongoing lesson or unit of study. There are opportunities for pupils to write poetry in each curriculum area. There can be unrhymed verse written such as free verse. Or poetry written may contain rhyme such as couplets, triplets, quatrains and limericks. Poetry written may also include a selected number of syllables per line such as Haiku (5-7-5 syllables for each of three sequential lines). Tanka contains 5-7-5-7-7 syllables per line for each of five lines.

It is quite obvious that there are many writing opportunities for pupil pertaining to each curriculum area and within each lesson taught. Pupils engage in much reading, re-reading and proofreading when engaging in writing experiences. Vocabulary development opportunities are numerous.

Seventh, pupils may engage in developing a dictionary. Even though there are pictured dictionaries, grade level dictionaries, unabridged dictionaries, as well as glossaries in basal textbooks, it can be highly profitable for pupils individually or in committees to develop their very own dictionaries. Why? Perhaps, there are many new words brought into the lesson or unit of study by teacher. It is good to alphabetize these new words and write meaningful definitions for each. Dictionary entries need to be functional so that they may be used as needed to obtain contextual information. It is good for pupils to be able to alphabetize and re-read the necessary entries.

Eighth, pupils and the teacher should engage in story telling activities. Content for the story needs to follow a certain order to be meaningful to the listener. Thus, sequence of ideas in story telling is important! A clear speaking voice with proper enunciation helps the oral presentation to be more effective. Having a pleasant speaking voice with quality eye contact with listeners assist in the communication of the story. When pupils hear stories told, especially pertaining to a specific library book at an interest center, interest in reading that book tends to be generated. Background experiences are also developed within pupils for reading additional books in ongoing lessons and units of study.

When engaging in story telling, pupils should be developing poise and gracefulness in the process. Pupils need ample opportunities to appear before others in informal and formal experiences. No doubt, skills and attitudes are being developed here that will have life-long values and worth. Shy pupils, in particular, need to appear before others in a variety of roles so that feelings of poise and worth are inherent. The confidence that can come from these experiences might well have carry over values to other endeavours.

Tenth, reading co-operatively in small groups can provide much enjoyment and interest in literature. Being with others is a favourite leaning style of selected individuals. They prefer to work together rather than working on an individual basis. Pupils too receive practice in reading. Cumulative practice should make for increased knowledge, skills and attitude toward reading. With co-operative reading, three or four pupils may take turns reading a library book. If one copy only of a library book is available. Sequential pupils may read aloud as the others in the group listen carefully to the contents. The contents may also be tape recorded so that individual pupils may re-read the library book. Then, if a word is not known in identification, the recorded voice provides the needed information.

If multiple copies of a library book are available, the small group of three or four pupils may follow along in their own library book as the sequential oral reading takes place. Thus, one person reads aloud as the others in the committee follow along in their own library book. Shared reading experiences has many intrinsic rewards for pupils. There should also be ample opportunities for those who like individual endeavours to read a book by themselves.

Eleventh, there should be many objects and items at an interest center whereby pupils may discuss each. I have observed many aquariums and terrariums in classrooms which provide stimulating situations for pupils to provide content for an experience chart. Sometimes a teacher has numerous potten plants in the classroom which may provide pupils an opportunity for informal conversation and also ideas for an experience chart. A rich learning environment helps pupils to think about the contents. The resulting ideas assist pupils to use oral language, engage in written work, read about similar situations or subject matter and/or listen to the thinking of others. A stimulating environment needs to be in the offing so that pupils have purposes for engaging in reading and language arts activities. For example, on the early primary grade level, pupils may observe and experience objects on an interest center. They may then provide content to the teacher who in return prints in neat manuscript letters what pupils have said and discussed. After the write-up of the contents, the pupils with the teacher pointing to words and phrases being read may comprehend the ideas presented into his experience chart. This approach is sound in that:

1. Pupils have the background information to begin with looking at and discussing objects at the center.
2. Pupils present ideas for the experience chart. Learners then have chances to speak and to listen to others. What is said should be meaningful since it is based upon personal experiences of pupils. When the teacher points

to words and phrases, he/she together with pupils read orally content from the experience chart. Here, young learners should be developing an enriched vocabulary with a larger basic sight vocabulary. These sight words become the building blocks for future reading activities. The contents of the experience chart may be re-read as pupils desire. Many pupils like to read over again what has been read previously. Practice here assists pupils to retain basic sight words better then would otherwise be the case.

Twelfth, a quality spelling program should help pupils to become better readers. There are numerous places where spelling words in vocabulary development may come from for pupils to master. Individualized spelling stresses learners mastering a reasonable number of words that come from what was missed in spelling words correctly from every day writing occurrences. The teacher needs to decide here how many of these misspelled words can be spelled correctly within a week or whatever the designated time would be. Words may also come from a quality basal spelling text, new words in a lesson for pupils to master as listed in the basal reader, words that research states are important for pupils to master in spelling such as the Dolch list (1955). As pupils practice the correct spelling of words, they are becoming involved in vocabulary development and reading, learners need to see print as often as feasible in order to become good readers. Spelling need not be dull and dry with memorization of words. Rather pupils should experience interesting activities by;

1. Using these words in writing letters to parents and friends, developing a related cross word puzzle and playing games with peers.
2. Working with peers in learning to spell words correctly. Co-operative learning may be a preferred style of learning for selected pupils.
3. Pantomiming the meaning of selected words. This could involve the playing of charades whereby a pupil chooses a word for spelling at random from a box, pantomimes it and then asks others in the classroom to identify which word is involved.

4. Dramatizing the spelling word. A pupils may select a spelling word at random and use puppets or marionettes to dramatize its meaning. Classmates may guess what the spelling word is. Creative dramatics may also be used. Here, the pupil chooses a word at random from a box and uses words and actions to indicate which word is being focused upon. The word wanted is not mentioned orally in the creative dramatic presentation. Several pupils could also be involved in this activity.

How much of the spelling curriculum should stress inductive and how much deductive thinking? We would suggest a balance between the two approaches. Thus, when using a spelling textbook in teaching, the teacher assigns words for pupils to master. This is a deductive approach. Furthermore, the teacher has pupils learn a strategy for learning to spell these words such as:

1. Looking at the spelling word carefully.
2. Saying the word accurately.
3. Saying clearly the parts of the word, such as pronouncing each syllable carefully and accurately.
4. Writing the new word without looking at it.
5. Comparing the written word with that contained in the basal spelling textbook.

The teacher here is emphasizing a deductive method of spelling words correctly. Why is this a deductive approach? The teacher has determined what and how pupils are to learn.

An inductive approach stresses pupils being involved in curriculum development such as, pupils seeing how many homonyms or synonyms to find in a homonym/synonym hunt. Pupils might have suggested this activity when studying a unit containing a few of these words. Also, the teacher may have suggested the activity and pupils individually or on teams volunteered to see how many could be found. The sky is the limit in the number to be located. Perhaps, the teacher needs to have a balance between deductive versus inductive approaches in having pupils learn in the area of spelling. If a basal spelling text is used and there are a few rhyming words in a weekly list, pupils could locate additional ones to go along with those given in an inductive approach in learning. With a deductive procedure, the teacher may challenge gifted learners with additional words to master in spelling in addition to those listed in the text. By studying the correct spelling of words, pupils should increase their skills in vocabulary development and reading.

Thirteenth, we recommend pupils learn to spell relevant words contained in computer packages. These are drill and practice activities, tutorial, gaming and games, simulation and diagnostic/remedial packages. Reading teachers need to evaluate each package carefully to determine which relevant words in spelling pupils should master. Use should be made of spelling words for retention to take place. Spelling words may be used to write:

1. Friendly and business letters.
2. Notices, announcements, plays, reports, poems and stories.
3. Names and addresses.
4. Birthday greetings and holiday messages.
5. Notes of sympathy and condolence.

As pupils participate in these writing activities, they need to proof-read content. The skills of reading are very much in evidence then. The spelling curriculum should be based upon words that pupils need to learn to spell. The needs of pupils are very important when developing any curriculum area. Beyond the goals of learning to spell words correctly are skills in reading for a variety of purposes that should be upper most in the minds of learners. Narrative, expository and creative writing should all be emphasized in ongoing lessons and units of study. Vocabulary development in an essential part in any listening, speaking, achieve as optimally as possible in vocabulary development and its related component—reading.

What then should be guidelines to use in assisting pupils in vocabulary development?

1. Word study should be integrated with prior knowledge and with learning in the content areas.
2. Word study should involve intensive "deep" study of some words, involving many exposures to the words in meaningful contexts, both in and out of texts.
3. Teachers should engage in direct teaching or modelling, talking explicitly about word meaning and structure.
4. Students should be actively involved in instruction; an important side effect of this involvement is the development of favourable attitudes toward words and word learning.
5. Students should be taught strategies for learning new words independently.
6. Teachers should introduce words in meaning "families" so that semantic and structural relationships among the words are made explicit.

These principles are more applicable at the intermediate grade levels and beyond, when student's cognitive development has advanced to the point where they can explicitly deal with increasing conceptual abstraction. Nonetheless, you will see aspects of these principles at work; in work study at the primary grade level as well .... (Templeton, 1997).

Conclusion

There are numerous opportunities for pupils to engage in vocabulary development. Each curriculum area provides these learning activities to increase proficiency in the use of vocabulary terms. The teacher needs to establish objectives, learning opportunities and evaluation procedures within individual academic areas to guide pupils in acquiring a rich listening, speaking, reading and writing vocabulary. The objectives of instruction need to stress relevant, functional words for pupils to master. Learning opportunities in vocabulary development should assist pupils to achieve the stated objectives. These activities need to be interesting, purposeful and meaningful. Evaluation procedures to appraise learner performance in achieving objectives need to be valid, reliable, varied and encourage further learning.

In evaluation Ph.D. theses for Sri Ramakrishan Mission Vidayala College of Education in India, the author of the study listed the following sequence in vocabulary development (Ayyappan, 1997):

The confrontation phase emphasizes the teacher presenting relevant data pertaining to the concepts as well as important related definitions. Students then generate questions pertaining to the concept or vocabulary term. Phase two is the concept information phase. Here, students compare the attributes given and relate them to form the concept of vocabulary terms taught. Learners discuss with other pupils the distinguishing features to identify the concept.

In phase three, the teacher obtains responses from pupils in a stimulating discussion. Pupils then identify similarities and differences from the information presented. Pupil hypotheses are then appraised involving the tentative concept. In phase four stressing the concept development phase, the teacher presents related tasks for pupils to complete pertaining to the concept stressed. Probing of pupils knowledge pertaining to a concept is important. References are also made to the textbook while discussing the concept. The major classroom interactions are:

1. Teacher interaction/introduction/information.
2. Activities for pupils include media interaction, consulting text, and peer interaction whereas feedback includes evaluation and teacher interaction (Ayyappan 1997).

One of the finest procedures in vocabulary development, one of us have observed in supervising student teachers and cooperating teachers, was the Hilda Taba inductive method used with a class of sixth graders. Here, the two teachers had pupils view a filmstrip on *Life on a Manor*. The teachers, after having pupils view the contents in the filmstrips, asked:

1. Tell us in a single word or phrase what you learned from watching the filmstrip. The following responses were given by pupils; castles, moats, draw bridge, the mill for grinding grain, oxen pilling a plow, peasants cutting wheat by hand, peasant cottages, the three field

approach in farming, fallow, boblemen, tournaments, page, knight, guilds, apprentice, master and wars.

2. How would you combine or join together the concepts you mentioned for number one above? Here, a variety of answers were given in and for an open-ended question. One grouping of vocabulary terms given by pupils was the following:

Oxen pulling a plow, peasants curring wheat by hand, the three field approach in farming and fallow were joined together.

3. What name would you give to the joined together vocabulary terms? The answer provided was "cultivating the soil".

REFERENCES

Ayyappan, R. (1997), *Concept Development in Electronics at Higher Secondary Level*. Coimbatore, India: Bharathiar University, Ph.D. thesis.

Templeton, Shane (1997), *Teaching the Integrated Language Arts*, Second Edition, Boston: Houghton Mifflin Company, 287-88.

Reading and the Structure of the English Language

The structure of the English language is important for pupils to know about. Knowing structural ideas can assist learners in getting the feeling of what comes next sequentially in oral or silent reading. Having objectives to achieve pertaining to these structural ideas can be quite abstract and difficult. We have observed in classrooms at different grade levels how learning key ideas and these structural ideas can be interesting and useful in reading. During the 1960s and 1970s, the structure of each academic discipline became major objectives for pupil attainment. However, educators must say that careful selection of what to teach is always important. The structure of knowledge emphasizes the selection of what is relevant and important to teach. It is ridiculous to think that the structure of knowledge movement was stressed only in the 1960s and 1970s. Determining key ideas and main ideas to teach is always important. Determining the structure of the English language, and any language for that matter, is very important. Much wasting of time occurs if teachers teach what is irrelevant and unimportant. The structure of knowledge movement also emphasized that pupils learn these ideas inductively. Inductive learning today is very important. Pupils like to discover rather than receive knowledge through lecture or heavy use of explanations. When pupils engage in problem solving, they are learning inductively. Thus, a problem is determined by pupils with teacher guidance in an ongoing lesson or unit of study. The problem is contextual and not outside the present learning activity being pursued. The problem indicates feelings of perplexity and uncertainty as to a course of action. The problem needs to be clear and unambiguous.

Pupils may then obtain information in answer to the problem. A variety of learning opportunities may be involve here when securing needed information or data. Sometimes, much time is needed in the solving of problems. At other times, instant decisions need to be made. Little time is then available to gather information. The information secured is used to develop an answer or hypothesis. The hypothesis is evaluated in a real life situation. Inductive learning then is used in problem solving, be it in literature or any curriculum area. Problem solving is always important in school and in society due to individuals facing problems in many facets of life.

Learning structural ideas can be quite complicated and lack purpose such as application. However, we have come to believe, after observing many student and cooperating teachers in the public schools, that enjoyable ways can be found to have pupils achieve key, major ideas in English as it relates to reading instruction. Listening, speaking, and writing are also involved here.

To emphasize the structure of knowledge approach in teaching, the teacher should:

1. Have an excellent knowledge of major generalisations in sentence patterns since these key ideas become objectives for learner attainment.
2. Sequence learning opportunities in that individuals experience the enactive (objects and items), the iconic (semi-concrete materials of instruction), and the symbolic (abstract ideas).
3. Appraise pupils to ascertain how many of these structural ideas are being attained by pupils in a spiral curriculum. With a spiral curriculum, pupils meet up again and again at increasing levels of complexity the structural ideas which serve as objectives of instruction.
4. Ask quality questions of pupils so that they may truly learn in an inductive manner. Inductive teaching then assist pupils to achieve the structural ideas.

5. Use enactive, iconic and symbolic materials in inductive approach in learning (Ediger, 1997).

Sentence Patterns

There are five sentences patterns, in particular, that pupils should have knowledge about in order to become more proficient in reading. These five patterns will come up again and again in oral or silent reading. Enjoyable, yet scholarly methods may be used to guide pupil achievement in attaining these five sentence patterns. The first pattern is the subject/predicate pattern. The reading teacher may take sentences from the basal reader or a library book read by children to illustrate sentence pattern. Sentence pattern number one—Boys swim. There are just two words here to express a complete thought or idea. Pupils in class can be asked for another word which would replace "Boys". There are numerous correct responses here. One word is "girls". A brainstorming approach can be very interesting for pupils to see how many words would fit in. The sentence pattern stays the same and yet the subject changed from "Boys" to "Girls".

Pupils may wish to do journal writing on different sentence patterns discussed in class. It is good too if learners reflect upon what has been written. Reflecting stresses thinking about diverse sentence patterns and using these win writing sentences in journal writing. Application of what has been learned emphasizes review, practice and use of sentence patterns in a multitude of ways. Pupils may wish to bring pictures to class which illustrate what is shown in an illustration. These illustrations are also good to indicate concepts stressed in sentence patterns, such as "Fish swim" for sentence pattern number one above.

A next sequential question could call for words that replace the predicate part "swim". Responses to be given by pupils might include the most obvious word "swam". Learners need to experiment with different words to take the place of "swims", such as using a singular subject with a singular predicate. Here, pupils could dramatize or use pantomime to illustrate a verb in a sentence. When verbs show action, it is relatively easy to dramatize/pantomime the contents.

A second sentence pattern for pupils to study and experience is the subject/predicate/direct object pattern, such as Bill hit the ball. Here again, pupils may suggest an endless number of words to substitute for the subject "Bill". Substitutions could also be made for the predicate "hit", as well as for the direct object "ball". Substitutions for each of these three words could be the following, as an example—Carl, caught and fish. Most pupils enjoy working with sentence patterns in this way. They also notice how the English language works, even with changes being made.

A third sentence pattern involves the subject/linking verb, predicate adjective pattern, such as "Flowers are beautiful". This sentence pattern brought on diversity of responses from a class of fourth graders when they noticed the many words that may be substituted and yet the sentence pattern stays the same. One pupil brought a vase of flowers to school, a concrete experience, to show the third sentence pattern mentioned. After the class discussed the vase with flowers, pupils added another learning activity not previously mentioned above. The activity emphasized using concrete materials in the classroom to show sentence pattern number three—Flowers are beautiful. What did pupils come up with? The following materials were used to show this sentence pattern:

1. The eraser was dusty. This sentence stressed what was observed at the chalkboard.
2. The food was delicious. This sentence came from eating in the school lunchroom.
3. The desk was dirty. A pupil observed his own desk in the classroom.

A fourth sentence pattern is represented by the subject/predicate/indirect object/direct object pattern such as, "Sally gave Sue a present. Sally gave what?" The answer is "present". "Present" is the direct object whereas to whom was the present given? The answer is "Sue". "Sue" is the indirect object.

At this point, pupils may be ready to experiment with what makes for a subject of a sentence. The subject will tend to be a noun or pronoun. A noun is a word that can be changed from singular to plural, such as girl/girls and woman/women. Singular refers to one whereas plural indicate two or more of something. This is relatively easy for pupils to access. Pupils may also experiment with the subject doing the acting, such as "caught" the ball. The subject may also receive the action such as the package was wrapped by Alice. Thus, something was done to the subject of the sentence which was "package".

In their journals, pupils listed nouns and checked these with the teacher. Pupils in committees drew pictures of nouns representing those which are singular as compared to those which are plural. Active and passive voice of subjects was dramatized such as—The boy was revived by two classmates. Here, a pupil lay motionless on the floor with two classmates. Applying artificial respiration! Pupils do like to dramatize and be creative in the language arts involving the study of sentence patterns.

A fifth sentence pattern is the subject/predicate/predicate nominative pattern, such as "Alice is a singer". Alice equals singer in this sentence. It names the same person. "Alice" is singular and needs a singular verb such as "is". "Alice is also the name of a person and thus comes under the traditional definition of what a noun is, such as a person place, or thing. The word "singer" is a noun too since it refers to a person. "Singer" is singular and when comparing that word with 'singers' where more than one person is in evidence.

Pupils can provide many responses as to substitutions that can be made for the words—Alice, is, singer; the sentence pattern of subject/predicate/predicate nominative would stay the same, *e.g.* Bob was a swimmer (Ediger, 1988).

In studying these five sentence patterns, pupils do not need to memorize content. In fact, when brain-storming, many correct responses are given by learners and they can experience much success inductively. Open-ended answers are given by pupils and these usually harmonize with the many possibilities that are necessary in terms of responses given. Pupils need to be successful learners so that they are increasingly more motivate. Pupils tend to develop knowledge and feelings pertaining to the structure of the English language which assist then to read in a more confident manner. For example, the subject/predicate sentence pattern indicates there are certain words that would fit into this pattern. Pupils then receive cues and clues as to which should follow in sequence (Ediger, 1997).

Higher levels of cognition might well be an end result when pupils engage in thinking about different sentence patterns. Sternberg (1997) has developed an excellent model for teachers to use when teaching and pupils are assisted to think at a higher cognitive level;

Memory: Remember what a gerund is or what the name of Tom Sawyer's aunt was.

Analysis: Compare the functions of a gerund to that of a participle, or compare the personality of Tom Sawyer to that of Huckleberry Finn.

Creativity: Invent a sentence that effectively uses a gerund, or write a very short story with Tom Sawyer as a character.

Practicality: Find gerunds in newspapers or magazine articles and describe how they are used or say what general lesson about persuasion can be learned from Tom Sawyer's way of persuading his friends to whitewash Aunt Polly's fence.

Let's consider sentence pattern number one—The subject/predicate pattern—"Boys swim". Using the Sternberg model, the lowest level of thinking would be *memory*. Here, pupils could recall "the subject/predicate sentence pattern. They might also recall what a noun is and what verb is. For *analysis*, pupils may be asked to explain the difference between the noun and the verb. To stress *creativity*, the pupils may be asked to write a sentence containing a noun and a verb. For *practically*, pupils might locate nouns and verbs in a very short story.

The Thornberg model provides guidance to teachers in having pupils move upward to higher levels of thought with four levels, namely memory, analysis, creativity and practicality in studying grammar as well as the structure of the English language.

Expanding Sentences

Pupils with teacher guidance enjoy making sentences longer or expanding them. For each of the five sentence patterns discussed above, the sentence can be expanded. If we take the first sentence pattern of subject/predicate—Alice is a singer, the word "Alice" does lend itself to expansion with single words, but it does better with phrases and clauses. One could say "Brave Alice is a singer". The single word "brave" describes "Alice". If a noun "girl" is substituted for "Alice". Then an endless number of single words may be given to describe "girl". The following are provided as examples: small tall, young, bashful, aggressive and hostile among others. There are many predicate nominatives that can take the place of "singer" such as older, younger, experienced, amateur, beautiful and tall among others.

Phrases are another way to expanding sentences. Generally, pupils learn rather easily that phrases contain more than one word and yet do not contain a subject and predicate. The following are phrases which modify "girl":

1. With a red sweater, such as "The girls with a red sweater was a singer".
2. Feeling well, such as "Feeling well, the girl was a singer".
3. On the pond, such as "The girl on the pond was a singer".

Later on, in sequence and when readiness is in evidence, pupils may study and learn if a phrase is adjective and modifies a noun or is adverb and modifies a verb, adjective or another adverb.

A clause can do much to clarify meanings in a sentence and at the same time the concept of expansion is being emphasized:

The girl who has black hair is a singer.

The dependent clause is underlined and contains a subject "who" and a direct object "hair". A clause has a subject and a predicate, but does not express a complete thought.

Pupils may provide words which take the place of the subject "girl" and the predicate nominative "singer". They may also give words that replace the direct object of the dependent clause "hair". Pupils should notice that a dependent clause does not make sense by itself, *e.g.* "who has black hair". The verb or predicate of the dependent clause "has" may also be changed to "had" and yet the pattern of sentence is the same. The teacher should make lessons interesting and meaningful on sentence patterns and no go beyond what pupils can possibly understand. The goal inherent in sentence patterns is for pupils to feel and understand similarities in a sentence pattern. Pupils will become better readers as a result. Pupils will know that the English language as unique routines which are predictable, such as each of the five sentence patterns. They will understand how to expand sentences and why this is done. When pupils read, they will notice these same patterns of expansion, such as single word adjectives and adverbs; adjective and adverb phrases and adjective, adverb and noun clauses. At the beginning in sequence, pupils will learn about single words modifying the subject and predicate pattern; subject predicate, direct object pattern; subject, linking verb, predicate nominative pattern; subject linking verb, predicate adjective pattern; and subject, predicate, indirect object, direct object pattern.

What about pupils using technical terminology such as "predicate nominative"? We would say the teacher may use these and other complex terms, but not require pupils to memorize them. Meaning, however, is very important for pupils as to what a predicate nominative is when sequencing learning opportunities (Ediger, 1996).

Evaluation of Pupil Achievement

There are numerous procedures to use in evaluating pupil achievement pertaining to knowledge and skills in the structure or patterns of sentences. Teacher observation can be an excellent approach, providing quality standards are used. With teacher observation, the philosophy of constructivism is in evidence. Thus, within context, pupils are applying what has been learned about sentence patterns. Within the framework of everyday lessons, pupils are indicating progression contextual situations.

Standardized and norm referenced tests may be used to ascertain pupil achievement. However, pupils are showing here how well they have achieved outside the context of learning.

Tests, no doubt, will always be with us and we can use results from these tests to indicate where pupils specifically need help. Diagnosis and remediation would then be involved.

Howard Gardner's (1993) theory of multiple intelligence has much to offer in terms of how to evaluate pupil achievement. As the name indicates, pupils have numerous intelligence, not just one only. Pupils individually may possess one or more of those intelligences:

1. Verbal/linguistic such as reading and writing well.
2. Logical/mathematical such as in strength of the left brain hemisphere with its logical thinking as well as the other component parts in mathematical proficiency.
3. Visual/spatial such as pupils excelling in art work, geometry and architecture.
4. Musical intelligence such as in composing, singing and playing musical instruments.
5. Bodily/kinesthetic such as in athletics, dance and pantomime.
6. Interpersonal such as pupils doing well when working harmoniously in group settings.
7. Interpersonal whereby pupils achieve well on an individual basis.
8. Scientific in which pupils use methods of objectivity in scientific knowledge obtained.
9. The human experience such as in coping well with the everyday problems that come about.

How then does the Theory of Multiple intelligences relate to pupil learning and evaluation in the structure of knowledge in reading and writing?

First, the heart of knowing about and using sentence patterns emphasizes verbal/linguistic intelligence. Here, pupils reveal their strength through oral use of and written work in sentence patterns. Using these patterns in oral and silent reading also stresses use of the structure of language. We must remember, pupils with other intelligences may not reveal what has been learned through verbal/

linguistic intelligence, although this must always be stressed in ongoing lessons and units of study. With logical intelligence, the pupils needs to realize, for example, that substitutions made for the subject/predicate/direct objective pattern of sentence need to be logical. We have noticed pupils who make illogical substitutions such as Bill (subject) caught (predicate) the "if". The word "if" does not fit in logically.

Bodily/kinesthetic intelligence may be used frequently since pupils can dramatize content in a sentence pattern and attach meaning in so doing. Interpersonal or interpersonal intelligence may be used in that the former stresses pupils working in committees whereas the latter emphasizes learners working individual on sentence patterns. We should add musical intelligence here since pupils individually who are talented in music may wish to put sentence patterns to an appropriate rhythm. A pupil even invented a dance to go along with syllabication related to a musical accompaniment. There are many possibilities here when stressing using multiple intelligences. Pupils individually may be able to reveal learning better through multiple intelligences as compared to using verbal/linguistic approaches only/largely when studying structure in the English language.

Conclusion

Pupils having knowledge and skill pertaining to the structure of the English language should become better readers and writers. There are sentence patterns which hold true again and again. There are ways of expanding sentences which are also very consistent. Learners need to enjoy learning opportunities emphasizing structure in the English language. In certainly need not be boring or dull and dry. Rather there are learning opportunities which fascinate pupils and motivate toward greater achievement.

As pupils study the structure of the English language, they should be better able to predict what will come in sequence in reading as well as in writing. Vocabulary growth and development should also be in the offing since pupils experiment with sentences, words, phrases and clauses. There should be much journal writing on the part of pupils when reading and writing are stressed as being interrelated. When pupils hypothesize as to which words might take the place of others in a sentence, individual differences are provided for and all may be successful learners because each pupil can present possible words in context.

The interests of pupils need to be focussed upon structural ideas and their component parts. The teacher needs to be certain that pupils are attaching meaning to these structure ideas. They are not be memorized for purposes of passing a test, but rather to use what has been learned in reading and writing. Thus, the level of application is very important since structural ideas have much use. We believe that teachers need to spend time in having pupils perceive how learning the structure of language is practical in reading and writing across the curriculum.

REFERENCE

Ediger, Marlow (1997), *Teaching Mathematics in the Elementary School.* Kirksville, Missouri: Simpson Publishing Company, 28.

Ediger, Marlow (1988), *Language Arts Curriculum in the Elementary School.* Kirksville, Missouri: Simpson Publishing Company, 8-18.

Ediger, Marlow (1997), *The Modern Elementary School.* Kirksville, Missouri: Simpson Publishing Company, 199.

Ediger, Marlow (1996), *Elementary Education.* Kirksville, Missouri: Simpson Publishing Company, 38-39.

Gardner, Howard (1993), *Multiple Intelligences: The Theory in Practice.* New York: The Basic Books.

Lakshmi, Bhagya L. and Bhaskara Rao, Digumarti (1999). *Reading and Comprehension.* New Delhi: Discovery Publishing House.

Thornberg, Robert J. (1997), "What Does it Means to be Smart"? *Educational Leadership,* 54 (6) 20-24.

Designing the Reading Curriculum

Teachers in the school setting need to be highly knowledgeable of how to design the reading curriculum. The design emphasizes the framework of teaching and learning situations as it relates to reading instruction. There are selected ingredients which should be inherent in the design. Each needs careful thought, deliberation, and attention. The design presents a vision of what will be stressed in reading instruction. Each pupil needs to achieve as optimally as possible. Thus, pupils individually should attain well in subject matter, in applying that which has been learned, and in evaluation results when using formal as well as informal means of assessment.

Separate Subjects Versus an Integrated Reading Curriculum

A first ingredient to discuss in developing the reading curriculum emphasizes the degree to which different curriculum areas should be related in teaching and learning. Reading then could be taught as a separate subject matter area from the other disciplines in the curriculum. Separate objectives of instruction would then be in the offing for reading instruction only.

In moving toward an integrated reading curriculum, the emphasis could be gradual. The first step might be *correlation* in which reading would be correlated with spelling instruction. Moving further toward the integrated approach, the reading teacher may stress the broad fields/fused approach in which reading might be related to the teaching of social studies. The objectives of instruction here should stress the two curriculum areas as being fused, not isolated from each other. The final stage of teaching diverse subject matter areas as being related might well be integration of content. Here, subject matter areas loose their boundaries and borders. Reading is then an inherent part of each curriculum area. There are definite advantages and disadvantages for stressing each plan of the separate subjects versus integration approaches. For example, in the separate subjects plan of instruction, the teacher may focus entirely upon reading instruction; the disadvantage of the separate subjects plan is a fragmented reading curriculum whereby the learner fails to perceive the relationship of ideas in the curriculum. The design of the curriculum then needs to take into consideration the separate subjects versus the integrated reading curriculum (Ediger, Marlow, 2001, Chapter Fifteen).

Scope in the Reading Curriculum

Scope pertains to the breadth of objectives to the emphasized in reading. Scope may stress a narrower or a broader breadth. Thus, a narrower scope may focus heavily upon a systematic procedure of teaching phonics. Inherent in teaching phonics might well be the following:

1. Grapheme/phoneme relationships as objectives for pupil achievement.
2. Syllabication skills to unlock unknown words.
3. Structural analysis to determine new words and their identification.
4. Identification of unknown words in context.
5. Development of a basic sight vocabulary in reading.

Toward the other end of the continuum, the scope of the reading curriculum may emphasize whole language approaches of instruction. For example, after background information has been developed for reading within learners, the inherent procedure of instruction might then pertain to the following:

1. Reading entire selections with the total class or a committee focusing attention upon the Big Book which has predictable content and which all can see clearly.

2. Pupils with teacher assistance reading the selection as the former points to the words and phrases as the oral reading continues.
3. The selection being reread as often necessary in its entirety so that pupils develop familiarity with a core of new words in reading instruction.
4. Subject matter read involves different academic disciplines such as social studies, science, and mathematics, among others.
5. The focus being upon ideas being read with pupils comprehending content in the selection read (Ediger and Rao, 2000, Chapter Fifteen).

A systematic approach in teaching reading emphasizes pupils learning to read whereby specifics are being taught such as sound symbol relationships and then eventually reading subject matter to secure ideas. Thus, the tools of reading are stressed first such as phonics and then reading for ideas becomes important. Whole language procedures emphasize pupils reading the entire selection, from the beginning of the young child's experiences in learning to read. The teacher might call attention to such factors in the selection as words beginning with the same consonant letters and/or words which end alike.

Sequence in the Reading Curriculum

Sequence answers the question, "*When* will each objective in the reading curriculum be stressed"? In answer to this question, the teacher may teach a selected initial consonant sound within a systematic sequence in phonics instruction. This may be followed by a different phoneme/grapheme construct and eventually include vowel letters/sounds as well as ending sounds within specific words. The sequence or order of the entire phonics program be then be placed in chart form to follow in reading instruction.

Whole language approaches might well involve a sequential listing of story content to cover, which contains content from all academic disciplines.

Sequence in the reading curriculum is based upon the following, be it systematic phonics or whole language approaches:

1. From the easier learnings to those which are gradually more complex. The teacher determines the sequence in systematic phonics instruction whereas the teacher, in whole language instruction, chooses story content to read for young pupils with increasingly choices being made by learners such as in individualized reading. Once readiness is in evidence, the pupil then may choose library books to read sequentially in individualized reading.
2. When state mandated objectives of instruction are in evidence, the order for their attainment may be determined by the teacher based upon knowledge of individual pupil achievement.
3. The teacher in a logical sequence arranges the order of objectives for pupil attainment. In a psychological sequence, pupils individually or within committees are rather heavily involved in determining what comes first, second, third, and so on, in objectives to be achieved.
4. Learning styles theory whereby the teacher emphasizes what harmonizes best with the pupil's appropriate way of achieving optimally, be it with direct or indirect teaching procedures (Searson and Dunn, 2001).
5. The teacher emphasizes diagnosis and remediation which stresses what a pupil needs to improve upon in reading achievement. The need may be phonics instruction to unlock unknown words or reading for meaning in which whole language instructional procedures are a necessity.

Not everything in reading can be learned at one time by a pupil. Thus, the teacher needs to spread out over time which ordered objectives learners should achieve in sequence. A teacher directed or learner choices made in context may well determine the sequence of activities in reading (Gunning, 2000, Chapter Eight).

Objectives in Reading Instruction

Objectives for pupils to achieve in reading should stress three broad categories. Knowledge objectives are important and usually come first in priority in the teaching of reading. Thus, the teacher desires pupils to learn much subject matter from reading. Important facts, concepts, the generalizations are selected as objectives for learner attainment. A second category—skills—emphasizes that pupils use or apply what has been attained be it ideas gained, word recognition techniques acquired, and/or higher levels of thinking. Attitudes are a third category of objectives which probably are least emphasized of the three categories. And yet, attitudinal ends may be as vital for pupils to achieve as the other two. With good attitudes, a pupil may achieve well in knowledge and skills ends. Thus, good attitudes go a long way in doing well in knowledge and skills achievement.

Objectives may be stated broadly as general objectives. The following are examples:

1. To develop within the pupil the ability to achieve main ideas in reading subject matter.
2. To develop within the pupil skill to think critically and creatively, as well as to be able to solve problems.
3. To develop within the pupil an attitude of *wanting* to achieve more optimally in reading.

General objectives provide guidance, in general and in a broad way, what pupils are to learn and achieve. These kinds of objectives were quite common in the 1950s and 1960s.

Presently, with the measurement and testing movement in vogue, objectives are stated in measurable terms. Each objective then needs to be stated precisely so that it can be measured if, after instruction, it has/has not been achieved by learners. With state mandated tests, test results from pupils are highly important for the following reasons:

1. Pupils may need to score at a certain level if they are to be promoted to the next grade level. Or a pupil may be denied a high school diploma if the individual test score is too low in high stakes testing.
2. A single test score describes what a pupil has learned. The every day accomplishments in schools do not matter when a single test score determines a pupil's future.

3. An assumption is that the state mandated test is valid and reliable. Statements need to be made by the developers of the state mandated test in terms of how it was validated and evaluated for reliability. There are state mandated tests which were not pilot tested to take out the kinks.
4. The same mandated test is given to all pupils in a state and yet there are tremendous differences among learners in terms of abilities, intelligences, and learning styles.
5. Accommodations for the handicapped are not made in most states with their mandated tests (Olson, 2002, pp. 6, 7).

In addition to specific, objectives being used in state mandated standards and tests to measure if these goals have been achieved by pupils, the ends of instruction too frequently stress factual recall of information. In school and in society, there is a greater need for objectives stressing critical and creative thinking, as well as problem solving, compared to the heavy emphasis upon factual recall with multiple choice items on each test.

Providing for Individual Differences

In designing the reading curriculum, individual differences need adequate consideration. When visiting any classroom of pupils, the author in supervising university student teachers in the public schools noticed rather soon how pupils differed much from each other. Pupils differed in being attentive in class, in interests possessed, in persevering in an ongoing learning activity, in working together diligently with peers on a given task, in responding to questions raised in class, and in attitudes, among others. Multiple Intelligences Theory (Gardner, 1993) emphasized that pupils individually possesses the following talents:

1. Verbal, such as in reading and writing.
2. Mathematical, as in reasoning and logical thinking.
3. Musical/rhythmical as in writing verse and setting it to music. Responding to music in a rhythmic manner also stresses this category of intelligence.
4. Intrapersonal intelligence whereby the pupil reveals achievement best in individual endeavours.

5. Interpersonal intelligence in which the learner shows leadership skills and cooperation in collaborative endeavours.
6. Bodily/kinesthetic whereby the pupils shows abilities in manual dexterity, and athletic prowess endeavours.
7. Scientific in which the pupil demonstrates quality abilities in objective thinking.
8. Artistic whereby the pupil indicates best what has been learned through creative work in art processes and products.

Individual differences may be provided through grouping pupils for reading instruction. The following may be used within a classroom depending upon the involved purpose:

1. Heterogeneous grouping which has mixed achievement levels in a specific group.
2. Homogeneous grouping whereby learners of a uniform ability group are taught together in reading.
3. Individualized plan in which a single pupil works alone, as in individualized reading.
4. Peer grouping as in two or three pupils discussing a self selected paperback by themselves.
5. Large group instruction in which the teacher provides background information to the total number of pupils in the classroom.
6. Cross grade grouping whereby a group of pupils from two grade levels are taught together such as in two third graders and two fourth graders being taught collectively.
7. Team teaching as in two or three teachers planning together the objectives, learning opportunities, and evaluation procedures for a given set of learners. These teachers then teach reading in large group instruction, in committees, and in individual pupil settings.
8. Nongraded grouping whereby pupils are taught collectively using reading materials harmonizing with the present reading achievement level of the involved

learners. The materials of instruction used may not be on the inherent grade levels of the pupils being taught.

9. Peer teaching in which one pupil teaches the others, specific items in reading.
10. Programmed learning involving the B.F. Skinner psychology of step by step reading with carefully and closely sequenced objectives of instruction (Ediger and Rao, 2000, Chapter Eighteen).

There are then a plethora of approaches which may be used in the teaching of reading. Each pupil needs to attain as optimally as possible. There are selected philosophies of teaching which may be used in reading instruction: *(i)* A basics approach stresses teachers selecting essential learnings for pupils to achieve. The basics in phonics and syllabication, as word recognition skills, as well as selected fundamental comprehension techniques are then taught systematically to pupils. *(ii)* A strong basal textbook, worksheet, and workbook approach provides major learning opportunities for pupils in reading. *(iii)* Essentialism may be contrasted with an activity centered procedure in teaching reading. A hands on approach may then be implemented such as pupils constructing object/items or doing art projects to reveal that which has been achieved in reading. *(iv)* Quite different is measurement driven instruction which focuses upon pupils achieving predetermined, specific objectives of reading instruction. Feedback from achievement, or lack thereof, on objectives achievement, is used by the teacher to make sequential instructional decisions. *(v)* An ungraded philosophy attempts to have pupils move forward as rapidly as possible in reading, depending upon readiness characteristics displayed. No grade levels are emphasized here. Pupils in groups move forward as rapidly as abilities and achievement permit. *(vi)* An interdisciplinary approach, as a different philosophy, emphasizes a reading curriculum which has all boundaries of academic disciplines eliminated. Literacy efforts here stress reading across the curriculum, regardless of the involved academic subject matter (Tiedt, 1983).

Philosophy of Assessment in Reading Achievement

Teacher developed and implemented informal means of assessment may be used. These include teacher observation of pupil achievement, use of rating scales and checklists, teacher written tests, anecdotal statements, diary entries, and journal writing, pertaining to pupil achievement and progresses in reading.

State mandated objectives and testing are used in 49 out of 50 states in the union to measure pupil achievement in reading. These tests are developed on the state level and provide a single numeral, such as a percentile, to indicate achievement. The amount of pressure on the teacher and pupils to attain high expectations depend upon each state. The following are used to meet high pupil standards within a state:

1. Annual testing to notice achievement.
2. Report cards showing how one district/state compares with the others. The results, called report cards, are printed/reported in the news media.
3. High stakes testing whereby a student may not be promoted to the next grade level due to a low test score. Also, a pupil may be denied a high school diploma due to not meeting state expectations from test results.
4. Education bankruptcy laws in which a state may take over a school or school system due to low average scores on these state mandated tests.
5. Teachers may be replaced if low pupil test scores are continually in evidence.

District wide tests may also be developed and implemented to assess if pupils are achieving school wide objectives of instruction. A variety of kinds of test items may be used here such as multiple choice, true/false, essay, matching, completion, and short response. Test items on any level, be it state mandated or district tests, need to be valid and reliable, pilot tested, and possess clarity in their writing (Ediger, 1998, 161-166).

Designing the reading curriculum needs to be done with much thought and deliberation. Each facet of the design is salient to emphasize so that pupils achieve as well as possible in reading!

REFERENCES

Ediger, Marlow (1998), "Why Don't Pupils Learn to Read"? *The Educational Review*, 104 (16) 161-166.

Ediger, Marlow, and D. Bhaskara Rao (2000), *Teaching Reading Successfully*. New Delhi, India: Discovery Publishing House, Chapter Fifteen.

Ediger, Marlow and D. Bhaskara Rao (2001), "Reading in the Science Curriculum," *Teaching Science Successfully*. New Delhi, India: Discovery Publishing House.

Ediger, Marlow and D. Bhaskara Rao (2000), "Psychological Foundations in Teaching Mathematics," *Teaching Mathematics Successfully*. New Delhi, India: Discovery Publishing House, Chapter Eighteen.

Gardner, Howard (1993), *Multiple Intelligences: Theory Into Practice*. New York: Basic Books.

Gunning, Thomas G., *Creating Literacy Instruction for All Children*. Boston: Allyn and Bacon, Chapter Eight.

Olson, Lynn (2002), "Idaho to Adopt 'Adaptive' Online State Testing," *Education Week*, 21 (19), 6, 7.

Searson, Robert, and Rita Dunn (2001), "The Learning Styles Teaching Model," *Science and Children*, 38 (5), 22-26.

Tiedt, Iris M. (1983), *The Language Arts Handbook*.

Englewood Cliffs, New Jersey: Prentice Hall, Inc. Chapter Eleven.

Reading in the Content Areas

Reading in the content areas is a basic in the curriculum. To learn and achieve optimally in any academic discipline, pupils need to be able to read well. The ability to read well involves a plethora of knowledge, skills and attitudes. There are numerous components then to the act of reading. Teachers need to be aware of what is involved in pupils learning to read and be able to analyze its specific parts. Reading is a complex whole to describe and it may be analyzed in different ways depending upon the philosophy of the teacher.

Content Reading and the Measurement Movement

Measurement of instruction involves the use of highly specific objectives in reading instruction. These objectives are selected prior to instruction. Precision of objectives is necessary so that the teacher may measure, if after instruction, learners have/have not achieved the stated objectives. If the pupil has not achieved an objective, a different teaching strategy needs to be used. The learning activities in reading are closely aligned with the objectives of instruction. Measurement is emphasized in terms of the stated objectives. Thus, the teacher measures if the pupil has/has not achieved an objective.

With a measurement philosophy of instruction, the following are important to consider:

1. Whatever exits, exists in some amount, and this amount then can be measured. The world of science stresses

measurability of elements in the universe. The planet earth is made up of some 107 elements and these can be combined to form molecules. Any molecule can be expressed in numerical terms of the number of elements in each. Water, for example, contains two atoms of hydrogen and one atom of oxygen, resulting in the formula—H_2O. The smallest unit of measurement for an element is the atom.

2. Achievement in student learning can be measured to determine what has been learned. For example, in state mandated tests, a pupil may be on the composite score of the fiftieth percentile, meaning that fifty per cent are below and fifty per cent are above that pupil from the total number of individuals who completed taking the test in the pilot study.
3. The standard error of measurement may be determined of the state mandated test. Thus, how consistently the test measures be it split half, alternative forms, or test/retest reliability and may be ascertained statistically with a standard error of measurement from pilot study data. A pupil's percentile score might then vary plus or minus depending upon the size of the standard error of measurement. Pertaining to one state in the union's test results involving margin of error or standard error of measurement, Keller (Education Week, February 6, 2002).

Wrote the following:

Montgomery Country (Maryland), the state's largest district with 130,000 students, was the first to raise the alarm about the scores. The percentage of students in the district just outside Washington scoring at a satisfactory level dipped last year to 51 per cent, about 4 percentage points lower than the year before.

But state officials have stressed that the margin of error for the scores ranges from 2 *percentage points* for the state to as many as *14* for a small school.

They also have suggested that the lack of test—score increases may be linked to the fact that schools across the state have more disadvantaged students and fewer experienced teachers.

4. Validity of the states' mandated test may be ascertained with pupils' results being correlated with results from the National Assessment of Educational Progress (NAEP). To increase validity, the teacher needs to align the local curriculum with the state standards or objectives of instruction.

It is quite obvious, from the above discussion, that testing pupil achievement stresses preciseness, statistical measurability, and quantification. With the testing and measurement movement, the teacher continually directs the reading activities for pupils in order that predetermined objectives are attained by learners.

Wiersma (1991) wrote the following:

> The term statistics has multiple meanings in educational research but probably its simplest meaning is "bits of information". If one says that 632 students are enrolled in a specific school, this can be considered a statistics. The salary schedule and the number of teachers at each salary level for a district are sometimes called salary statistics.

Statistics has a much broader meaning than simply bits of information, however. It also refers to the theory, procedures, and methodology by which data are summarized. It has been suggested that to some people, the terminology of statistics seems like a foreign language; although this may be true, the understanding and use of statistics is not so much a matter of identifying new terminology and symbols for already known concepts as it is a way of reasoning and drawing conclusions. Although the lay person often views statistics as an accumulation of facts and figures, the researcher sees statistics as the methods used to describe data and make sense out of them.

Content Reading and Problem Solving

Problem solving stresses flexible steps in the identification and finding solutions to a problem (Dewey, 1916). In context, pupils in a committee setting identify a problem. The problem is open ended and requires a solution. Deliberation is involved in problem solving activities. The problem needs to be clearly defined so it is possible of being solved. This is done in a discussion setting.

Reading is one avenue of securing information to solve the problem. The content chosen from reading must relate directly as a solution to the problem. An hypothesis or tentative answer to the problem is developed. The hypothesis is evaluated in a life like situation involving a variety of life like experiences, including reading. If the hypothesis stands up in the evaluation process, it is accepted. If not, a new hypothesis may be developed and evaluated. The steps of problem solving given here are flexible, not an absolute.

Problem solving approaches in learning are based on pupil's experiences, not externally determined objectives of instruction nor from testing. Thus, pupils with teacher guidance are heavily involved in determining and solving the identified problem.

Problem solving emphasizes the following:

1. Pupils with teacher guidance helping to determine the curriculum with flexible steps of identifying and securing solutions to problems.
2. Pupils being assisted to obtain information to arrive at solutions.
3. Pupils being involved in practical learning opportunities.
4. Pupils having adequate chances to apply that which has been learned.

Throughout problem solving activities, reading is one experience for learning along with others. School and society are not to be separated, but integrated. What is useful in society provides objectives and experiences in the curriculum. In society, too, committees and groups are involved in problem solving experiences; thus, pupils need to learn to work harmoniously with others in the school setting.

In problem solving philosophy in reading, the teacher assists, encourages, and motivates pupils to engage in the identification and finding solutions to dilemma situations. Evelyn Dewey (1919), daughter of John Dewey, wrote the following:

The development of a democracy demands that nothing be done to interfere with the fluidity of the population: there must be no barriers built between different groups and occupations; everything must be kept as open as possible to promote free and sympathetic communication. This demands common interests among all the people; and the strongest common interests between people widely separated by space and occupation is the evaluation of their government to the satisfaction of them all.

Content Reading and the Individual

Individualized instruction is advocated by selected educators in that optimal opportunities be given to the pupil to select and sequence his/her very own learning activities. Content reading may then be stressed in personalized reading curriculum. Here, there are an adequate number of content or expository materials from which the pupil may select what to read in a sequential manner. Purposes for reading reside within the learner. The teacher may assist the learner to develop background information for reading by discussing a few illustrations in the library book or related pictures from a CD ROM. Otherwise, motivation for reading comes from within the pupil, not from externally imposed sources. The pupil may reveal comprehension from reading by choosing from the following procedures, among others:

1. Writing a summary covering subject matter read.
2. Doing a related art project.
3. Making objects, such as a diorama, to show main ideas acquired.
4. Participating in a dramatization experience to reveal major concepts obtained.
5. Video taping a personal research project based on subject matter read in the content areas.
6. Cassette recording of expository selections from books being read aloud.
7. Planning and implementing a bulletin board display pertaining to thematic books read.
8. Having a conference with the teacher to appraise oral reading and comprehension quality.

9. Choosing others to do a mural on collaborative reading completed.
10. Self selecting a way to indicate comprehension such as journal writing of ideas acquired by the pupil (Santman, 2002).

Individualized procedures of reading instruction emphasize the pupil as the major person in developing the curriculum. The teacher stimulates and assists in pupil learning and achievement. Individualizing the reading curriculum is open ended and is quite opposite of the measurement movement. It stresses the importance of the learner being the focal point of instruction. Societal needs are of lesser importance then meeting the needs of the individual pupil. The interests and needs of the pupil come first in developing a reading curriculum. The teacher is a supporter of learning of the pupil. Pupils need to

1. Become skillful in the art of choosing and decision making.
2. Assume responsibility for decisions made.
3. Accept others as having extreme worth.
4. Realize self fulfillment in terms of goals, learning opportunities, and evaluation procedures stressed in reading content (Ediger, 1995, p. 153).

Content Reading and Perennialism

Perennialism emphasizes pupils reading the classics to achieve knowledge, skills, and attitudinal objectives of instruction. The classics represent literature which has stood the test of time. Recently written literature does not come under the topical heading of the classics. The writings of Plato, Aristotle, Nathaniel Hawthorne, Henry Wadsworth Longfellow, Robert Louis Stevenson, among other examples, represent classical writings. Perennialism stresses a highly academic program of reading. Thus, a stimulating academic reading program needs to be in evidence emphasizing vital, enduring ideas of the past. Cultivation of the intellect or mind becomes a major objective in reading instruction. Pupils need to read and reflect upon worthwhile ideas of great minds and writers of the past whose enduring ideas stimulate thinking. Perennialists believe in pupils reading the classics for the following reasons:

1. They have stood the test of time and place. These writings are still very salient presently.
2. They remain important today whereas recently written literature may not survive in terms of being salient.
3. They are written by the best of minds.
4. They provide pupils with common background information which all need as general education, before moving on to an area of specialization.

Pertaining to Mortimer Adler's *Paideia Proposal* (1990), Tanner and Tanner wrote the following:

> The perennialist's refusal to consider the nature of the learner in developing the curriculum is reflected in the *Paideia Proposal*. Instead of seeing childhood and youth as a distinct phase of human development requiring uniquely appropriate experiences for effective growth, childhood and youth are regarded as obstacles to be gotten over with as quickly as possible. "Youth itself is the most serious impediment—fact, youth is an inseparable obstacle to being an educated person," declares the Proposal. The Proposal goes on to call for twelve years of basic schooling for all, capped by the Socratic study of great literary works and other works of art. This kind of learning "aims at raising the mind up from a lesser or weaker understanding to a stronger and fuller one," and the "art of the teacher depends upon an understanding of how the mind learns by the exercise of its own power," declares Adler, as though the mind exists as a separate entity.

Perennialists advocate, pupils studying the great ideas of the ancient world, the renaissance, and the age of the enlightenment. These ideas have endured as being worthwhile whereas recent writings may soon end up in oblivion. The changeless and the eternal are to be preferred to the transitory and changing ideas. A non-vocational curriculum needs to be in evidence. Vocational and professional training comes after the great ideas of the past have been studied. Reading and reflecting Socratically upon the classics provides pupils with what will remain in time and space. Reading in the content areas then emphasizes that which is vital and relevant subject matter.

With different philosophies of instruction, it behooves the teacher to study each diligently and come up with what will assist pupils individually to achieve as optimally as possible.

REFERENCES

Dewey, John (1916) *Democracy and Education*. New York: The Macmillan Company.

Dewey, Evelyn (1919), *New Schools for Old: The Regeneration of the Porter School*. New York: E.P. Dutton and Company, p. 336.

Ediger, Marlow (1995), *Philosophy in Curriculum Development*. Kirksville, Missouri: Simpson Publishing Company, p. 153.

Ediger, Marlow and Digumarti Bhaskara Rao (2002), *Philosophy and Curriculum*. New Delhi, India: Discovery Publishing House.

Keller, Bess (February 6, 2002), "Controversy Surrounds Release of Maryland Test Results," *Education Week*, 21 (21), p 19.

Santman, Donna (2002), "Teaching to the Test?: Test Preparation in the Reading Workshop," *Language Arts*, 79 (3), 203-211.

Tanner, Daniel, and Laurel Tanner (1990), History of the School Curriculum. New York: The Macmillan Publishing Company, p. 133.

Wiersma, William (1991), *Research Methods in Education*. Fifth Edition. Boston: Allyn and Bacon, pp. 306-307.

Making use of Ideas Gleaned from Reading

It is important for pupils to make use of ideas obtained from reading subject matter. A lack of retention occurs if use is not made of ideas presently possessed. The reading teacher then needs to gather information on the plethora of ways to emphasize pupil comprehension and application in the reading curriculum. Tenets from educational psychology need to be followed in teaching and learning situations to assist pupils to achieve as much as individual abilities permit. Thus, the reading teacher needs to

1. Engage pupils in learning. Passive recipients of knowledge is not adequate, but active involvement is desired so that intrinsic pupil motivation is in evidence.
2. Cultivate the interests of pupils in achieving. Interested pupils achieve more optimally as compared to those who lack interest. The teacher then needs to use learning opportunities which stimulate feelings of interest within pupils.
3. Secure purposes for learning, developed within pupils. Purpose involves pupils perceiving reasons for achieving. Taking time for clarity in purposes for learning is time well spent. Pupils need to be clear on what this to be studied any why.
4. Assist pupils to attach meaning to ongoing activities and experiences. Non-sense subject matter acquired has little value for pupils, but that which possesses meaning

makes sense to each pupil. Meaningful learning provides understandable subject matter acquired. What does not make sense to the pupil is soon forgotten (Emery, 1992).

5. Use alternative teaching strategies for those pupils who have not been successful with a previous procedures. Pupils individually differ from each other in a plethora of ways. The teacher needs to possess a repertoire of methods and approaches of reaching each pupil in learning and in achieving.
6. Meet the learning styles of pupils individually. Individual and committee endeavours need to be used in teaching and learning situations (Searson and Dunn, 2001).
7. Use multiple intelligences theory adequately when designing the curriculum. Pupils individually have talents which need to be cultivated. These talents or intelligences may be used by pupils to reveal that which has been learned in an ongoing lesson or unit of study (Gardner, 1993).
8. Indicate the relationship of knowledge from diverse academic disciplines. Thus, subject matter should not be compartmentalized into component categories, but rather become interdisciplinary in nature (Ediger, 1993, 17-20).
9. Help students develop wholesome attitudes toward the reading curriculum. The attitudinal dimension is vital to achieve in a positive manner since pupil achievement in reading depends so much upon affective predispositions learners possess in learning to read.
10. Guide learners to use and apply what has been attained in subject matter and skills acquired. How can the reading teacher assist pupils to make use of ideas gleaned from reading?

Writing Poetry

From content read, pupils with teacher guidance may write poetry. There are diverse kinds to write. Rhymed verse offers interest in learning opportunities for selected pupils. The simplest form of rhyme in poetry is the couplet. The couplet has two lines, somewhat uniform in length. Many pupils with appropriate background information enjoy writing a couplet by the self or cooperatively with another, one giving the first line and the other learner the second line. From a single reading selection, pupils might think of diverse possibilities in using subject matter to write a poem. Whichever type of poem taught needs to be modeled by the teacher (Ediger, 1998, 74-77). The teacher may then

1. Read aloud the kind of poem being emphasized.
2. Write on the chalkboard the kind of poem being taught in order that pupils may discover and notice essentials contained therein, such as in a particular kind of rhymed verse, be it couplets, triplets, quatrains, and limericks, among others.
3. Have library books on the specific type of verse being taught for personal and for pupil use.

In supervising student teachers in the public schools, a couplet written by two third graders, pertaining to a story on fishing, wrote the following:

Three boys with hook, line, and sinker

loved to catch fish in a pond and then tinker.

A second type of rhymed verse for pupils to write is the triplet. A class of fourth grade pupils read and discussed a story on mining for minerals. They collectively brain stormed a poem on that topic and wrote the following triplet containing three lines of rhymed verse:

A miner in moving westward ho!

came upon a mound along a row

found fortune, fame, and treasure to tow.

A separate set of three fourth graders cooperatively wrote the following triplet:

Brave miners with pick, shovel, and effort

walked and ran a long way to the distant port

hoping to find gold, silver, and a precious sort.

Poetry written by pupils needs to be on their individual developmental levels. They need to experience challenge and high expectations, but success in achievement is also very important. There are selected readiness factors which pupils need to possess in order to write the type of poem being stressed as an objective of reading and writing instruction. If a pupil cannot do the writing of the intended poem, he/she may dictate the contents to the teacher or a peer for the actual writing. When necessary, accommodations need to be made for handicapped learners. Each pupil needs to attain as optimally as possible. Background knowledge is vital when poems are written. Thus, each pupil must possess knowledge which provides content for the written poem. The knowledge may come from the basal reader, library books, AV aids, specialists, as well as from internet sources.

A fourth type of rhymed verse for pupils to write is the quatrain. A quatrain contains four lines with all ending words rhyming or lines one and two as well as lines three and four rhyming. In observing a student teacher/cooperating teacher teach a set of fifth graders, a committee of four pupils brain stormed and then wrote the following quatrain:

The girl with a bright colored cap

sat down quietly to read a large map

into the room came a small kitten

carrying a broom, mop, and a mitten.

A fifth type of rhyme in poetry is the limerick. Motivated pupils tend to like all forms of rhymed poetry, but the limerick seems to add an interesting dimensions. In limericks, lines one, two, and five rhyme (making for a triplet), as well as lines three and four rhyme which make for a couplet. The following limerick was written by two sixth graders:

The bells were ringing a merry tune

Along came a boy with a silver balloon

He walked fast and quickly

At the beginning he looked sickly

But he soon leaped as if to touch the moon.

It is soon apparent that pupils may make use of ideas read by writing diverse kinds of poetry. In addition to rhymed verse, pupils may also write unrhymed poetry, based on syllables. Haiku is a well known form of poetry which has three lines with a succession stressing five, seven, and five syllables per line respectively. Pupils, as a readiness factor, need to hear and divide words into syllables. A sixth grader wrote the following haiku, based on a social studies unit titled "The Middle East:"

The Dome of the Rock

Stood neatly on a steep hill

With a minaret.

A second haiku was written by a different set of sixth graders resulting in the following:

The wide Western Wall

Near to the Mosque el-Aksa

Appear beautiful.

By adding two more lines to the haiku, the writer has completed a tanka. Each of these additional two lines contains seven syllables, as in the following tanka, also on "The Middle East:"

The old stone tall church

called the Holy Sepulcher

aged and well renown

has many tourists each day

to show history.

Pupils need to make use of knowledge ready by varying the kinds of learning opportunities provided. A good variation, from rhymed poetry and verse containing a certain number of syllables per line, is free verse. Free verse is quite open ended and also has no particular ascribed length. The following, also pertaining to the social studies unit on "The Middle East," was written by a fourth grader:

The wall around Jerusalem is

two and one/half miles in length

forty feet high

enclosed with eight gates or entrances

filled with tourists when peace prevails

a busy place for buyers with its many small shops

Alliteration may be added to any written poem. With alliteration, two or more consecutive words in a poem need to start with the same beginning sound: busy buyers; small stalls (for shopping in the walled city); peaceful places. Poets use in device of alliteration frequently in written work.

Echoic sounding words, called onomatopoeia, may also be included in a poem: splish, splash, splush (as in rain falling from November to April in the Mediterranean climate in the Middle East). These three words also indicate alliteration.

Then too, many poets use imagery in writing poetry. Imagery emphasizes the use of creative comparisons in writing verse: The clouds look like fluffy pillows roaming up high. The creative comparison pertains to "The clouds look like" and "fluffy pillows roaming up high," (Ediger, 2000, Chapter Twelve).

What Make Application of What has been Read?

There are a plethora of reasons why pupils need to use and apply that which has been read. Among others reasons, the following are important:

1. It aids in retention and remembering with continued use.
2. It makes learnings practical.
3. It helps to expand learnings acquired to a new contextual use.
4. It assists pupils to perceive value in what has been learned.
5. It guides pupils to use words in diverse kinds of written work be it in creative, narrative, and/or expository writing.

Teachers need to help pupils use content acquired in reading by introducing new objectives, learning opportunities, and assessment procedures. Each of these three components of the curriculum need to be in evidence. Thus in assessing pupil achievement pertaining to what has been read, a portfolio may be implemented and developed. The portfolio used in assessing pupil achievement may contain the following selected items by the involved learner with teacher guidance:

1. Entries of different types of poetry written by the learner.
2. Art products used to illustrate the different kinds of poems written.
3. Snapshots of construction projects made to model selected poems written.
4. Illustrated book covers and jackets made to enclose the portfolio.
5. Cassette recordings made of the pupil reading aloud his/her poems to classmates.
6. Video-tapes made of the involved learner working within a committee setting to plan and do dramatizations of written poems (Ediger, 1998, 4-8).

The teacher needs to assist pupils to use what has been learned. A variety of methods and learning opportunities need to be in the offing. Definite objectives of instruction need to prevail to emphasize pupil application of content learned. Evaluation techniques need to be used to indicate if the instructional objectives have been achieved.

REFERENCES

Emery, Donna W. (1992), "Children's Understanding of Story Characters," *Reading Improvement*, 29 (1), 2-9.

Ediger, Marlow (1993), "The Integrated Reading Curriculum," *Education Magazine*, nr. 107, 17-20. Published by the Qatar National Commission for Education, The Persian Gulf.

Ediger, Marlow (2000), *Teaching Reading Successfully*. New Delhi, India: Discovery Publishing House.

Ediger, Marlow (1998), "Reading Poetry in the Language Arts," *The Progress of Education*, 73 (4), 74-77. The Progress of Education is Published in India.

Ediger, Marlow (1998), "Intonation, the Student, and the Language Arts," *Oklahoma Reader*, 34 (1), 4-8.

Gardner, Howard (1993), *Multiple Intelligences: Theory Into Practice*. New York: Basic Books.

Searson, Robert, and Rita Dunn (1993). *The Learning Styles Teaching Model*, Science and Children, 38 (5), 22-26.

Improving Teacher Questions in Reading Instruction

There are a plethora of reasons why teachers need to be able to ask high quality questions in the teaching of reading. Among the many reasons, the following are salient:

1. Questions raised need to assess pupil comprehension of what has been read in an ongoing lesson.
2. Questions raised need to stimulate interest in reading.
3. Questions raised need to enable learners to engage in higher levels of cognition such as critical and creative thinking, as well as problem solving.
4. Questions raised need to assist pupils to perceive purpose or reasons for reading a given selection.
5. Questions raised need to provide for optimal achievement levels in reading instruction.
6. Questions raised need to help pupils clarify content read (Emery, 1992).
7. Questions raised in reading instruction need to encourage pupils to become life long learners.
8. Questions raised need to help pupils engage in meaningful reading experiences.
9. Questions raised in reading need to guide pupils to perceive content as being holistic and related, not in terms of isolated ideas.

10. Questions raised need to diagnose and remediate pupil difficulties in reading (Ediger, 2000, Chapter Six).

How might to above enumerated broad objectives be achieved by pupils in ongoing lessons in reading? Which specific kinds of questions might then be asked of pupils in reading instruction?

Specific Questions to Ask Learners in Reading

Pupils do need to clearly differentiate facts from opinions. When reading expository materials in reading, pupils might well be assisted in making the differentiation. For example, a date given for the establishment of Jamestown Colony in the New World is 1607. This date, if factual, can be verified by using another or several reputable reference sources. The factual statement may be written on the chalkboard. In contrast, the teacher may say, "In my *opinion*, all the colonists who came in 1607 were brave individuals". Learners may then discuss how the colonists *felt* as they came to and settled in the New World. Pupils may then notice likenesses and differences of ideas presented here. With adequate background information, there will tend to not be agreement on how the settlers felt as they came to and settled in the New World. Being able to separate facts from opinions will involve sequential growth of skills on the part of pupils. For example, on the kindergarten and first grade levels, pupils will agree on the number of learners in their classroom. This can be verified with repeated counting by different pupils. If asked which kind of food is liked best, there, of course will be variation in responses. Attempts to verify the one favorite food by all classmates is impossible and therefore represents an opinion.

A second kind of developmental question in reading for teachers to raise is to have pupils detect persuasive language. A good current events program, for example, will emphasize reading and Letters to the Editor section of a newspaper. The Letters will tend to emphasize persuading others to follow a certain line of thinking. Thus, a writer of a letter may emphasize that environmental laws are too strict and more land needs to be developed for oil drilling purposes such as in the Arctic Wild Life area. In response, a writer to the Letters to the Editor may attempt to persuade people of the need for more land being devoted to wild life and conservation purposes. A democracy tends to stress the importance of people debating the pros and cons of an issue. Perhaps, the issue of economic development versus conservation of the natural environment might be compared with the textbook author's purpose or goals.

Third, an important kind of question for teachers to raise of pupils is to have the latter draw a conclusion. With a discussion of the pros and cons of conserving the natural environment versus business concerns, as well as, Letters to the Editor, and the author's textbook perspective, pupils may be guided to develop a conclusion of the issue. The conclusion will summarize the major ideas presented during the discussion. Pupils need to be asked if they see any weaknesses in the ongoing as well as in the developed conclusion (Ediger, 2002, 16-19). The following questions are important to ask:

1. What is not in the conclusion which in valuable to include?
2. Have too many things been put into the conclusion to make it too lengthy rather than to summarize main points?
3. What should then be taken out, if it is too lengthy?

Fourth, pupil need to detect bandwagon approaches in advertising. Selected ads may state that everyone uses shaving cream number one, which is then identified by name. The feeling may result in that the hearer feels he should *also* use shaving cream number one. It is good for pupils to bring advertisements to class and these may then be analyzed to notice if and how bandwagon approaches are being used. Questions to ask pertaining to pupil collected advertisements from the printed media are the following:

1. What products are being advertised?
2. What is being said about each product?
3. What approaches are being used to influence buying of *the* one product as compared to the others?
4. Which product named appeals to you most, if any, and why?

5. What would you recommend to make the *for sale* product even more appealing to customers? (Ediger, 1998, 74-77).

Fifth, pupils need to use relevant information in problem solving. Ideally, pupils with teacher guidance should identify the problem in a contextual situation. Clarity in problem statement is important. Thus, a meaningful problem is chosen for solving. The next flexible step is to have pupils locate data sources to use in solving the problem. The information gleaned needs to be relevant and pinpoint solutions to the identified problem. Critical thinking is necessary to separate the relevant from the non relevant. Needed information to solve the problem becomes an hypothesis and is subject to evaluation in a live like situation. If the evaluation upholds the tentative hypothesis, well and good. If not, a new hypothesis needs to be selected as a tentative answer to the problem. Again the hypothesis is tested in a life like situation and remains as is, unless evidence warrants this not to be the case. Stated hypotheses are always viewed as tentative and to evaluated contextually (Ediger, 1996, 145-161).

Sixth, pupils need to experience locating the author's purpose(s) in writing. What are the author's reasons for writing? These reasons are purposes for writing. The author may wish to inform or present information to readers. Additional purposes are the following:

1. To present biased information which leads pupils to a single point of view. The teacher's task then is to guide pupils to perceive other perspectives and points of view.
2. To propagandize an idea or set of ideas. To do this, a writer will repeat in highly favourable terms a line of thinking. Generally, propaganda is perceived as being highly negative in a democracy. Companies, corporations, religious organisations, and governments may use propaganda to promote their cause or causes. The New Right, the conservative Christian movement, and the Aryan Nations white supremacy groups, certainly do have their agendas of indoctrination. Pupils, when ready, need to be able to detect

indoctrination efforts and analyze the efforts to impose these efforts. In a democracy, it is important to think critically pertaining to ideas in propaganda efforts.

Seventh, quality questions need to be asked to evaluate pupil achievement. This is an informal means of assessing learner achievement. In a discussion group, the teacher may ask a plethora of good questions to assess learner progress. For example, a teacher might ask questions such as the following pertaining to a literary selection read by pupils:

1. What can you say about the main character(s) in the story?
2. Where did the story take place? How does the setting relate to the main character(s)?
3. Who is telling the story? What is the theme of the story teller?
4. What happened in the story? Was the plot different than what you thought might happen?
5. Was here irony in the story. The concept of *irony* might well need to be explained here (Ediger, 2001, Chapter Seven).

Eighth, the teacher needs to raise questions to help pupils focus attention upon the new words being presented for reading. Pupils benefit much when they see new words on the chalkboard or computer monitor prior to reading a new selection. The teacher needs to help pupils view each new word carefully so that they will be identified correctly in silent and oral reading. There are teachers who write the new words within a sentence so that pupils may identify them in context. Questions raised by the teacher to notice if the presented new words can be identified correctly, as these are being practiced in word recognition from the chalkboard, might well include learners giving a meaningful definition of each. The definition for each new word must be correct, contextually, in subject matter read. This will assist pupils to understand subject matter sequentially in reading. If definitions are difficult or nearly impossible to give, pupils may use each in a sentence. Related to word recognition and meaning attached, the teacher also needs to guide pupils to ask questions covering content to be read so that a purpose or reason is there for reading the selection. Questioning skills need to be developed within pupils. It is salient for each person to be able to ask quality questions so that curiosity is an end result (Ediger, 1993, 17-20).

Ninth, guest speakers need to be invited into the classroom to enrich an ongoing lesson or unit being taught. The need to have specialized information to share with pupils in the classroom. The community is then brought into the local educational setting whereby school and society are integrated, not separate societies. With adequate background information, pupils should possess curiosity and ask relevant questions of each speaker.

Speakers with skills and knowledge pertaining to the following may be brought into the classroom (Parker, 2001):

1. Persons with special skills: weavers, potters, jewelry makers
2. Exchange students
3. Persons with interesting hobbies
4. Members of the local historical society
5. Newspaper reporters, editors and staff writers
6. Members of service organisations
7. Country agents
8. Representatives of environmental and conservation groups
9. 4H and other club leaders
10. Early inhabitants of the community
11. Professional persons: doctor, lawyer, software developer
12. Members of the local business community: bankers, shop owners
13. Union officials
14. Representatives of local industries (docks, timber, manufacturing)

15. Travel agents (think of them as "applied geographers")
16. Recent immigrants or other newcomers in the community
17. Artists who work on public murals or public sculptures
18. Commercial pilots (more "applied geographers!")
19. Community helpers: firefighters, police officers, librarians
20. Government officials representing the three branches...

It is vital that teachers and pupils be able to ask relevant questions in the classroom setting so that the latter become curious and interested in learning to seek answers.

Pupils do need to raise important questions in order to learn from diverse sources of subject matter in formal as well as informal settings. Pupils might then become increasingly proficient in

- Informing in providing information to others.
- Connecting the self with the text, or putting the self into the shoes of others.
- Raising questions, speculating, and pondering.
- Positing hypotheses and possible answers.
- Interpreting by making sense of what has been read.
- Recalling information.
- Judging the worth, merit, and accuracy of content and actions (See Roser and Keehn, 2002).

REFERENCES

Emery, Donna W. (1992), "Children's Understanding of Story Character," *Reading Improvement*, 29 (1), 2-9.

Ediger, Marlow and D. Bhaskara Rao (2000), *Teaching Reading Successfully*. New Delhi, India: Discovery Publishing House, Chapter Six.

Ediger, Marlow (2002), "Developing a Reading Community," *Edutracks*, 16-19. Published in India.

Ediger, Marlow (1998), "Why Don't Pupils Learn to Read?" The *Educational Review*, 104 (16), 161-166.

Ediger, Marlow (1996), *Technology in the Curriculum* Australian Journal of Educational Technology, 12 (2), 145-161.

Ediger, Marlow (1993), "The Integrated Reading Curriculum," *Educational Magazine*, nr. 107, 17-20.

Parker, Walter S. (2001), *Teaching Social Studies in the Elementary School*, Eleventh Edition. Upper Saddle River, New Jersey: Merrill, Prentice Hall, pp 292-293.

Roser, Nancy L., and Susan Keehn (2002), Fostering Thought, Talk, and Inquiry: Linking Literature and Social Studies, *The Reading Teacher*, 55 (5), p 419.

Testing and Evaluating Student Achievement in Reading

Teachers and administrators desire to know how much students have achieved in reading instruction. There are a plethora of ways which may be used to ascertain learner achievement in reading. Educators need to work continually in attempting to find the best ways to measure and evaluate student reading achievement. Selected procedures will now be discussed.

Teacher Observation of Reading Achievement

Perhaps, the oldest form of assessing learner reading achievement is to use comprehensive teacher observation. Quality criteria used by the teacher can be an excellent way to assess reading progress. The emphasis here is upon using careful teacher observation with inherent criteria of excellence. The reading teacher may wish to devise a checklist with the involved student's name on each. He/she may then observe and record objectives which learners should attain on the checklist. The teacher's impressions for each student may also be written in journal form. Each entry should be dated. Which are selected criteria to be used by the teacher to assess student behaviour in reading (Ediger, 1999, 38-40)?

1. Word recognition. There are diverse skills which students need to use in identifying unknown words. Highly proficient readers, no doubt, have mastered these skills when reading fluently with excellent

comprehension. Others, regardless of grade levels will be selected deficiencies in identifying words. There are appropriate categories to list on the checklist such as students using

(a) Phonics successfully to unlock unknown words. Specific problems may be listed which cause these difficulties including lack of associating grapheme/ phoneme relationships, learning to read words by sight which do not follow a sound/symbol correspondence, as well as being able to identify parts within words which do/do not follow a pattern of spelling involving phonetic elements.

(b) Structural analysis to identify unknown words. Structural analysis skills need to be understood and known by the student to make it easier to identify unknown words. Thus, there are common prefixes and suffixes to be taught which when met up with in print discourse, the reader can separate these prefixes and suffixes from the base word, making it possible to recognize the unknown. Common prefixes are "un," "ir," "ex," "trans," among others.

(c) Syllabication skills in that when a student cannot identify a word while reading, he/she may divide the unknown into syllables. May times, the student can then identify the unknown word in print.

(d) Context clues in that the reader may try a word which may fit in as a possible choice for the unknown. The word chosen must make sense with the rest of the words in the sentence being read. Sometimes, more than one sentence needs to be read to ascertain the unknown word.

(e) Pictures clues, especially for young readers, may provide the know word to fill in for the unknown. If a student does not known a word, he/she may look at the picture on the page with the print discourse. The picture may then give away what the unknown word is. On the upper elementary school levels, it may be more difficult to use pictures

located on the same page as the related print to identify unknown words. Why? There are fewer pictures on sequential pages of text as compared to those written for the early primary grade levels.

(*f*) Configuration clues may be helpful to some students in that the shape/form of a word unknown to the reader may provide the necessary clues for identification of an unknown word met up within print discourse (Ediger and Rao, 2000, Chapter Six).

The reading teacher may record how well each student is achieving in the above six named categories of word recognition. What students individual are weak in needs to be diagnosed. Careful paying of attention to the diagnosed provides new objectives to the teacher as to what needs to be stressed in the reading curriculum as objectives of instruction. Based on diagnosis, the reading teacher selects areas of weaknesses. Those weaknesses are followed by remediation as learning opportunities. The learning opportunities assist students to achieve objectives of instruction.

If students are taught to identify words only, then comprehension in reading might well be lacking. As supervisor of student teachers in the public schools for thirty years, the author has noticed individual pupils calling words and even doing this correctly, but not knowing or comprehending that which has been read. After all, the purpose of teaching/using word identification skills is to have students read with meaning (Ediger, 2001, 61-66).

There are different levels of complexity in guiding students to engage in more difficult kinds of thinking. Certainly, students need to read factual subject matter in a meaningful way. There are salient facts which students need to glean from ongoing reading activities. Facts may be acquired for their very own sake and/or for building blocks in reading ensuing materials and thus engage in more complex levels of thought.

Second, understanding of facts then becomes a salient level of sequential complexity in reading. Understanding subject matter read indicates that meaning is being attached to ongoing selections in reading. Meaning theory is very important to stress in reading. To comprehend and to make sense of what has been read is of utmost importance! Otherwise, why read?

Third, using what has been learned is a doing approach. To use means to apply learnings acquired to a new situation. The level of application is used here in that what has been learned is used to achieve something else (Ediger, 2001, 59-66).

Fourth, an analysis of content read becomes important. To analyze is to separate into component parts such as facts from opinions, fantasy from reality, and accurate form inaccurate content. It is always good to analyze subject matter read to divide into relevant segments. Never is everything read of equal value because certain ideas are more salient than others, or main ideas are separated from subordinate content. Thus, the subordinate ideas support the main ideas read.

Fifth, creative reading is very valuable in that new, novel ideas result to the learner. Unique ideas accrue due to the student, for example, brain storming possible answers to identified problems pertaining to the new subject matter acquired. School and society expect originality of content to come about so that new inventions, procedures, and ideas accrue to improve the human condition.

Sixth, assessing the worth of ideas read is also a valuable objective to attain in higher levels of cognition in the ongoing reading process. Each reader will draw selected conclusions on what value(s) the achieved ideas have in school and in society. Valuing the worth of something read will depend much upon how the reader will remember subject matter read. What is prized highly, then, will have its enduring values in remembering subject matter read. Vital ideas should be retained longer as compared to what is perceived to be unimportant (Ediger and Rao, 2000, Chapter Seven).

Through teacher observation, the teacher may notice how well students individually are reading on each of the different levels of cognitive complexity. What is observed may be recorded on the individual student's checklist and/or through journal writing. Entries need to be dated for each student. The reading teacher may then teach and students must learn to overcome deficiencies. It is up to the student to shoulder responsibilities to become a better reader.

Portfolios and the Reading Curriculum

Informal appraisal results may become a part of the portfolio procedure in guiding more optimal student reading achievement. Portfolios, too, are also non-formal approaches to use for diagnoses and remedition, as well as determining sequential experiences for students. Diagnosis and remedition, initially, are non-sequential activities for students whereas a high quality reading curriculum stresses a student centered set of objectives, learning opportunities, and assessment procedures which are more seamless and make for *continuous* progress in reading. Both, however, are necessary to aid student development and achievement in reading. Diagnosis and remedition must be emphasized when a student just did not get it, and before more optimal progress can be made, what is lacking must be made up. Portfolio items to be included in reading might well include the following:

1. Cassettes of oral reading to notice fluency in reading.
2. Snapshots of art work, construction projects, bulletin board displays, murals, dioramas, dramatizations, friezes, among others, to show comprehension of and in reading.
3. A video-tape indicating how well a student does in discussions, within the reading curriculum.
4. Written products as indicators of reading achievement including outlines, summaries, conclusions, and notes taken on reading lesson content.
5. Illustrations drawn to show comprehension of subject matter in reading.
6. Diverse kinds and forms of poetry written to reveal what has been learned from ongoing lessons in reading. These poems may include rhymed verse (couplets, triplets, quatrains, and limericks), poetry involving syllabication (haiku, tanka, and septolets), as well as open ended poetry such as free verse. Poetry may

increasingly emphasize complex items including alliteration, similes/metaphors, and onomatopoeia (Ediger, 1999, 278-279).

7. Student journal writing to indicate what has been learned, what is left to learn, impressions from reading a given selection, as well as indicating values acquired from reading.
8. Notes pertaining to conferences conducted with the teacher after the completion of reading a library book when implementing an individualized reading program.
9. Purposeful worksheets completed, dealing with reading instruction, during class time.
10. A sampling of homework activities such as writing a book report (Ediger, 1999, 41-45).

Viewers and readers of portfolio items may then notice student achievement in reading. The entries in the portfolio provide a random sampling of the kinds of work done by students in reading to indicate achievement and progress. They provide data on specifics in terms of strengths and weaknesses in reading. Parents may have a much better opportunity to notice learners achievement here as compared to looking at a single test score given to indicate student achievement on a state mandated test (Searson and Dunn, 2001, 22-26).

State Mandated Reading Tests

State mandated tests in reading are given in most states to students to notice if satisfactory progress is being made in achievement. Generally, the objectives for the test are available to teachers unless these are standardized tests, published by a commercial company. These mandated tests are developed and written, usually, under the auspices of the state department of education. Teachers then need to select learning opportunities which assist students to achieve the stated objectives. The tests are aligned with these objectives. Thus, students may have experienced test items which relate directly to the stated objectives. Strengths given for using state mandated tests to ascertain student achievement in reading include the following:

1. They provide some information on how well a student is doing in reading.
2. They make comparisons on reading achievement among learners.
3. They give a numerical value on how well students are doing in reading. The numerical value is generally provided as a percentile. Grade equivalents, standard deviations, quartile deviations, and/or stanines may also be given as indicators. Percentiles, generally, are the easiest for parents to understand of all the statistical terms just mentioned to reveal learner progress.
4. They provide trend data on how well students do over a period of years when making yearly comparisons.
5. They may show an average weakness of students such as the latter being low in comprehension as compared to phonics in reading test results (Ediger, 1999, 12-16).

Items which need to be strengthened in the state mandated testing arena are the following:

1. Validity may be quite weak in that the tests do not cover what has been taught.
2. Reliability reveals a rather high standard error of measurement (SE Meas). This means there are definitely more weaknesses within a test as the SE Meas increases.
3. Inadequate pilot studies of these tests have been made. Pilot study results pinpoint weaknesses within a test involving a random sampling of students taking the test, before it is used statewide. Printouts of student results in the pilot study might well reveal what needs to be corrected in terms of deficiencies in multiple choice items on the test.
4. A lack of information to the users/implementers as to how the norms of the test were determined.
5. Special accommodations are lacking for the handicapped when taking the state mandated test.
6. Vague, hazy test items are in evidence on the state mandated test.

7. Averages from student test results are used to make comparisons among schools within a state. Averages do not tell about the individual student in terms of strengths and weaknesses faced in learning to read.
8. Comparisons made among schools within a city may be very unfair due to lower income level schools achieving at a much lower level as compared to those in more affluent areas of a city.
9. Test results are not too useful for teachers unless there is precision provided in terms of what the teacher should emphasized in teaching and what students need to learn for the latter to improve in reading.
10. Students and teachers cannot go over the multiple choice test items in which incorrect responses were given by the learner.

State mandated tests have much need for improvement based upon the above named weaknesses. Each kind of error needs to be diagnosed and remedied in order to update and strengthen the testing movement. The testing of young children is being considered strongly and being implemented, in selected schools, on the kindergarten level of instruction (Allen, 2001, p. 1).

How should test results be used from mandated testing? Too frequently, punishment is used to get" chools in line with upping student achievement". There are a plethora of problems involved with this line of reasoning including

1. Testing is only one way of students revealing that which has been achieved. Gardner (1993) lists eights different intelligences possessed by diverse individuals. These are the following:
   (a) Verbal such as in reading and writing as required in traditional testing situations.
   (b) Space/artistic as in art products and processes to show what has been learned.
   (c) Mathematical/logical with its implications for student revealing reasoning abilities in ongoing experiences.

(*d*) Musical/rhythmical. Here, students with this intelligences indicate learnings through the writing of lyrics and setting the words to music.

(*e*) Interpersonal with the *individual* showing what he/she has learned due to this intelligence possessed.

(*f*) Interpersonal intelligence whereby these individuals reveal strength in *collaborative situations* to show what has been learned.

(*g*) Bodily/kinesthetic intelligence involve those who best reveal learnings acquired through the use of the gross and finer muscles as in games played and in athletic prowess.

(*h*) Scientific in which the student reveals objective, not subjective, thinking in school experiences as well as in evaluation situations.

In viewing the above named intelligences, a reader might show what has been gleaned from reading by doing and making an art project, intelligences number two listed above, instead of responding to multiple choice test items as is true of most state mandated tests. The author when supervising student teachers in the public schools noticed a plethora of art projects developed by learners to show comprehension in what had been read such as an illustration completed by a student showing a farm scene pertaining to subject matter read. Or, three students having read the same short story from paperbacks developed a mural or urban life after having completed the related reading activity. A student made and used two sock puppets to do a dramatization, based on library book content read. There are many possibilities then in students doing art projects to portray characters in stories read.

2. Test results for a single test should not determine a student's future such as in an exit test whereby a student may never receive a high school diploma for having failed a test. Even if the test can be taken over again, the stigma of failure can be great.

3. Publishing schools for being educationally bankrupt penalizes low income area schools (Ediger, 1999, 280-285).

REFERENCES

Allen, Rick (2001), "Cultivating Kindergarten, the Reach for Academic Heights Raises Challenges," *Curriculum Update.* Alexandria, Virginia: The Association for Supervision and Curriculum Development, p 1.

Ediger, Marlow (1999), *"Affective Objectives in Reading Instruction," Reading Matters,* 2 (1), 38-40.

Ediger, Marlow (1999), "Teacher Education and the Public Schools, Making the Connections—Writing Poetry," *The Progress of Education,* 73 (12), 278-279. Published in India.

Ediger, Marlow, "Evaluation, The Language Arts, and the Student," *Focus,* 25 (2), 12-16.

Ediger, Marlow (1999), "The Pupil in the Rural School," *The Journal of Instructional Psychology,* 26 (4), 280-285.

Ediger, Marlow, and D. Bhaskara Rao (2000), *Teaching Reading Successfully,* New Delhi, India, Discovery Publishing House.

Ediger, Marlow (2001), "Assessing Student Progress," *School Science,* 39 (1), 62-66.

Ediger, Marlow (2001), "Assessing Inquiry Learning in Science," *Experiments in Education,* 29 (4), 59-65.

Ediger, Marlow, and D. Bhaskara Rao (2000), *Teaching Mathematics Successfully.* New Delhi, India: Discovery Publishing House.

Ediger, Marlow and Digumarti Bhaskara Rao (2002), *Improving School Administration.* New Delhi, India: Discovery Publishing House.

Ediger, Marlow (1999), "Spelling Words Correctly," *Bhasa,* 1 (4), 41-45. Published in India.

Gardner, Howard (1993), *Multiple Intelligences: Theory Into Practice.* New York: Basic books.

Searson, Robert, and Rita Dunn (2001), "The Learning Styles/Teaching Model," *Science and Children,* 38 (5), 22-26.

Handwriting and the Pupil

The teacher of handwriting must select vital objectives for learners to achieve. The concept of relevance is important to emphasize in selecting ends for pupil attainment. Thus, much thought and careful consideration needs to be given by the teacher in selecting these handwriting goals. Too frequently, pupils have developed trivial and insignificant learnings. There is much to be learned during the elementary school years. In society, the "explosion of knowledge" has been a definite reality for some time. The knowledge explosion societal trend has important implications for the classroom teacher. The teacher must select educational purposes, carefully. Pertaining to writing skills, Petty wrote:

> Writing involves many skills and abilities. The most fundamental of these are the thinking skills or abilities, which are basic to the expression of feelings and thoughts, whether the medium is speech, movement, art, or writing. In relation to writing, these skills include collecting and organising data; classifying, comparing, and summarizing ideas and feelings; choosing the most appropriate words and phrases for conveying expressions; organising these expressions into sentences that are clearly understandable; and sequencing the sentences into a meaningful whole. All of these thinking abilities are used to compose a piece of writing, with the effectiveness of any composition largely dependent on the quality of the thinking ability or skills of the composer. No written expression, not even a single sentence or a label or a short memorandum, will be effective expression unless it is well thought out.

In addition, of course, skill in forming letters and words, in spelling correctly, in punctuating sentences properly, and in those matters of form and custom in the appearance of various types of writing are also very much a part of effective written expression. And each of these general skills or abilities consists of specific lesser ones: in handwriting, the strokes needed to make the letters, spacing, rhythm of movement; in spelling, making sound and symbol associations, affixing, capitalizing; the punctuation, the strokes needed to form the punctuation marks. All of these skills require teaching and thorough practice so that they become automatic to writers and permit them to use full thinking power for composition.

The Child and Handwriting

Certainly, the teacher must give careful consideration to child growth and development characteristics when selecting objectives. If pupils cannot achieve stated objectives, modification of stated ends is in order. Handwriting objectives selected by the teacher for learners to achieve should be attainable. At the same time, the chosen objectives represent new learnings for pupils to acquire.

The length of time devoted to handwriting instruction needs careful evaluation. Early primary grade pupils need relatively short periods of time devoted to learning activities involving handwriting. Generally, their attention span is not as long as compared to older pupils. First, grade pupils become tired rather soon from handwriting experiences because the finer muscles, involving the use of the arm, hand, and fingers, are being developed gradually. The teacher needs to observe individual pupils to determine if learning activities need to be changed from handwriting to a different curriculum area which does not require use of the finer muscles. Intermediate grade pupils generally write for a longer period of time to finish a given reasonable assignment without excessive fatigue and tiredness setting in. However, for any age level, expectations from any individual can be too high in activities involving handwriting. If pupils perceive reasons for developing selected understandings, skills, and attitudinal objectives, energy levels of the involved persons generally increase in wanting to further pursue a given learning activity. Varying approaches in teaching may also assist learners to maintain a longer attention span pertaining to teaching-learning situations involving handwriting experiences.

The teacher must remember that each child is unique in many ways and that includes rate of achievement in handwriting. Pupils feel frustrated and may learn to dislike handwriting experiences if they cannot achieve to the level expected of them. Pupils should enjoy handwriting experiences as well as have feelings of satisfaction in all curriculum areas of the elementary school.

In determining educational objectives pertaining to handwriting, the teacher needs to consider and answer the following questions:

1. Can learners satisfactorily achieve the chosen aims?
2. Will pupils feels successfully in their accomplishment?
3. Can interest be developed and/or maintained within pupils in achieving desired objectives?
4. Are the stated objectives in handwriting in harmony with neuromuscular skills that learners presently possess?
5. Do the objectives guide learners to develop appropriate attitudes, as well as skills and understandings?
6. Are the objectives stated so that it can be determined if achievement in that direction is taking place?
7. Will learners feel that purpose is involved in achieving the desired objectives?

For initial instruction in handwriting, Lee and Rubin wrote:

> Most things we learn to do, we learn largely through imitation and experimentation, giving special attention to the more troublesome aspects. We usually arrive at our own personal adaptations and idiosyncrasies. Handwriting can be learned the same way.
>
> Many children learn to write their names and perhaps much more before they come to school. In school, each can have a card with his or her name on it in good, clear manuscript writing, so that it is readily available for copying. When children begin dictating sentences for the teacher to write for them, they will soon want to write for themselves. Thus begins their first significant writing "lesson".

The teacher can write the sentence in good, clear manuscript on a strip of paper the appropriate length for the child's picture. The child takes both the strip and the picture to the writing center, places the strip just above the blank space reserved for the sentence, and copies the sentence directly below the teacher's writing.

When this procedure is repeated many times and combined with discussion during dictation, no other writing "lessons" are needed. When a few children have difficulty with a certain letter, the teacher can group these children for a few minutes, explain the problem, and provide a good model for them to copy. They can solve the problem quickly by keeping this model in front of them as they write.

Teachers must be aware that there is a great difference in the small muscle coordination of children of this age. When a child is trying, the writing must be accepted with appreciation for progress, regardless of imperfections. If it is really illegible, perhaps larger writing—or smaller writing—would help.

Society and Handwriting

What does society expect of pupils in handwriting achievement? It is imperative that individuals exhibit legible handwriting when communicating with others. Time is wasted in reading content if it is difficult to determine what others have written due to poor handwriting. Individuals like to read meaningful content which is easy to decode. This is true of content written in friendly letters, business letters, announcements, plays, poems, stories and in letters of application in applying for jobs or positions. Legible handwriting must be in evidence. The employer generally, all things being equal, will be more influenced with content in a letter that has good handwriting as compared to illegible handwriting. It is true, of course, that letters of application in applying for positions and jobs are also typed. However, there are other numerous writing occasions in which legible handwriting is a definite asset as compared to illegible handwriting. Society does place value upon individuals exhibiting quality legible handwriting.

The teacher needs to answer the following questions pertaining to what society might expect pupils to learn in handwriting:

1. Will the curricular learnings that pupils develop be useful in society?
2. Are the chosen objectives relevant pertaining to what pupils may need in terms of learnings now as well as in the future?

General Objectives in Handwriting

General objectives in handwriting state the direction of behaviour that teachers want learners to achieve over a relatively long period of time. The teacher needs to determine which understandings, skills, and attitudes are to be developed within pupils at the end of a designated interval of time. General objectives may not be achieved during the time a unit is taught or perhaps even during a school year.

Pupils should exhibit continuous progress in handwriting. They need to be taught at their present level of achievement and guided in progressing at their optimum rate of achievement as they progress through diverse years of schooling.

The following, among others, might well be important general objectives for pupils to accomplish in handwriting.

A. Understandings Objectives:

1. To develop within the pupil an understanding of how to form letters legibly.
2. To develop within learners an understandings of how letters may be aligned properly.
3. To develop within the child understandings pertaining to appropriate spacing of words and letters.
4. To develop within the learner an understanding of the necessity of having proper proportion of letters.
5. To develop within the child appropriate generalizations in achieving legibility in handwriting.
6. To develop within the learner an understanding of approaches to self-evaluation in the area of handwriting.
7. To develop an understanding within pupils of the necessity of exhibiting neatness in handwriting.

B. *Skills Objectives*

1. To develop within the pupils skill to form legible letters in handwriting.
2. To develop within learners skill to use proper alignment in handwriting.
3. To develop within children skill to use appropriate proportion of letters in handwriting.
4. To develop in children skill to utilize proper spacing of letters and words.
5. To develop within the child skill to evaluate his/her own achievement in handwriting.
6. To develop within pupils skill to exhibit neatness in handwriting.

C *Attitudinal Objectives*

1. To develop within pupils a desire in wanting to improve achievement in handwriting.
2. To develop within learners a feeling of wanting to improve in the formation of legible letters.
3. To develop within the child an attitude of wanting to reveal proper proportion of letters.
4. To develop within the learner a desire to space words and letters properly.
5. To develop within the child a desire to assess his/her own achievement in handwriting.
6. To develop an attitude within learners of wanting to reveal neatness in handwriting.
7. To develop an attitude of respect within learners toward quality in handwriting as revealed by others in society.

It is important to emphasize balance among understandings, skills, and attitudinal objectives in teaching handwriting. Desirable attitudes assist in achieving understandings and skills ends. Greene and Petty wrote the following:

The major reason for teaching handwriting is its role in communication. Handwriting is the principal tool of written expression; for this reason it must be legible. Thus the principal objective of handwriting instruction is legibility.

Considering this objective, a teacher should not stress meaningless drill on handwriting but should strive mainly to have pupils produce legible copy. The misapplication of the principle of use and need so frequently evident is a result of the neglect of sound procedures in instruction. The principal factor overlooked is that handwriting is a developmental process that requires more than just a few years of the child's total period of growth. Simply permitting children to write as they have the need is not giving handwriting instruction nor can handwriting be taught once and then dropped from the instructional program. Production of legible writing at a reasonable speed can be achieved and maintained only as a result of constant and meaningful practice. Thus the handwriting program should be built around these basic goals:

Encouraging pupils to use writing as a means for effective expression.

Helping each child to discover how skill in handwriting aids expression.

Having all pupils strive for neatness and legibility with moderate speed in their writing activities.

Establishing practice periods as appropriate at all grade levels.

Analyzing the handwriting faults of individual pupils and seeking their correction.

Developing in each pupil a sense of personal pride and self-appraisal and a desire for self-improvement.

Developing correct posture and the proper use of writing tools.

Specific Objectives

Selected teachers, principals, and supervisors wish to have clearly stated objectives, as advocated by behaviourists, in teaching-learning situations. The teacher then may need to write measurable objectives in handwriting. There is relatively little leeway in determining what is to be taught when viewing specific objectives. After instruction, the teacher may determine if learners have or have not achieved the precise objectives. It is vital to have pupils achieve relevant handwriting objectives. Reasonable specific objectives need to be written for learners. Learners might then be successful achievers. Learning activities to achieve specific objectives in handwriting should be interesting, have purpose, and be on the understanding level of pupils. Provision must be made to provide for individual differences when measurably stated objectives are used in teaching handwriting.

The following are examples of specific objectives for pupils to achieve in handwriting.

1. The pupil will write three sentences using recommended alignment of words and letters.
2. The pupil will write the lower case cursive letters "a," "b," and "c" correctly as presented in class by writing a sentence.
3. The pupil will write five sentences using proper spacing of letters within each word.

The teacher after instruction may assess if pupils have or have not achieved stated objectives. It is important to correlate the teaching of handwriting with other curriculum areas in the elementary school. There are many learning activities in handwriting which correlate well with writing activities in social studies, science, mathematics, reading and other language arts areas, health, music, art, and physical education. Pupils need ample opportunities to practice quality handwriting in other curriculum areas in the school/class setting.

Yelon and Weinstein wrote:

> Reinforcement, in a behaviorist view, is the single most important factor in learning. The low of reinforcement, sometimes called the law of effect, defines the shaping of behaviour through reinforcers. A common example is the laboratory situation in which pigeons are trained to press levers for food; the training is accomplished by providing food each time the lever is pressed. Similarly, the law of reinforcement applies to human behaviour; children may learn polite table manners, for instance, if their parents smile approvingly each time they eat correctly.
>
> Every element of human thought and feeling, according to behaviorist learning theory, may be defined in terms of

reinforcement—not just table manners but good study habits and socially approved behaviour of all kinds, even love itself. Techniques which manipulate reinforcement alter the learning process.

Learning Activities in Handwriting

There are a variety of learning activities that may be provided for learners in handwriting. Individuals differences must be provided for in any classroom. Pupils will vary much from each other in handwriting achievement. The teacher must consider the present achievement level of each child in handwriting before learning activities are selected to achieve new stated objectives. The kinds of learning activities that are selected in handwriting may well depend upon the way the school curriculum area is organised. For example, the classroom teacher may decide to teach handwriting as a separate subject with no relationship being emphasized with other curriculum areas in the elementary school. The teacher then assumes that pupils automatically will use acquired handwriting understandings, skills, and attitudes in new writing situations involving the social studies, science, mathematics, the language arts, health, music, physical education, and art. The writer definitely feels that classroom teachers must assist learners to see the uses of what has been learned previously. Thus, learners must perceive that what has been learned earlier can be utilized in ongoing learning activities.

The teacher of handwriting will definitely wish to correlate handwriting with other areas in the school curriculum. If the teacher is teaching spelling, he/she will also wish to emphasize quality handwriting. Handwriting errors can make for incorrect spelling of words. For example, learners who do not cross the "t" in cursive writing and leave a loop in that same letter are actually writing the letter "l" when the letter "t" was intended to be written. The teacher then may definitely want to correlate handwriting with spelling.

Handwriting may be taught as being related to any curriculum area in the elementary school. For example, in the final product that is written in a health unit of study, a learner may exhibit improved handwriting in a report on proper dietary habits. The quality of handwriting exhibited may be assessed in terms of what the learner can reasonably well achieve. Additional examples of relating handwriting to different curriculum areas will now be discussed.

Mathematics and Handwriting

Products of learners in mathematics become difficult to evaluate if the written work is slovenly done and illegible. Thus, the teacher has an important responsibility in guiding learners to write numerals and symbols in mathematics legibly. The learner may then communicate ideas more effectively if this is done. Individuals communicate content in many different ways. Writing numerals and symbols pertaining to mathematics is a form of communication of ideas to others. It is imperative then that numerals and symbols be written legibly so that effective communication of ideas may take place. Neatness in these written products is also important.

Occasionally, learners will be writing reports in mathematics based on research. If pupils are studying the Roman system of numeration, they may wish to gather information from different reference sources and complete a written report on this topic. The best handwriting of the individual pupil needs to be expected in the final product.

Science and Handwriting

There are numerous opportunities for pupils to utilize handwriting in the science curriculum. Among these important learning activities might be the following:

1. A committee of pupils or individual learners may write up the findings of a science experiment.
2. Individually or within a committee, pupils might write a method of procedure to follow in order to conduct an experiment.
3. A report may be written on a chosen topic related to an ongoing science unit. Topics, such as "magnetism," "Electricity," "atoms," "electrons," "protons," and "neutrons" might well make for quality content in written reports.

4. Temperature readings could be recorded on a daily basis in a unit on "Climate in Our Community".
5. Notes may be written pertaining to a selection read from an encyclopaedia or science textbook.
6. An outline might be written from content read using a variety of reference sources.
7. Criteria or standards ought to be written on being an effective member and/or leader of a discussion group.
8. Summaries could be written or main ideas presented in a filmstrip or film presentation relating to the science unit being studied.

Science teachers must always think of variety of learning activities for learners in order to provide for individual pupils within a class.

Social Studies and Handwriting

In a self-contained classroom or in a departmentalized plan of teaching, the teacher can stress the importance of handwriting pertaining to writing activities in the social studies. The following, among others, might provide quality learning activities for pupils:

1. Business letters could be written to order free charts, pictures, and other audio-visual aids related to the ongoing social studied unit.
2. Friendly letters might be written to pen pals. These pen pals may come from countries presently being studied in social studies, or having been studied in the past.
3. Generalizations and main ideas may be written on content read from diverse reference sources.
4. Important facts read relating to a relevant question raised by learners in an ongoing social studies unit may be recorded.
5. Announcements can be written inviting another class to observe culminating activities for a specific unit in social studies.
6. Speaking parts for a play may be written cooperatively by a committee of pupils relating to a specific part of a

social studies unit. In a unit on "Discovering New Lands" learners might write a play to interpret how explorers felt when new lands were being discovered. The play can be presented to other members of the class and to other classes of children.

7. Directions could be written in making relief maps which relate to a unit being studied. For example, if pupils are studying a unit of Australia, they might make a relief map on that country.
8. Standards can be developed by the class on giving effective oral reports. Reports may be given to the entire class by individual pupils or by a committee of children. Reports given could be assessed in light of these written standards.
9. An outline may be written relating to important conclusions reached in reading an important selection in social studies.
10. When pupils are engaged in presenting hypotheses pertaining to content in a picture, object, or problem, handwriting experiences then become a reality in functional situations in the classroom.
11. Learners may take notes relating to a discussion that has taken place.

Handwriting and the Language Arts

Handwriting is a part of the language arts curriculum in the elementary school. Handwriting thus becomes an inherent part of language arts as well as the other curriculum areas in the elementary school. Selected learning activities, among others, that pertain to handwriting in the language arts could be the following:

1. Pupils with teacher assistance might label objects in the classroom in a reading readiness program using manuscript writing.
2. Handwriting textbooks can be utilized in lessons as the need and purpose arises.
3. Experience charts might be developed with teacher guidance in a reading readiness program. Learners may

notice what is said orally can be written down in manuscript letters. Cursive writing will be introduced later on.

4. Learners can write ideas over content that has been read pertaining to different purposes in reading. These purposes involve critical reading, reading to follow directions, factual reading, reading for a sequence of ideas, creative reading, reading for main ideas, and reading to develop generalizations.
5. Pupils need ample opportunities to practice forming letters correctly, writing letters and words with recommended alignment, slanting letters properly, spacing words and letters legibly, and using proper proportion of letters.
6. Pupils with teacher leadership may write news items. The resulting newspaper could be sent home weekly, biweekly, or monthly on important happenings in class.

Health and Handwriting

Many interesting learning activities provided for pupils in the area of health could also help learners achieve important goals in handwriting. The following learning activities in health education may assist learners to improve in handwriting:

1. Learners may take notes over a talk given by a physician pertaining to improved health practices in everyday living.
2. Main ideas could be written covering a set of slides or pictures presented by a registered nurse related to improving healthful living in the community.
3. Each pupil might write a personal experience chart pertaining to contents from a filmstrip relating to a facet of healthful living.
4. Letters can be written to members of the city council making recommendations on improving polluted areas.
5. Menus for a week may be written pertaining to balanced diets for individuals.

6. Business letters can be written to order free materials relating to health units of instruction.

In Summary

When writing objectives for learners to achieve, it is of utmost importance for the teacher to consider each pupil's present achievement level. The teacher also must consider trends in society and their importance in determining handwriting goals. Objectives may be stated broadly as is the case of general objectives in curriculum area of handwriting. Specific objectives can also be written which may be achieved in a relatively short period of time. General objectives are achieved over a longer period of time. The teacher must determine rational balance among understandings, skills, and attitudinal objectives that learners are to achieve. Each category of objectives is vital to emphasize in teaching-learning situations.

The teacher must think of various methods to use in teaching handwriting. These varied approaches are necessary to provide adequately for each learner in class. Handwriting correlates well with each curriculum area in the elementary school. The pupil must exhibit improved handwriting in the final product that has been written. The child generally may not reveal improved handwriting at the time that content is being written. Ideas come first when writing content. However, the learner can always show improved handwriting in the final written product. Legibility in handwriting must permeate and be emphasized as being important in all curriculum areas in the elementary school.

REFERENCES

1. Dawson, Mildred A. *Guiding Language Learning*. Second Edition. New York: Harcourt, Brace and World, Inc., 1963. Chapter Seventeen.

2. Ediger, Marlow. "Essentials in Teaching Handwriting," *Education* (September, 1965), 37-39.

3. Ediger, Marlow. "Handwriting in the Elementary School," *School and Community* (April, 1972), 46.

4. Ediger, Marlow. "On Teaching Handwriting, "Illinois *Schools Journal* (Fall, 1971), 156-157.

5. Greene, Harry A., and Walter T. Petty. *Developing Language Skills in the Elementary School*. Firth Edition. Boston: Allyn and Bacon, Inc., 1975.

6. Lee, Doris M., and Joseph B. Rubin. *Children and Language*. Belmont, California: Wadsworth Publishing Company, 1979.

7. Myers, Emma Harrison. *The Whys and Hows of Teaching Handwriting*. Columbus: The Zaner-Bloser Company, 1963.

8. Petty, Walter T. (Editor). *Curriculum for the Modern Elementary School*. Chicago, Illinois: Rand McNally College Publishing Company, 1976.

9. Rose, Karel. *Teaching Language Arts to Children*. New York: Harcourt, Brace and Jovanovich, 1982.

10. Strickland, Ruth G. *The Language Arts in the Elementary School*. Boston, Massachusetts, 1957. Chapters Twelve and Thirteen.

11. Tidyman, Willard, and Marguerite Butterfield. *Teaching the Language Arts*. Second Edition. New York: McGraw-Hill Book Company, 1959, Chapter Fifteen.

12. Trauger, Wilmer K. *Language Arts in Elementary Schools*. New York: McGraw-Hill Book Company, 1963, Chapter Five.

13. Yelon, Stephen and Grace Weinstein. *A Teacher's World, Psychology in the Classroom*. New York: McGraw-Hill Book Company, 1977.

Writing in the Language Arts Curriculum

The reading and writing curriculum correlate well with each other. Why? Very often, reading experiences provide the springboard for writing. Thus, a variety of kinds of poetry may be written based on content acquired from reading. Diverse kinds of rhymed and unrhymed poems may then be written. Literary elements such as characterization, setting, plot, irony, theme and point of view many be rewritten or elaborated upon by pupils from having read a given story or selection. Creativity should be a major objective of pupil writing. Novelty, uniqueness and originality of content from pupil writing, should be wanted. Written work should emphasize cutting across all academic disciplines. Written work then has no single academic discipline to stress but writing across the curriculum should be the objective of instruction (Ediger, 1997).

There are definite assumptions pertaining to writing. These assumptions are the following:

1. Pupils learn to write by writing.
2. Proficiency in oral language assists the learner to do a better job of writing.
3. Success in writing helps pupils to extend major goals to improve continuously in written work.
4. Writing seemingly is the most difficult of the four areas of vocabulary development—listening, speaking, reading and writing, but each needs to be emphasized to assist pupils to achieve as optimally as possible.

5. Pupils individually learn to write, but each pupil may learn much through collaborative endeavours in writing. Pupils learn from each other in writing.
6. Writing needs to be taught as being interrelated with grammar, punctuation, spelling, vocabulary, syntax, semantics, structure in the English language, handwriting, whole language and phonics.
7. Written work cuts across all academic disciplines whenever print discourse is used.
8. Pupils need to write for a variety of audiences such as the teacher, parents, friends brothers and sisters among others.
9. Sequence in writing improvement begins with the pre-school years, including scribbling and occurs throughout adulthood.
10. Written work should be useful whereby application is made of print discourse, as well as be creative for leisure type and utilitarian activities.

The teacher needs to focus upon the above named objectives in teaching writing and their inter-relationship with the other areas of the language arts. Writing must be related to all academic disciplines when written work is being stressed. These ideas are expressed further in basic goals that pupils need to acquire in on-going lessons and units of study. Pupils are to:

1. Write frequently to record ideas in print discourse.
2. Experience the relationships among listening, speaking, reading and writing.
3. Expand literary experiences in incorporate written expressions.
4. Use a variety of purposes to convey meanings in writing.
5. Experiment with diverse genres and subject matter when engaged in writing.
6. Attend to conventions in writing such as quality punctuation, capitalization and grammar.

7. Edit personal work and the work of others in writing by using collective endeavours.
8. Appreciate writing skills possessed and enjoy what has been written.
9. Utilize reading and children's library books as springboards in writing in their diverse manifestations.
10. Indicate pride in being successful in listening, speaking, reading and writing.

Leadership from the principal is vital. The principal and the teacher need to work together for the good of the child in attaining more optimally in the school setting (Ediger, 1998).

Creative Writing and Poetry

An important source for writing is to use content from basal texts and library books, among other print discourse sources, to engage pupils in written work. Through reading, viewing objects, items, illustrations and audio-visual materials directly related to what is/has been read, might well encourage creative poetry writing by learners. Discussions pertaining to what has been read might also impress pupils to apply what has been learned in poetry writing.

First of all, let's take a look at writing poems which rhyme. Many pupils like to write poetry which contains rhyme. There are numerous patterns in rhyming poetry. Early primary grade pupils who can hear rhyme may wish to write couplets, individually or in a small committee. A couplet contains two lines with ending words rhyming. These young learners may wish to dictate the couplet for the teacher to print in neat manuscript letters. Dictated poems may be saved for re-reading by pupils in class. Later on, and for all pupils, learners may wish to write triplets containing three lines. With a triplet, all ending words rhyme. A slightly more difficult poem to write is the quatrain. Here, with four lines of verse, all ending words need to rhyme or lines one and two as well a lines three and four should rhyme.

The limerick has five lines with lines one, two and five rhyming as well as lines three and four rhyming. Limericks generally begin with "There once was. . . . The limerick may be written as follows:

There once was a man of great height

He always seemed to be up tight.

He swatted a bee

and landed in the sea

That wonderful man of great light.

There are pupils who cannot hear rhyme or may wish to write unrhymed poetry. The haiku is a favourite of many people to write. The haiku contains three lines with the following sequence: five syllables for the first line, seven for the second line, and five syllables for the third line. The following haiku is an example:

Birds

Birds fly without rest

Where do they get the power?

I do not know why.

A tanka is a slight variation of the haiku and has a total of five lines with the following number of syllables for each line: five, seven, five, seven, and seven. The following tanka presents a model:

The Arctic in Winter

The blasts of cold air

Keep the polar bear on ice

Whither the young cubs?

Walking on the tall iceberg

Never mind the cold weather.

The haiku and the tanka above were written by elementary age pupils whom we observed when supervising students teachers and one of us cooperating teachers in the public schools. We find that pupils like to write poetry when background information has been experienced and motivation to write is there.

Free verse has no rhyme and no syllabication involved for writing. One pupils whom one of us observed in the classroom wrote the following free verse:

The horse
gives us rides when wanted
is fed well in the barn
exercises much during the day time
loves to be petted
wants to be noticed
desires to be comfortable all year long
hates flies and gnats in summer
eats grass in summer and grain/hay in winter
wants to please others
may ever be grateful for good care.

In the writing of poetry, pupils need to use elements that poets apply in writing verse creatively. One element is onomatopoeia which stresses words written to make echoic sounds. The following emphasize words making their very own sounds: splish, splash, swoosh and slash. The relationship will not always be sound made in the environment. These words also bring in a second element poets use in writing and that is alliteration. With alliteration, two or more sequential words start with the same sound. In this case, the "s" sound is made. A third element is imagery. Imagery has two dimensions and these are similes and metaphors. Similes connect two phrases, in general, such as in the following example of a poem written by a pupil: The cloud of a smoke looked like a billowing lion. Thus, the 'cloud of smoke' is compared with "a billowing lion". The word *like* connects the two phrases. Another word used in similes to make these creative connections is the word as e.g. "The crow caws as a coughing giant. Metaphors, as a second element of imagery, do not have the words "like" or "as" to make these novel connections. For example, the following imagery pertains to a metaphoric approach: "The egg in the pan bubbles tiger like in the water". There is no connector, such as *like* or as between. "The egg is the pan" with "bubbles tiger like in the water".

Writing in Journals

Journal writing is quite popular as an activity for children in the elementary school. There are numerous items that might be written in a journal. Here, many pupils record with they have experienced in a reading lesson such as summaries of content read and discussed in the classroom, vocabulary terms learned in a lesson or unit of study, results discussed from a test taken, and/or impressions acquired from a study of characterization, setting, plot, theme, point of view and/or messages of the writer of stories and literature in general.

Some pupils write journal items each day. Others write once a week or biweekly. We suggested encouraging pupils to write each day, but at least once a week. Pupils need to do much writing in order to become proficient in written work. Practice makes for proficiency in writing. We do much writing of manuscripts for publication and at the beginning, our written work left much to be desired. With effort put forth, we have been quite successful in having our manuscripts published in educational journals. We are convinced that most pupils can communicate effectively in writing if there is adequate practice, assistance from the teacher and from parents in the home setting, encouragement from many, a stimulating environment to provide ideas for writing and a designated place for writing with the necessary materials.

Journal writing should have important purposes such as the following for the writer: to be more observant of happenings in every day life, to keep record of ideas and events, to use models that stress quality writing and to establish meaning in life's endeavours. It is important for the pupil to carry his/her journal and a pencil along, in order to record important things in life. What might go into journal writing?

1. Happenings in class that were of interest.
2. Content read from library books as well as the basal textbook.
3. A sketch of something that is difficult to write about.
4. Poems that were of personal interest.
5. Letters written and received.
6. Frustrations felt in writing.
7. Descriptions on items and objects that fascinate the writer.

8. A creative description of a modified setting, characterization, plot, theme, point of view and other elements of a story read.
9. Statements on what you would like to be or become in the future.
10. Play parts of a story in literature or unit in the social studies.

Writing A Personal Experience

Pupils tend to like telling incidence about their own life and times. The personal experience involves a part of the person's life time. The learner needs to choose what is personally relevant and what might be important to the reader of the essay. Sometimes, pupils have so much to write about that the reader feels overwhelmed in its reading. At the opposite end of the continuum, selected pupils just cannot get started in writing a personal experience. Readers like to know which events truly shaped the history of the writer. The pupil also needs to write how he/she fits into wider social roles in life.

A narrative account of events then needs to be shared with peers. The account actually involves a part of the history of the individual doing the writing. Some important pointers for the writer of the essay are the following:

1. Think of what is truly relevant to write about in your life and times.
2. Select an event that is clear and distinct. The event(s) should be written about in detail.
3. Describe each incidence carefully so that readers may role play selected characters in the story of life. There needs to a character, setting and plot in the historical account.
4. Sequence the order of events in the writing so that it makes sense to the reader.
5. Write details with assist the reader to be an inherent part of the story.
6. Use depth coverage in writing about the major events or characters in the writing.

7. Emphasize dialogue in the writing to breath life into the personnel experience.
8. Build the major events or incidences of a story up to a climax.
9. Write for a target audience and identify this audience.
10. Give each person in the essay should have a name.

Writing An Outline

Outlining salient subject matter may be a good way to learn about main ideas, subordinate ideas and details. When a person reads, he/she needs to sort out what is of major importance as compared to that which is less salient. To view each sentence as having the worth of others, robs the reader of securing important ideas. With the explosion of knowledge, it behooves the reader all the more to arrange content read in terms of major versus minor ideas. Otherwise, the reader is bombarded with ideas which do not lend themselves to remembering effectively what has been read. The teacher needs to model good outlining habits to pupils. Peers may also assist each other in outlining subject matter read.

When pupils outline content read or the spoken voice listened to, careful attention needs to be paid to major as compared to more minor ideas. Let us suppose we are reading/listening to an essay on *Bears*. The first major division of the presentation is, "Looking for food". The first major division of the presentation is, "Looking for food", is a phrase. A subdivision may indicate the kinds of food being looked for. The pupil doing the outline may write the following kinds of foods—fish, rodents, seals and birds. The latter animals emphasize details. A second major division under the heading *Bears* might be, "Finding shelter". A subdivision here might be the kinds of shelter which are acceptable, such as caves, an old deserted building, the side of a mound of dirt and among intertwined branches.

Questions that might the raised pertaining to outlining include the following:

1. How long should the outline be? This depends upon the length of the reading selection being outlined. Or a teacher might assign the length of the outline.

2. How many main major division are there in an outline? This depends upon how many broad ideas there are in a selection that in being read and outlined. We would say that a reading selection of 250 words will generally have two major divisions. Rules in outlining say that there need to be two major divisions at least under one title or topic. There also need to be two subdivision, at least, under a major division. There also should be a least two details under a subdivision. What if two of each (such as main divisions, subdivisions and details) cannot be found? Then put the data within the statement preceding the two items of lesser value.

3. Should there be a sentence outline or a phrase outline? This depends upon the teacher and the pupils involved in writing the outline. We prefer the sentence outline since each sentence says something that is complete in meaning. In my thinking, phrases lack the clarity that sentences possess. The above examples emphasized a phrase rather than a sentence outline. We will now write a model sentence outline:

The Holy Land

A. A region that is scared to Muslims, Jews and Christians.

 1. There are Five Pillars of the Muslim religion.

  (a) The Hajj at Mecca, Saudi Arabia is made at least once during the life time of a devout Muslim.

  (b) The Holy Book of the Muslims is the *Koran*.

 2. The Pentateuch, the first five books of the Old Testament, is holy to devout Jews.

 3. The Church of the Holy Sepulcher is a holy place to devout Christians inside the walled city of Jerusalem.

B. A region made up of the Mediterranean climate has rainy whether from October to April.

The above outline contains two major divisions, such as in A and B. It has three subdivisions such as the numerals 1, 2 and 3. Two details are in evidence such as a and b under the first subdivision. As more content is read, additions may be made to this outline.

Writing An Opinion

A personal perspective of a writer contains a point of view or an opinion. Generally, the writer wants to be understood in terms of what is believed in the opinion. The writer may challenge his/her own point(s) of view in the writing. Sometimes, through writing, the writer wants to understand the premises better of his/her own ideas. By writing about personal beliefs, the writer may also clarify and critically evaluate thoughts brought forth. The following are selected pointers for the pupil in writing about his/her opinions.

1. Choose something that has been on your mind for a long time.
2. Assist readers to comprehend and understand your beliefs.
3. By yourself in the written content. . . Do not write about someone else's opinion.
4. Use your own distinct style in writing.
5. Write in the first person.
6. Use examples and details in your writing to make meaningful the opinions expressed.
7. Write on what "bugs" you.
8. Take a point of view which represents your thinking on an issue.
9. Give your thinking on capital punishment, the creation story or the evaluation of the universe or the pros and cons of governmental spending on social projects.
10. Write about your favourite pet peeve.

Proofing your writings provides numerous opportunities for reading ideas and content. The final copy should be one that you are very proud of.

Writing on How Something Should be Done

There are numerous occasions when we are asked to provide information on how something is to be done. Directions need to be given frequently on assembling a mower, repairing a kitchen appliance, installing a door bell and building a deck, among other items. People tend to be curious on how something works as well as why something does not work. We believe children find it interesting and challenging to write about something within their area of readiness involving how to do something. The "how to" essay may also involve providing explanations about an event or reasons for an occurrence or happening. There are a plethora of writings that stress how to do something. We would want pupils individually to be involved in determining content for developing the how to essay. Pupils do need to be ready in terms of subject matter acquired so that writing on how to do something is possible.

We have the following suggestions when pupils write the "How To" paper. The pupil needs to choose a topic that he/she understands well and can explain it to pupils. It is truly frustrating when one is asked to do something that is not conceivable. Second, the content should relate to what others do not understand and need assistance in its doing. Third, the writer should have an audience that needs to have this information conveyed. This means that content needs to be written on the understanding level of the target audience. The writer needs to determine what it is that the reader might lack in understanding. There might be something in the how-to-essays that clarifies that which makes for confusion on the part of the reader. Proper sequence needs to be in offing when writing clearly and distinctly the order of steps involved in how to do something. The ordered steps should not be isolated from each other, but rather follow a related set of ideas. Thus, the sequential steps follow a relationship, not an isolation from each other. Step one is related to step two while step two is related to step three and so on.

The following additional pointers are salient in an How To Do It paper, as well as in all written work:

1. Eliminate redundant ideas.
2. Modify vague statements that are relevant otherwise, so that the reader may follow directions carefully and implement successfully what was given in the essay.
3. Try the steps written in the 'How To' paper to see if they work.

4. Proofread very carefully that which was written.
5. Have a peer try out what is written in the easy.

Writing and Problem Solving

Developing problem solving skills is important for elementary age pupils presently as well as in the future at the work place. Seemingly, problems are with us continually. Selected problems may be solved rather quickly. Others are much more time consuming in solving. What is important is that pupils learn to identify and solve problems. The first flexible step is to identify the problem. Clarity is involved when identifying problem areas. Data is then gathered in order to offer solutions to the problem area. Information then is available for an hypothesis. The hypothesis is a tentative answer to the problem. The hypothesis is tentative and subject to testing. A real live situation needs to be used for testing the hypothesis. If evidence warrants, the hypothesis is rejected. New data or information then need to be gathered. This results in a new hypothesis which is again subject to testing in a life-like situation. If results indicate, the hypothesis may then be accepted.

There are numerous reasons pupils need to learn to write information essays. New information has come out on a topic and the learner believes others need to be informed of the new content. Perhaps, there is a need to inform individuals about the necessity of selected current events items that have just come off the news network. The major purpose here being to inform learners and others about the newness of the situation. Information then is being shared. There is so much new information coming out that it is difficult to stay abreast of what is new. We certainly do live in an information age and individuals feel so limited when they can only learn to know a small amount what is new content. If we think to internet and all the information that is therein, it baffles the individual who thinks of possible ways to learn as much as possible. Newspapers and news magazines attempt to keep individuals informed as to what is going on. But the amount of information coming there from is overwhelming. There are selected pointers that may be provided pupils when writing the information essay. These are the following:

1. Try to be as objective as possible when reporting information. The information does not represent opinions, feelings and subjective thoughts.
2. Remember that the writer is writing for human beings and not automations.
3. Write facts, not opinions, to be presented in an appealing way.
4. Delimit the topic to what can be accurately covered and in detail. Overly broad topics may be too complex to cover as compared to a more delimited approach.
5. Cover your delimited topic in a comprehensive way to discussing the five w's—who, want, where, when and why. Shallow and survey methods of reporting information may not stand up under scrutiny. Depth coverage of information will influence the reader much more so as compared to survey procedures.
6. Be as accurate as possible in reporting information. Sources of information need to be checked for reliability and accuracy.
7. Make certain that the information being reported is new and not something that is a rehash of previously presented ideas.
8. Have pupils perceive the new information being reported as related to what was known previously.
9. Sequence ideas presented effectively so that readers perceive the relationship of new knowledge to what was presented previously.
10. Use drawings, diagrams, figures and illustrations to report information, clearly and accurately.

In an information age, pupils need to be able to present content accurately and in depth. The information needs to be as factual as possible and yet it needs to be presented in an appealing manner. It is always important to secure learner attention in reading written work.

Writing to Describe

Descriptive writing is very important to a pupil. Why? Each pupil needs to learn to describe something as accurately as possible.

In conversing with others, individuals are asked to describe something such as a car, bicycle, house, and/or a place, among others. When pupils are ready, they should have sample opportunities to describe something that is purposeful in their lives. When going to the doctor's office, we are asked to describe how we feel, what the pain is like and the kinds of foods we like to eat frequently. When engaged in descriptive writing, the writer needs to be as accurate as possible when describing an object a musical performance and/or a delicious meal at a banquet, among other things.

Generally, a good conversationalist can converse well and in conversing, decisions enter in. There are selected excellent pointers that may be given in order that pupils write well in descriptive writing:

1. Have something worthwhile to describe. Worthwhileness is an important concept to stress in writing since pupils do better in writing when a purpose or reasons are involved in written work.
2. Have a peer evaluate the descriptive writing product to notice accuracy, in particular, in the written product.
3. Appraise the sequence of ideas in the descriptive writing. Good sequence or order of sentences can assist to clarify the descriptive writing product.
4. Have major ideas be supported with details, whose ideas are of lesser value but do add emphasis upon the major ideas.
5. Use adjectives wisely in your writing since these words describe nouns used as subjects and objects.
6. Develop pupil interest as much as possible when writing to describe. Due to interest factors, the reader might continue to pay attention to the entire written product.
7. Use adverbs effectively to describe. The descriptive adverbs modify verbs, adjectives and other adverbs within the framework of descriptive writing.
8. Check for meaning within the written product. Meaningful statements assist in improving any descriptive writing product.

9. Pay careful attention to the mechanics of writing such as correct punctuation, capital letters, spelling of words and indentation of paragraphs among other items.
10. Proofread and modify weaknesses in the descriptive writing paper.

Narrative Writing

Narrative writing tells a story. Pupils need to do much reading of narrative stories so that they will understand the elements that go into this type of writing. Thus, there needs to be good models of narrative writing for pupils to emulate. Much interest then might be developed in the writing of narration. Interest is powerful factor in learning. Interest in writing might well propel children to pupil forth effort in narrative writing. Pupils, too, need to perceive reasons for writing narrative content. These reasons should be stated deductively by teachers as well as inductively. There are times when prizes and awards in extrinsic motivation allow a pupil to really buckle down to write narrative forms of stories.

When readiness factors permit, the pupil with teacher guidance may begin using the elements of writing narrative accounts.

There are definite pointers for the teacher to point out to pupils when narrative writing is in the offing:

1. Have pupils understand the important ingredients of narrative writing by reading stories that clearly point out what narrative writing is.
2. Permit pupils to use a familiar story for revision and thus stress, heavily, sequence of happenings in the story.
3. Provide quality continuity when pupils are heavily involved in writing sequential happenings in narration.
4. Read aloud narrative accounts so that pupils understand sequence in narration.
5. Guide pupils to choose a character that will be fully described in the narrative account.
6. Assist learners to write a setting for the character that will interest the reader.

7. Help pupils write a theme for the story. The theme will be the underlying message in narrative writing.
8. Let pupils develop a point of view in terms of someone telling the sequential events in the writing.
9. Have pupils write a plot which tells what actually happened in the story. The plot must keep the reader reading to find out what really happened in the story.
10. Use conversation in the story whereby quotation marks indicate what a character said at a specific time.

As is true of all writing done by pupils, the teacher needs to have conferences with pupils individually and collectively so that optimal progress for each pupil is possible. A writer's workshop might assist individuals to improve in the area of writing.

Writing to Assert

Information written by the learner, at times, will need to be backed up with logic and evidence based upon research. Assertions go beyond opinions, feelings and subjective knowledge. The assertion attempts to prove selected ideas, concepts and generalizations. Quality reasons given by the writer to make these assertions include strong and consistent logic, as well as good research which is accurate and reliable.

Sometimes, a writer believes that too many people have inconsistent ideas are based on partial truths and poor research. The record then needs to be straightened out. There are selected pointers for pupils to become more proficient in developing written content which does hold water:

1. The central idea of the essay must be the assertion, not opinions, feelings, attitudes and subjective thoughts.
2. Vocabulary terms in the essay should be clear and meaningful. Peers and the teacher who proof-read may need to point out the fallacy in logic used as well as terms that are vague and fail to communicate.
3. With critical thinking, the essay may need to be analyzed into important parts which then make it possible to take out and weaknesses in the assertion.

4. Ample evidence must be given to substantiate the assertion.
5. The evidence presented at diverse places in the essay needs to be sequential and related, not in terms of isolated fragments.
6. Evidence presented needs to be written in a manner readable to the audience or target group.
7. Research information may be presented in terms of graphs, charts, illustrations, tables and figures.
8. The summary of the essay needs to present a generalization which draws conclusions, supporting the assertion.
9. The assertion made will need to be written in a serious manner, but in a way which facilitates the reading thereof.
10. Clarity in writing and direct communication is necessary.

Oral discussions whereby pupils need to defend statements made, could be a pre-requisite in writing assertion essays. These learning opportunities provide background experiences for pupils in being able to defend statements made. Assertions should be backed up with supportive information which is logical and research based.

Evaluation Within an Essay

Individuals seemingly are always evaluating ideas, objects and statements made. Their worth and accuracy is then being evaluated. Quality criteria need to be used in the evaluation process. Otherwise, the evaluative statements may have little worth. There are definite pointers that may be given to assist the writer in writing an evaluation essay:

1. There needs to be clarity on what is being evaluated.
2. Comparisons need to be made between and among comparable items. Apples and oranges should not be compared since they are different fruits and the

comparisons a writer makes depend upon the feelings and subjective ideas of the evaluator.

3. Evaluative statements should be valid in terms of the topic presented in the essay.
4. Clarity in the criteria used to judge the worth of something is a must.
5. There seems to be an opposite and equal reaction to many statements made in society. The writer must allow for other points of view, presented by listeners, that may have much merit.
6. Statistical devices should be used to support evidence in the evaluation process, such as tables, charts, graphs, figures and research data.
7. Sequential statements should be made to support the evaluation process.
8. Evidence to support an evaluation should be significant, not minor ideas not trivial content.
9. Bias and prejudice need to be avoided in the evaluative statements.
10. Defend what has been written, based on logic, reason and objective data.

Writing Business and Friendly Letters

Business and friendly letter writing and two kinds of written work which have high utilitarian values. Most people write both kinds of letters to serve personal needs.

The business letter needs to have a heading to show where it came from such as the street and its number, the city and state as to its origin and the present date. Convention indicates these items should be on upper right hand side of the business letter. The inside address should be located on the left hand side of the letter. The inside address indicates to whom the letter is written, street address, city and state with zip code number. The greeting is directly below the inside address. The body is the major part of the business letter and pertains to what is being ordered in terms of merchandise or other requests, followed by the closing and the signature. Thus, a model business letter might look like the following:

Heading

D–43, S.V.N. Colony
Guntur 522 006
Andhra Pradesh
India
August 15, 1996

Inside Address

Bowen Book Company
1849 Skyview Hall Drive
Kansas City, Missouri 69981
Greeting

Dear Sir

Body

I would like to request a price list of current books you have on education. Your prompt attention to this would be greatly appreciated since our class is studying the educational systems of different countries.

Thank You

Closing
Sincerely Yours
Signature
D.B. Rao

The friendly letter has the same format as the business letter above, except the inside address is not necessary. The reason for this is that in friendly letter needs to contain personal experiences of the writer which would be of interest to the receiver of the letter. I would suggest here that the writer of the friendly letter include such items as the following:

1. Hobbies and interests being pursued.
2. Vacations that were taken.
3. Weekend trips experienced.
4. A new addition to the family.

5. Gifts given and received during holidays, birthdays and other special events during the year.
6. An unusual event or happening.

Before a letter is sent, careful proof-reading needs to be in the offing. Politeness is involved when business and friendly letters are carefully and accurately written. Receivers of letters need to be clear as to the meaning of content written. Writing in long hand needs to be proofed in terms of clarity in handwriting. It is difficult to write legibly in long hand. Pupils should have ample experiences in using the word processor when conveying information in business and friendly letters.

Writing to Persuade

There are occasions when individuals need to persuade others in writing as well as orally. Selected educators have stated that persuasion is the most important kind of essay writing. Frequently, there are not right or wrong positions on an issue. Therefore, the individual, having strong feelings about one side of the issue, may use persuasive powers to have others, who initially disagreed, change their minds. When voting for officers at any level of government, the candidates running for office take different positions on an issue. Each candidate attempts to persuade voters to accept his/her position when voting. Liberals versus conservatives, agriculture versus business, pro-choice versus pro-life, as well as pro-labour versus pro-business provide opportunities to hear and determine how each person stands on an issue. The position taken may represent how the candidate will vote in an election.

Some pointers that may assist pupils in being able to persuade others include the following:

1. Select a position on an issue which you agree with whole-heartedly. Write a persuasive essay to support your contention. Attempt to influence others to accept you point of view.
2. Write the essay for a selected audience. The audience should tend to believe the other side of the issue.
3. Do possess clarity in terms of where you stand. Your position should be very clear in the essay.

4. Argue, using logic, to substantiate your thinking on the issue.
5. Focus on the one issue so that your argument will be stronger and more influential.
6. Provide evidence which strengthens your point of view.
7. Appeal to the feelings and emotions of the reader when presenting your argument(s).
8. Establish credibility in your writing so that readers will wish to share your position on the issue.
9. Sequentially, order your statements to support your point of view on the issue. The best supportive statement comes toward the end of the essay. The attention of the reader must be kept so that the most powerful influence comes toward the end of the essay.
10. Clarity in the writing of ideas is important with a variety of vocabulary terms used to convince others. Redundancy in writing makes for less influence over the unconverted reader. Arguments given must be direct, logical and used to obtain converts from the uncommitted.

Being able to influence others is very important in a democracy. There are may ideas and points of view on the many issues in society. Peaceful means of resolving these issues is important. Too frequently, violence is resorted to in society to influence others toward a certain position or point of view. The pro-life versus pro-choice issue is a good example. There needs to be rational means with debate and persuasion used to convince others to join a particular group having a specific point of view. Democracy in society emphasizes the freedom to express and listen to diverse sides of an issue. The atmosphere here must be such that listeners and readers might make up their own minds, after hearing the different points of view on an issue.

Finding Time to Write

If pupils are to become proficient writers, when will there be time to do much teaching of writing? I have noticed student teachers and cooperating teachers use different time schedules to permit increased time for writing. Numerous elementary school teachers indicate that there needs to be a scheduled period of time to have pupils be actively involved in writing for different purposes. Perhaps, two to three thirty minute periods and then given to teaching writing each week. Here, pupils are provided guidance and direction in writing. A definite type of writing might then be emphasized such as narrative or expository writing.

A second approach in finding time to teach writing is to relate writing with all curriculum areas in the elementary school. For example, there are many writing activities then that can be stressed in the social studies. Poetry writing might then be correlated with a thematic unit in the social studies (Ediger, 1997).

Third, before the school day begins, there could be writing instruction as well as writing projects for pupils. Pupils may write collaboratively or individually. It is good to provide choices for pupils as frequently as possible.

Fourth, pupils need to be encouraged to write in the home setting. Through parent/teacher conferences, a way may be worked out whereby the home setting becomes conductive to pupil writing. Definite goals in writing for pupils to achieve might be discussed with parents.

Fifth, writing clubs have been successful in many schools. These clubs meet after school. The Writing Club has specific goals for learners to attain in writing. Sharing of written products might be an end goal to stress. Pupils may learn from each other and challenge learners to achieve at a more optimal level in writing.

Sixth, pupils should definitely be encouraged to write when assignments and tasks have been completed. Some of the finest writing comes from pupils when they write in their spare time during the school day!

Conclusion

There are many kinds of writing activities for pupils. Pupils need to develop proficiency for a variety of types of writing.

Hopefully, pupils individually will achieve more optimally in writing. With writing experiences, pupils engage in reading also. Writing and reading cannot be separated. What is written will be read. Sometimes the re-reading is done many times since the end product needs to be proofed and become a quality written product.

We would like to end the writing and reading connection by indicating ways to motivate writers to increase proficiency in print discourse. How might pupils then be motivated to increase writing skills and products?

1. Developing a classroom that is very rich with materials which encourage writing by pupils.
2. Encouraging pupils to write content pertaining to their very own interests and purposes. The content then for writing comes from the learner.
3. Providing rich experiences from which pupils enjoy writing in their diverse manifestations.
4. Showing interest and respect for pupil's writings.
5. Building on the interests of pupils to encourage participation in many purposes in writing.
6. Building a classroom environment for writing that is free from ridicule, embarrassment and fear.
7. Giving adequate time before, during and after the school day for pupils to truly become proficient in writing.
8. Assisting pupils to use the merchants of writing well without losing out on quality ideas for written expression.
9. Helping pupils to feel confident when sharing ideas from writing.
10. Evaluating pupils progress in writing which encourages, but does not destroy interest in written work (Tiedt, 1983).

A quality program of evaluation needs to be in evidence to appraise pupil progress in the language arts and reading. This is true also in appraising pupil achievement in motivation. The teacher needs to evaluate, continuously, pupil progress in motivation. Motivation needs to be there to have pupils attain worthwhile objectives in the language arts/reading curriculum (Ediger, 1996).

REFERENCES

Ediger, Marlow (1997), *Teaching Reading and the Language Arts in the Elementary School*. Kirksville, Missouri: Simpson Publishing Company, 135-44.

Ediger, Marlow (1997), *Social Studies Curriculum in the Elementary School*, Fourth Edition. Kirksville, Missouri: Simpson Publishing Company, 168-83.

Ediger, Marlow (1996), *Elementary Education*. Kirksville, Missouri: Simpson Publishing Company, 107-17.

Ediger, Marlow and Bhaskara Rao, Digumarti (1996), *Science Curriculum*. New Delhi: Discovery Publishing House.

Ediger, Marlow (1998), "The Principal of the School", *Reading Improvement*, 35: 45-48.

Tiedt, Iris M. (1983), *The Language Arts Handbook*. Englewood Cliffs, New Jersey: Prentice-Hall, 184.

Writing Achievement in Education

There are deficiencies in English achievement, consisting of reading and writing, whereby high school students have done poorly. Ninety four per cent of Putnam, Massachusetts tenth graders failed the English section of a mandated test in an article entitled, "A Quiet Crises: Unprepared for High Stakes Testing" (Education Week, April 18, 2001). Certainly, students need to be better prepared for doing well in English in order to communicate effectively with others.

Education students also need to be able to communicate clearly in writing presently and at the future work place. They have a plethora of purposes to be good communicators in written endeavours for the following reasons:

1. Receivers of messages expect clarity to be involved in the education arena. High expectations for quality communication are then in the offing.
2. Politeness and consideration for others are involved when clarity of ideas are communicated in written endeavours.
3. Rules of grammar and sentence structure are involved in meaningful writing.
4. Proper punctuation needs to be exhibited so that clarity of content and distinct ideas are being communicated.
5. Appropriate indentation of paragraphs needs to be emphasized to indicate that a new coherent set of ideas is being expressed.

6. A sequence of ideas within a paragraph, as well as among paragraphs, assists the reader to understand what is being read.
7. Agreement of subject and predicate is a foundational concept in written communication.
8. Rules for capitalization of words are necessary ingredients in writing to enhance meaning and vocabulary in interpretation of written work.
9. Modifiers, such as adjectives and adverbs, need to be placed correctly within sentences so that the reader may interpret ideas appropriately.
10. A variety of kinds of sentences need to be incorporated into written products, not only for meaningful writing, but also to prevent boredom or sameness in sentence structure (Kausalya, 2001).

Education students need to realize high expectations and goals in writing. Hazy, vague communications make for errors and lost time when communicating content effectively to others.

Ideas Expressed in Writing

Education students need to be certain that vivid messages are communicated in writing. What the messages are to contain will depend upon the purpose in writing. These purposes, for example, include writing necessary information in

(a) all course requirements;

(b) business letters and personal correspondence;

(c) written reports, note taking in class, summaries, outlines, essays, and conclusions;

(d) projects involving print discourse developed individually and/or collaboratively;

(e) diagrams with accompanying related neat labels;

(f) journal writing, logs, and diary entries to reveal achievement in ongoing lessons and units of study;

(g) narrative, expository, and creative writing in technical education;

(*h*) written work in current events and new developments in technical education;

(*i*) rubrics to be used in appraising achievement in student written work;

(*j*) self-evaluation standards in assessing in achievement and progress in different facets of education (Ediger, 1994, 23-24).

Ideas contained in the above named purposes in writing need to contain topic sentences where applicable for each paragraph, possess order in writing the sequential paragraphs, and express content in a manner of clarity so that the reader might comprehend what is being communicated in writing. For example, complete information in personal correspondence needs to answer questions of when, which, why, what, and where—the five w's of clearly written communication. It is surprising how many writers omit one of the five w's, such as "when" a meeting is to be held. Thus, a vital item has been left out. Receivers of the written communication then need to e-mail, fax, or call by telephone to obtain this bit of vital information. There may be no e-mail number given in the written communication, and a voice recorder might respond to the telephone call. These kinds of problems could certainly be eliminated by having clarity to begin with in the written communication.

Quality communication could involve students' being actively involved in writing the class newsletter on a weekly basis, designing a web page for important notices for class members, as well as developing a bulletin board display containing salient information for technical education classmates.

Modern means of communication also require that technical education students become proficient in the use of the word processor. The word processor makes it possible to secure an excellent final document for communication purposes (Ediger, 1994, 76-77). Spell checkers have been a godsend for those who do not spell words correctly. However, writers in using word processors and spell checkers, still need to be good spellers. Why? A word needs to be spelled in a manner close enough to the correct word since "ngbil" cannot be determined correctly by spell checkers for "night". Nor will spell checkers be able to ascertain if an incorrect homonym has been used in written communication, among other deficiencies in writing. Technical education students always must be good proof readers. This is the responsibility of the sender of messages (Ediger, 1999, 183-191).

The Mechanics of Written Communication

Education students need to use necessary rules of grammar in written communication. Grammar becomes a *tool* to improve clarity in writing. Agreement of subject and predicate must be in evidence in the written communication. In the sentence, "Technical education students in class needs to attend sessions regularly," lacks agreement between the subject "students" and the predicate "needs". "Students" is plural in number and requires a plural predicate "need".

Modifiers of the subject (adjectives) and or predicates (adverbs) need to be positioned correctly. For example, the following sentence lacks clarity: The technical education student types rapidly with a red sweater; rather it should read: The technical education student with a red sweater types rapidly. The phrase "with a red sweater" is an adjective and modifies the subject "student". Clearness in writing also requires proper punctuation in written work. In a class newsletter, for example, if the following item is contained therein, how many students worked on the class project? Dale Lee Martin Lindsey Douglass and John developed a very informative bulletin board display. There could be as many as six persons or as few as three if Dale Lee Martin, Lindsey Douglass, as John are separate beings. If so, the end person listed should also contain the last name, such as John Mark. It then becomes vital for commas to be used correctly when words in a series occur in written communication (Ediger, 2000, 59-68).

Proper indentation of paragraphs are musts to indicate that a new coherent set of ideas are forthcoming. The new paragraph indicates that there is a change of emphasis from one sequential paragraphs to the next. The sequence indicates a relationship of paragraphs, but the direction of expressed content has been changed. The first word in any paragraph is always capitalized as is true of the first word in any sentence. Proper nouns always appear in capital letters, e.g., Martha (the name of a particular person), Paris (the name of a city), Belgium (the name of a nation), the Nile (the name of a particular river), January (the name of one of the twelve months of the calendar year), and Europe (the name of a continent), among others. These are a few uses when capitalizing words is salient in written communication. Technical education students should become well versed in using capital letters properly in *all* written communication (Ediger, 1978, 412-416).

Varying Sentence Variety in Writing

A variety of sentences need to be written to develop and maintain reader interest in what is being communicated in written form. Simple sentences, such as in the following five patterns may be written:

1. The man wrote a letter (subject—predicate—direct object).
2. Jay studied (subject—predicate).
3. Alicia was tall (subject—predicate—predicate adjective).
4. The man was a carpenter (subject—predicate—predicate noun).
5. Albert gave Judy the newsletter (subject—predicate—indirect object—direct object).

Each of the above named simple sentences should be expanded to be more meaningful to the reader. For example, in sentence pattern number one above, the following expansions may be added: The man wrote a highly informative letter on education. The word "highly" is an adverb and modifies an adjective "informative". "Informative" is an adjective since it describes "letter;" "on technical education" is an adjective phrase and describes what kind of "letter" it was. Expanding a sentence then can be done to any of the five sentence patterns in English with adjectives and adjective phrases describing nouns, whereas adverbs and adverb phrases describe adjectives, verbs, and other adverbs (Ediger, 1999, 33-42). With practice and purposeful writing activities, education students can master.

1. Different sentence patterns.
2. Expansion of sentences in ongoing written work.

Variety in written work should also include using compound sentences whereby to simple sentences are combined to form one sentence. Compound and complex sentences may be expanded the same way as was true of simple sentences. Complex sentences contain an independent clause and one or more dependent clauses.

As a fourth kind of sentence, compound complex sentences as the name indicates contain a compound sentence component as well as one or more dependent clauses. Technical education students then need to practice varying the kinds of sentences written by using

1. Simple sentences.
2. Compound sentences.
3. Complex sentences.
4. Compound complex sentences (Ediger, 1999, 109-115).

Time, effort, and quality sequence are necessary for the technical education student to be able to write meaningfully using a variety of kinds of sentence patterns and different kinds of sentences.

In Closing

The authors would like to emphasize also that education students should understand the different types of sentences in communicating ideas in writing. There are

1. interrogative sentences whereby questions are raised and the end punctuation mark is the question, mark;
2. declarative sentences that state facts or opinions ending with a period;
3. imperative sentences are those with the understood "you" as the subject that issue a command or a request, also ending with a period;
4. exclamatory sentences that indicate strong feelings and end with an exclamation mark.

Education students, to do well in class and at the workplace, need to achieve optimally in writing. Instructors in education and supervisors at the workplace desire quality communication from all. In education classes, students need to practice writing within a utilitarian framework.

REFERENCES

Education Week. April 18, 2001. A Quiet Crisis: Unprepared for High Stakes Testing. Marion. Ohio: Education Week, p. 12.

Ediger, M. 1994. Reading in Science. *Science Education News*, 43 (4): 23-24.

Ediger, M. 1994. Teaching Science and the Learner. *The Progress of Education*. 79 (4-5): 76-77.

Ediger, M. 1978. Issues in Curriculum Development. *College Student Journal*. 12 (4): 412-415.

Ediger, M. 1999. Spelling and the Language Arts. *Experiments in Education*, 26 (11): 183-191.

Ediger, M. 1999. Writing and the Student. *College Student Journal*. 34 (1): 59-68.

Ediger, M. 1999, Reading and the Structure of the English Language. *Reading Improvement*. 36 (3): 109-116.

Ediger, M. 1999. Technology in the School Curriculum. *Journal of Research in Educational Media*. 3 (4): 33-42.

Kausalya, J. 2001. *Cognitive Ability, School Environment, Socio-Economic Status, Teacher Effectiveness, and Performance in English Among Standard 9 Pupils*. Chennai, India: University of Madras, Chapter Two. Ph.D Thesis.

Reading Poetry in the Language Arts

An important type of leading for elementary age pupils is to read poetry. There are pupils who love to read poetry and unfortunately others either are neutral or react negatively to its reading. My hope in this writing is that all pupils will read and react more positively to diverse forms of verse and their contents. Pupils in classrooms where I have supervised student teachers and cooperating teachers are somewhat eager to express their opinions about the study and writing of poetry. Some of the recorded comments we have written down of these opinions include:

1. I do not understand what is written.
2. I would rather read stories from library books.
3. The language used is confusing.
4. I like to read poems that rhyme.
5. I would rather do something else than read.
6. I like poetry that has animal content.
7. I like to read poetry and other literature.
8. I do not like to memorize poetry.
9. I feel that the words used in poems are difficult to understand.
10. I wish more time would be given to the study and reading of poetry.

From the above comments, it is quite obvious that there are mixed feelings toward the reading of poetry. Certainly, the teacher will need to establish objectives in which each pupil learns to love the studying and reading of poetry. This can be a difficult task and yet the teacher needs to try to get pupils actively engaged in units of study pertaining to poetry in the elementary school. We would suggest that a major goal of instruction should be to assist pupils to love and appreciate poetry. Additional objectives include obtaining meaning and understanding of poems read, desiring to write different forms and types of poems, working harmoniously with others in reading and writing of poems, increasing vocabulary development through poetry writing, improving reading skills in word recognition and comprehension (Ediger, 1997), relating poems read to different curriculum areas in the elementary school, building and developing background information to use in diverse subject matter areas in the curriculum, as well as in increasing in the desire to learn, grow and achieve. To write quality poetry, the pupil needs background information. The teacher needs to have a rich learning environment in the classroom. We believe in having many learning centers in the classroom so that learners may look at what is at each center. Objects, items, audio-visual aids, realia and library books with other print materials need to be located at each of these centers. The teacher needs to introduce each center briefly as well as motivate and assist pupils to move forward with achievement in poetry writing. Pupils need to browse through books containing poetry. First, lets take a look at how the poetry curriculum may be organised.

Organising the Poetry Curriculum

Teachers need to think of how to organise the poetry curriculum so that more optimal pupil achievement is in evidence. We have observed teachers teach entire units on poetry as a separate subject. The unit involved here may be entitled "Reading and Writing Poetry". Why do selected teachers teach separate units on poetry? Depth teaching might then be involved in that the focus is upon poetry only in its many forms. Here, the teacher may have pupils concentrate on rhymed, unrhymed but with a certain number of syllables per line and no rhyme and no specific number of syllables per line. When readiness is in evidence, pupils may compare and contrast diverse forms of poetry studied and written. Ingredients in poetry writing may also be emphasized here with imagery, alliteration and onomatopoeia. In the separate subjects approach of units on poetry in the elementary school, pupils may focus in depth upon what goes into the different forms of verse to emphasize poetry in its diverse manifestations.

For example, in studying imagery, pupils may learn in depth what is involved here with metaphors and similes. Thus, pupils need to understand that metaphors do not require words including *like* and *as*. Creative comparisons may then be made: The moon, a yellow flame of gold, moves rapidly in space. Here, the moon is compared creativity with, "a yellow flame of gold". This is a metaphorical comparison.

A second form of imagery is to use similes whereby the words "like" and "as" are used to make creative comparisons: The clouds in the sky look like sheep walking on blue grass. The smile her is "like sheep walking on blue grass". Thus, a creative comparison is made between "The clouds in the sky," and "sheep walking on blue grass".

In addition to the separate subjects poetry curriculum, the teacher may also wish to correlate reading and writing poems with different curriculum areas. Here, the teacher attempts the best possible to have pupils directly relate each poem studied to social studies, science, mathematics and the language art areas. Thus, if a social studies unit on the Civil War is being taught, the teacher may assist pupils to read and study literature written during this war. Social Studies and literature are being correlated. Perceiving relationship of knowledge by pupils is a major goal of the correlated curriculum. There are fewer separate subjects to be taught in a given day. The elementary school curriculum tends to be crowded as it is and teachers do welcome certain curriculum areas to be correlated.

In correlating social studies and poetry, one pupil in the fifth grade wrote the following quatrain containing patterns of rhyme:

The Holy Land

Moslems, Christians and Jews

Each have their own unique views

Mosque, Church or Temple

Religion is taught as an example.

When pupils perceived that knowledge is related, it becomes easier to remember what had been learned. Why? One idea obtained triggers, off others that are related. In a separate subjects poetry curriculum, the pupil may perceive content in isolation and thereby not sense that facts, concepts and generalizations can be learned as a unity or as ideas related to each other. There are fewer separate subjects to teach if correlation of content is in evidence.

A third way of organising the poetry curriculum is to stress an integrated curriculum. Here, the teacher learns upon social studies, science, mathematics and literature, among other academic disciplines, to provide content for poems written by pupils. Each academic discipline tends to become blurred with the integrated curriculum. Pupils then have even greater chances of understanding how knowledge can be related. Many educators would argue that pupils here should retain subject matter in memory longer due to using it and in this case not being a separate subject.

How the teacher wishes to organise the poetry curriculum depends upon many factors. These include the number of curriculum areas taught which can be emphasized satisfactorily as related by the teacher. Sometimes the integrated curriculum is also called the interdisciplinary approach for organising instruction.

One pupil wrote the following triplet with all ending words rhyming and indicating an inter-disciplinary curriculum:

The Dome of the Rock in the Holy Land

The Dome of the Rock has an octagonal design

(mathematics)

It is used for worship by the Moslems as a sign

(social studies)

With all of its beauty viewed by yours and mine

(art).

The poetry curriculum needs to be carefully developed with quality, objectives, learning opportunities and evaluation procedures. In making these three decisions, the teacher also needs to think of organisations such as the separate subjects, the correlated and the integrated approach in teaching and learning.

Alliteration and Onomatopoeia in Poetry Writing

Pupils with teacher guidance should learn to use alliteration in poetry writing. Poets use this device frequently in writing. Alliteration tends to stress two or more sequential words that begin with the same sound. Learners find it fascinating to create verse whereby the two or more initial sounds are the same in an ordered way. A Committee of three children collaborated on writing the following containing alliteration:

The Dead Sea in the Holy Land

With salty sea water at sight

And low level elevation of land

I find to dear Dead Sea to lack life.

We feel that writing poetry with alliteration assists pupils in recognizing the role of phonics in reading. Creatively determining words that start with the same sound stresses sounds, not spelling. For example, the words *cent* and *sent* have identical sounds but these words are spelled differently with the initial consonant sound.

Another device that poets use in writing poetry is onomatopoeia. Here, words used must make the sounds that one hears in the natural environment. If one throws a rock into the water, the sound made is similar to splash! Thus, the word splash makes that sound, in degrees, when a rock is thrown into the water. A pupil I observed while supervising student teachers in the public schools wrote the following containing onomatopoeia in a science unit of study:

The Sound of Wind

Why does the wind sound like *swish, swoosh, slosh, slash* and *spash*? The unequal heating of the earth's atmosphere makes for movement of air.

The movement of molecules through the air say travel, move and go!

The underlined words in the above poem seem to indicate in degrees the sound of wind. The pupil has included onomatopoeia in the first line only of this poem.

Poems That Rhyme

One important kind poetry does rhyme. Others do not. The following are examples of rhymed verse which pupils may write when readiness is in evidence (Ediger, 1988). Couplets contain two lines with ending words rhyming, such as in the following poem:

The Forty Niners

The Forty niners went to the West

The look for gold with great zest.

One teacher mentioned to one of us while supervising student teachers that the whole word method only or largely was used when she attended public schools. Major learnings came from studying rhymed verse. In her school, the teacher would have pupils brain storm ideas on how many words would rhyme with a particular word printed on the chalkboard. These listed words were then to be used in poetry writing.

Triplets have three lines with all ending words rhyming. From a brain storming session on ideas about the zero, a committee of three wrote the following triplet:

The Zoo

I like to visit the zoo to see large lions

We have studied these animals in science

They live in a few nations with different biomes.

The quatrain was discussed above and needs a little review. Quatrains have four lines with lines one and two rhyming as well as lines three and four rhyming. Sometimes, all ending words rhyme of the four line poem. A dyad of two pupils wrote the following within a unit of study:

An Inventor

Thomas Edison invented the light bulb with much work

His efforts helped all to see better at night little quirk

The light bulb was here to stay

And make life better with more pay.

Selected pupils like to work together with others in the classroom in writing a poem. The number here needs to be kept small so all may participate such as a dyad of two members of a maximum of four pupils writing collaboratively.

Limericks are a very popular kind of poem for pupils to write. Generally, this poem starts with the words "There once was a— The limerick has five lines comprised of a couplet and a triplet. Lines 1, 2 and 5 form a triplet whereas lines 3 and 4 form a couplet.

Kindness

There once was a man in a large city

Who felt sorry for poor people in a pity

He raised much money for the poor

And felt he needed much more

That wonderful man worked on a committee.

It is excellent if pupils volunteer to write poetry; however, there are learners who do not participate with intrinsic motivation and may need to be assigned to a committee which is highly accepting and provides for all pupils to succeed.

Unrhymed Verse

Many pupils are surprised that there can be unrhymed poetry which provides for interest and purpose on the part of the learner. They find free verse to the challenging and relatively easy to write. After all, pupils should enjoy reading and writing poems. Intrinsic motivation is important in all learning as an ideal. Many pupils are motivated from within and do not need inexpensive prizes as rewards for learning. For those lacking intrinsic motivation, the teacher may need to use an award system and, hopefully, pupils will wean themselves from extrinsic motivation as time goes on. We do not count verbal praise as extrinsic motivation. Honest praise is good for pupils and should be used judiciously. We believe that quality learning takes place best with intrinsic motivation, but a few pupils will need rewards and prizes as motivators. Two pupils wrote the following haiku containing five-seven syllables for each of three lines:

The Goat

The goal is a joy (five syllables)

In the grass among the trees (seven syllables)

A lovely sight seen!

A tanka has two more lines, each having seven syllables.

The Tall Camel

I like to see far	(five syllables)
Where camels roam in deserts	(seven syllables)
And chew scarce rare feed	(five syllables)
Up, away go the camels	(seven syllables)
Where grass and water abound.	(seven syllables)

Writing Free Verse

Free verse is a very open-ended kind of poetry. There does not have to be any rhyme nor syllabication. Many pupils enjoy brain storming lines for free verse. The following free verse was composed by four pupils collaboratively:

The Shepherd

Alone with the sheep in the field

plays on the flute to maintain entertainment

watches and cares for each and every sheep

is careful with the little lambs

herds the animals to good grass

throws stones at cement fences

does not mind being alone

relishes time with the sheep

ever faithful and kind

Conclusion

Pupils need to experience reading and writing different kinds and forms of poetry. There are rich meanings and messages in poetry. The novel use of words adds to the learning repertoire of pupils. There should be poems for pupils to read that deal with diverse topics and genres. The poems should be on appropriate reading levels of individual pupils for maximum achievement to take place. The teacher needs to read poetry frequently to pupils in an enthusiastic way. Each pupil may wish to collect his/her favourite poems for enjoyment and future reference. Pupils need to become motivated through the use of different stimuli in order to read and write more poetry. For selected pupils, reading much poetry has been a way of increasing skills in learning to read more proficiently.

REFERENCES

Ediger, Marlow (1997), *The Modern Elementary School*, Kirksville, Missouri: Simpson Publishing Company, 206.

Ediger, Marlow (1988), *Language Arts Curriculum in the Elementary School*. Kirksville, Missouri: Simpson Publishing Company, 29-36.

Rao, Digumarti Bhaskara and Pushpa Latha, Digumarti (1993). *Achievements in English*. New Delhi: Discovery Publishing House.

Poetry in the School

Pupils should develop a thorough appreciation for poetry. Many words are generally used in novel and unique ways in poetry. Thus, a study of poetry should aid pupils in vocabulary development. Of utmost importance is that pupils read creative ideas and thoughts when studying poetry. Pupils can then be aided in developing their own creative ideas when writing poetry.

Poetry comes in many forms. Generally, pupils have felt that rhyming words are inherent in all poetry. However, this is not always the case. Poetry may be either rhymed or unrhymed.

Trauger writes the following pertaining to objectives in the poetry curriculum:

> Maintaining children's native responsiveness and maturing their poetic understanding to keep in abreast of their chronological age are worthy long-range objectives in teaching poetry. Between the two, the balance in delicate; there is danger of strangling the former through fumbling efforts at the latter.
>
> The preservation of responsiveness is a delicate undertaking influenced by diverse factors, some deriving from the complexity of poetic art, some due to marginal circumstances which superficially might seem only slightly related to liking or disliking poetry. More than any other form of literature, poetry is sensitive to influences which prevail around the edges of a classroom lesson. The teacher believes that she is teaching one thing. She actually may be teaching it, but at the same time, because of manner, attitudes, and the classroom climate, she, unawares, teaches

something else. That something else may either enhance or eclipse what she thought she was teaching.

The project of maturing a child's understanding of poetry hinges on discovering more and more in the snug package of a poem. This becomes a great consequence in junior and senior high school years. The understanding of poetry needs to grow apace with the pupil's progress in other subjects. His understanding should be as grown up in relation to poetry as to science or social studies. If comprehension is in the young adolescent stage in those latter studies but still infantile in approaching verse, the pupil can be expected to dismiss poetry as childish or irrelevant. If maturation keeps pace with chronological age, the young person can interpret poems appropriate to his grade and in them find delight and wisdom.

Poetry in the School Curriculum

Poetry may be correlated with different curriculum areas in the school. The teacher may have pupils study and write poetry as it relates to units of study in science, social studies, mathematics, health, as well as in other language arts areas. Poetry might also be taught as a separate unit of study. An ultimate goal for pupils to achieve is to enjoy reading and writing poetry. Poetry should not be analyzed when it destroys pupil interest in learning.

Poetry Correlated with Other Curriculum Areas

It is proper teaching procedure if pupils perceive that subject matter from diverse academic disciplines is related. For example, if pupils on the first grade level are studying a unit on the city, they might dictate content to the teacher who in return writes the resulting poem. Pupils must understand the kind of poem being emphasized in teaching-learning situations. The teacher needs to set the stage so that pupils have an inward desire in wanting to write a particular kind of poem. Using discussions, pictures, filmstrips, and/or slides should provide background information for pupils in desiring to write poetry. If first grade pupils have an adequate writing vocabulary, they may write their own poem. An interesting kind of poem for pupils to write is a couplet. Couplets contain two lines of verse. The two lines are somewhat uniform in length with ending words rhyming. The following are examples of couplets.

1. The city is filled with people
   And the church has a tall steeple.
2. The sidewalk is broad and wide.
   The boy rides a bicycle on the side.
3. The children play in the house
   Where there is no mouse.

If pupils are studying an elementary school science unit on magnetism and electricity, the following couplet may be developed by pupils individually or in committees:

We made some magnets in the room
Then we cleaned the room with a broom.

Pupils individually or cooperatively may also write triplets. Thus, three lines are to be written with ending words rhyming. The three lines should be somewhat uniform in length. Again, the stage must be set for pupils so than an inward desire exists to write poetry. A stimulating environment must be present to aid pupils in developing background information for the writing of poetry. The following is an example of a triplet as it relates to and integrates with a specific social studies unit entitled "Westward Movement".

The forty niners went to the West
To look for gold with great zest
Hoping to gain much wealth at best.

Pupils may wish to write free verse with teacher guidance. No rhyming of words is required in the writing of free verse. In the writing of free verse, there are no standards pertaining to the length of each line and for the entire poem. A writing center in the class setting could contain selected pictures pertaining to an ongoing unit of study. The pictures, of course, need not necessarily relate to an ongoing teaching or resource unit. Learners may choose and write about a picture. The written content could pertain to free verse. The following is free verse as it relates to a picture on frame animals:

The cow
can be a beautiful animal
provides us with milk and cream
eats grain and hay eagerly
may also provide a good supply of meat
is interested in the pipeline milker
misses her calf much
does not get along well with pigs
is eagerly waiting for the long winter to
end and have summer arrive
likes the roam in the shed with other cows
does not like the big dog in the yard
would rather be in a warm shed as compared to
the cold outdoors.

Each pupil needs to determine the length of his or her free verse. Pupils should be creative in thinking of unique ideas in writing any type of poem.

There are definite advantages in having pupils write free verse. Learners are not restricted in using rhyming words. Uniformity in length of lines also is not a restriction. The writing of free verse can be related to many unit titles in diverse curriculum areas. If pupils are studying a science unit on prehistoric life, the following free verse could be written by a child individually or in a small group:

The Tyrannosaurus Rex dinosaur
ate many other kinds of dinosaurs
had serrated teeth
was the king of dinosaurs
was ferocious
was taller than other dinosaurs

lived during the Mesozoic era

might have been cold-blooded like fish and turtles are today.

Limericks are an enjoyable type of poetry for pupils to read and write. Limericks consist of a couplet and a triplet. The first, second, and fifth lines in a limerick make a triplet. The third and fourth lines comprise a couplet. Generally, it is important for pupils to understand and attach meaning to a couplet and triplet before limericks and introduced. From an anthology of children's literature, the teacher may read limericks to children. These limericks must e chosen carefully to capture interests of listeners. Enjoyment of poetry is of utmost importance! The selected limericks must be on the understanding level of children. Learners with teacher guidance could select which limericks they like best. These may be written on the chalkboard or on a transparency. Pupils inductively need to arrive at meaningful generalizations pertaining to what ingredients are necessary in the writing of limericks. Thus, learners may write their own limericks once the inherent pattern is understood. The following limerick pertains to a unit on magnetism and electricity:

There once was a man called Thomas Edison

Who invented a bulb which gave a bright light in the long run

He liked to invent things

From which American and the world benefits and sings

And made life easier, more enjoyable, and much more fun.

Haiku poetry can also be enjoyable for pupils to write. Rhyming words are not necessary in haiku poetry. Pupils, however, do need to be able to divide words into syllables when writing haiku poetry. The first line of a haiku poem has five syllables. The second line has seven syllables, followed by five syllables in the third line. Haiku poetry may discuss nature. The following haiku poem might be written by observing rain falling in the out of doors:

The rain pattering

on the window with great speed

swish, slosh, swoosh, slash, spash.

Pupils need to be praised and encouraged to present novel ideas in writing poetry. Pupils should be encouraged to invent new words. The last line of the previously written haiku poem has unique words which give sounds made by drops of rain. Onomatopoeia is a term given to words which make sounds similar to those in the natural environment. Alliteration is also prevalent in the last line of the haiku poem in that the beginning sound of each word is the same. Numerous poets use alliteration as a poetic device in the writing of poetry.

Imagery in Poetry

It is important for pupils to understand imagery in the writing of poetry. Thus pupils may understand meaningful concepts and generalizations pertaining to metaphors and similes. This can be achieved utilizing approaches such as the following:

1. Reading poetry containing metaphors and similes to pupils.
2. Discussing with pupils meanings of metaphors and similes.
3. Developing poems with learners that contain metaphors and similes.
4. Having pupils find and read poems that contain metaphors and similes.
5. Having pupils individually or in committees write poetry which contains metaphors and similes.

Wolfe writes the following pertaining to pupils developing sequential learnings in imagery:

> Children can make comparisons, too; once set in motion in an expectant classroom their originality astonishes both them and us. Perhaps they have already described boys and girls in the class. One girl, like Jane, has golden hair; a boy, like Will, has blue eyes; still another pupil has brown eyes or black hair.

We may put some comparisons on the board for completion, naming pupils our class has described:

1. Joe's eyes are as blue as—
2. Fred's eyes are as brown as—
3. Fran's dress is as green as—

From these we may go on to other comparisons to be completed:

4. The house was as dark as—
5. His face was as red as—
6. The wind made a noise like—
7. Jimmy stood as still as—

In a later lesson we may begin with several comparisons like this:

As soft as a kitten's paw

As soft as a feather

As soft as a pillow

Pupils with teacher guidance might then write lines of verse containing imagery such as in the following examples:

1. The rain sounded like fairies dancing on the window sill.
2. The train roared like a giant in the sky.
3. The wind blew like a sneezing ogre.

In each of these lines of poetry, similes are used. Something is compared to something else joined by the word "like". In sentence number one, for example, the sound of "rain" is compared to the sound of "fairies dancing on the window sill". In sentence number two "The train roared" is compared to "a giant in the sky," while in sentence three "The wind blew" is being contrasted with "a sneezing ogre". The word "as" is also used in imagery. He came as a thief in the night.

In the case of metaphors, the words "like" and "as" are not used in making creative comparisons. Notice the use of metaphors in the following lines of verse:

1. The cat, a swirling mass of colors, runs in the yard.
2. The dog, clawing feverishly in the garden, finally found a bone.
3. The clouds were fluffy pillows racing across the sky.
4. The house appeared to float on fairies' wings in the sky.

Otherwise, similes and metaphors have similar functions in making creative comparisons.

Creative Writing in the Pupil

Creative thinking is an important skill and attitude for all learners to develop in greater depth as they progress through the school years. In everyaay living, it is important to think creatively so that one's own problems may be solved. Too frequently, solutions that have worked for others in the solving of problems may not work for us. Unique solutions in many cases are then needed to solve problems. Progress in American society and the world has come about due to individuals having been creative. Thus, progress in medicine, manufacturing, dentistry, education, agriculture, and other facets of life, has come about through creative efforts of individuals and groups. It is of utmost importance for students to engage in creative thinking.

Donoghue described creative behaviour in the following paragraph:

> A creative person is one who relies on the aspects of memory and cognition (which are most often measured by IQ tests) and so may sometimes be labelled as less intelligent and hence, in educational settings, an "over-achiever". He approaches learning situations in unstandardized ways and appears offbeat or inferior at times in his thinking. He is not highly success-oriented. What he is, however, is curious, original, self-directing, sensitive, secure, flexible, persistent, humorous, and productive. He needs to meet challenge and to attempt difficult ... tasks just as he needs to give himself completely to a task and to become fully absorbed in it.

The teacher must provide a psychological environment whereby students feel free to explore and experiment. Learners need to feel relaxed in the class setting to think of ideas which are different and unique. Thus, a student can present a contribution which is novel based on previously acquired learnings. It is difficult to come up with ideas which are unique for all learners in a class. However, it is possible for a pupil to come up with original content on an individual basis.

Pupils with teacher guidance need to plan a rich learning environment. Students must have experiences which stimulate creative thinking. Stimulating bulletin boards, learning centers, reading materials, and audio-visual aids aid in setting the stage for creative endeavours. Students will then acquire subject matter which might be utilized to write a creative story, poem, essay, letter or other form of written work. The teacher must think of learning activities which will stimulate creative thinking.

Too frequently, the teacher has assessed student progress in writing based on spelling words correctly, demonstrated neat handwriting, using punctuation marks properly, and using capital letters correctly. Very little emphasis may have been placed upon ideas that students have expressed. To be sure, students need to make continuous progress in correct spelling of words, legible handwriting, correct punctuation, and proper capitalization of letters. Students may reveal their achievement in the mechanics of writing when they proofread their final written product. At the time ideas are written on paper, students may not be able to concentrate on the mechanics of writing. Donoghue writes:

> Factors identified as the most inhibitive to creative expression include: (1) tests based on detailed memorization; (2) discouragement of fantasy and imagination; (3) stereotyped sex roles; and (4) social expectation, including peer censure.

The teacher must give careful consideration to praising students for being creative. Most students like praise for work that reveals improved performance. If creative products are praised by the teacher, students generally will feel that creativity is what is wanted and desired. If the teacher, criticizes students' creative behaviour, learners might feel that this is not an approved way of approaching learning activities. A smile of approval, saying "that's tremendous," or "that's terrific," among other means, can certainly stimulate students in desiring to express content creatively.

There needs to be time set aside whereby students can share completed work. Students individually may perceive how content differs between and among finished products. When sharing thoughts, students learn from each other pertaining to ways of expressing unique ideas as well as creativity contained in ideas in and of themselves. They may learn about new vocabulary terms which can be used in writing as well as creative ways in which these terms can be used. Students may also learn about inventing words to use in writing.

The teacher certainly needs to be well acquainted with characteristics of students revealing creative behaviour. There are teachers who have confused creative behaviour of students with misbehaviour. That is most unfortunate! Teachers then should become well versed in approaches to *(a)* setting the stage for learners to exhibit creative behaviour, *(b)* rewarding creative behaviour of students, and *(c)* being highly knowledgeable about characteristics of individuals who are creative. Green and Petty write the following.

> Poetry is (or should be) a vital part of the literature program, yet too often it is neglected or poorly taught in today's schools. Some teachers simply do not know how to present poetry to children; others feel it has little place in the modern science-oriented world; a few, unfortunately, spoil children's appreciation by poor reading or prolonged analysis of form and style. Yet children love rhythm, rhyme, and the sounds of words.

In Summary

The teacher must set the stage to have pupils develop feelings of desiring to express ideas creatively. A variety of rich learning experiences can aid pupils in creative thinking and creative writing. These experiences must be challenging and interesting. Pupils can then be encouraged to participate in a wide variety of creative activities.

Learners should have ample opportunities to engage in the writing of poetry. Learners may then write couplets, triplets, free verse, limericks, and haiku poetry. Pupils' ideas in creative writing need to be accepted and respected by the teacher as well as by learners.

Greene and Petty write the following teaching methodologies in the writing of poetry:

> Although the presentation of poetry should be almost exclusively oral, visual aids cannot be omitted altogether. The teacher should be constantly on the watch for pictures which will make suitable illustrations of poems; these may be used when a poem is

presented orally, or occasionally a bulletin board may be centered around a few lines or a short poem, either new or already known to the children. Once in a while, a bulletin board display may honor a poet whose work the children have particularly liked, but these should be few in number; attention should be centered primarily on the poems themselves.

No teacher should feel any compulsion to teach particular poems because they are in the suggested course of study, because they are in the anthology available to the class, or because they are reputed to be classics. There are enough "good" poems to suit anyone's taste. An invaluable asset is a file of titles, with notations as to where the poems may be found. These may be arranged by subject (or in whatever manner the teacher finds convenient) and they should include a generous assortment of poems suitable for holidays, the seasons of the year, and any other subjects which seem appropriate to the grade level and backgrounds of the children.

REFERENCES

1. Arbuthnot, May Hill (Ed.). *Time for Poetry*. Chicago: Scott, Foresman and Company, 1959.
2. Arnstein, Flora J. *Poetry in the Elementary Classroom* New York: Appleton-Century-Crofts, 1962.
3. Burns, Paul C. *Diagnostic Teaching of the Language Arts*. Itasca, Illinois: F.E. Peacock Publishers, Inc., 1974. Chapter Five.
4. Chambers, Dewey W. *Children's Literature in the Curriculum*. Chicago: Rand McNally and Company, 1971.
5. Donoghue, Mildred R. *The Child and the English Language Arts* Dubuque, Iowa: Wm, C. Brown Publishers, 1971. Chapter Two.
6. Donoghue, Mildred R. *The Child and the English Language Arts*. Second Edition. Dubuque, Iowa: Wm. C. Brown Publishers, 1975.
7. Greene, Harry A. and Walter T. Petty. *Developing Language Skills in the Elementary Schools*. Fifth Edition. Boston: Allyn and Boston, Inc., 1975.
8. Kim, Eugene, and Richard D., Kellough. *A Resource Guide for Secondary School Teaching*. New York: Macmillan Publishing Company, 1987.
9. Lamb, Pose (Ed.). *Guiding Children's Language Learning*. Dubuque, Iowa: Wm. C. Brown Publishers, 1971. Chapter Six.

10. Mangieri, John, et al. *Teaching Language Arts*. New York: McGraw Hill Book Company, 1984.

11. Petty Walter T. (Ed.). *Issues and Problems in the Elementary Language Arts*. Boston: Allyn and Bacon, Inc., 1968. Chapters Tan and Eleven.

12. Shane, Harold, et al. *Improving Language Arts Instruction in the Elementary School*. Columbus: Charles E. Marrill Books Inc., 1962. Chapter Thirteen.

13. Trauger, Wilmer K. *Language Arts in Elementary Schools*. New York: MaGraw Hill Book Company, 1963.

14. Wolfe, Don M. *Language Arts and Life's Patterns*. Second Edition. New York: The Odyssey Press, 1972.

Grouping Pupils for Instruction

There are numerous means of grouping pupils for instruction. Each approach needs to be appraised in terms of providing for pupils individually to realize optimal achievement. Teachers, principals, and supervisors need to study, appraise, and implement that which assists each pupil to achieve optimally.

> Groups have common properties. All groups have a *background* or lack of background which influences their behaviour. If children have worked together before, that joint work becomes part of their background. If not, this lack of prior contact will influence their interaction. People, including children, always approach group involvement with some kind of expectation. They may look forward to the experience, believing other people will contribute greatly to their investigation, or they may be unsure of how the group will work because they have little or no data on the members of the group.
>
> In addition to background, all groups develop a *participation pattern* that exists over time and can be described at any particular moment. In a group of three children, for example, a pattern might emerge in which one child dominates the discussion with the other children listening attentively; in another group of three, there may be an equal exchange of views by each child.
>
> All groups have the property of *communication*, which refers to how well members understand each other and how well they express their feelings, attitudes, and information. Children with very different cultural and/or experiential backgrounds may have difficulty making themselves understood by others in the group.

All groups exhibit *cohesion*, the bonds uniting the individual parts. Team spirit and group morale are outward signs of group cohesion.

Groups have the tendency to create *standards*, or rules of conduct necessary for remaining in the group. In social classes, the teacher may establish the standards and responsibilities for the group members. For example, he may appoint a group leader to keep notes that can be shared with the rest of the class. It is essential that everyone who participates in a group understand its standards, the expectations others have for each person's performance.

People in groups of three or more are often assigned particular roles that define the relationships among members. In these cases, the group has a particular *structure and organisation*. Sometimes the teacher assures a formal structure by assigning roles, and at other times allow the structure to remain informal, with roles and tasks shifting during different lessons. Sometimes the children's backgrounds and varying abilities determine group structure.

The Self-Contained Classroom

In the self-contained classroom, one teacher generally teaches all curriculum areas (except perhaps, music, art, and physical education) to a single set of learners. Thus, the teacher selects objectives, learning activities, and evaluation procedures in the curriculum areas of language arts, social studies, science, mathematics, and health.

Critics of the self-contained classroom concept believe that subject matter becomes too complex to have one teacher teach the majority of curriculum areas to a single set of pupils. This might be true on the intermediate grade levels, in particular. It follows that no teacher may have the competency or skill to teach so many diverse curriculum areas. Teachers then cannot acquire the needed skills to specialize in teaching a specific area of the curriculum in the self-contained classroom.

Advocates of the self-contained classroom believe that a teacher can do a good job of emphasizing correlated, fused, and integrated means of curriculum organisation. These opportunities exist due to the self-contained teacher teaching most of the diverse curriculum areas to a single set of pupils. If the self-contained teacher wishes to, the separate subjects curriculum may also be emphasized. The self-contained classroom may emphasize a flexible means of scheduling for different curriculum areas. The teacher can divide the school day in terms of time needed specifically for each subject matter area. The self-contained teacher may also divide the school day into an even amount of time devoted to each curriculum area, as is true of departmentalized teaching. Flexibility certainly is possible when thinking of time given to each curriculum area in the self-contained classroom.

The teacher in a self-contained classroom has ample opportunities to get to know each pupil well. This knowledge should be utilized to increasingly do a better job of teaching, and thus more adequately provide for each individual learner.

There are selected facets of the self-contained classroom which need criteria to guide their effective implementation. The teacher needs to evaluate if he/she is keeping abreast of recommended procedures in teaching the language arts, social studies, mathematics, science and health units. Pupils need to achieve optimally in each of these curriculum areas.

Departmentalization and the Teacher

There are elementary schools which departmentalize diverse curriculum areas starting with the first grade level. Generally, departmentalization is emphasized more so on the intermediate grade levels. In departmentalization, the teacher may specialize in the teaching of a specific curriculum area. Thus, the teacher can become highly proficient in teaching language arts, science, mathematics, or social studies. Junior and senior high school teachers over the many years, in general, have taught in departmentalized schools.

Criticisms that have been hurled departmentalization include the following:

1. Pupils may perceive diverse curriculum areas as being fragmented and isolated rather than related to each other.
2. Teachers may emphasize the teaching of subject matter to the minimizing of attempting to get to know each pupil well.

3. Teachers may not plan with other instructors to correlate, fuse, or integrate subject matter.
4. Diverse periods in the school day may compartmentalize to an excessive degree that which is taught.

There are selected guidelines which need to be followed when implementing a quality departmentalized plan of instruction:

1. Each teacher needs to study and implement recommended trends in his/her area of speciality in teaching pupils.
2. Each teacher needs to plan with other instructors when it is feasible and good to correlate, fuse, and integrate diverse curriculum areas.
3. Each teacher must attempt to get to know pupils well in order to assist each learner to achieve optimally.
4. Depth teaching of content in a specific curriculum area is recommended; however, learners should also develop generalizations pertaining to relating diverse curriculum areas.

Team Teaching and the Teacher

More minds are better than one mind in selecting objectives, learning activities, and appraisal techniques for a given set of pupils, according to the thinking of advocates of team teaching. A team must have at least two teachers as members. The emphasis here must be upon teachers in a team planning together the objectives, learning activities, and evaluation procedures for teaching-learning situations. Teachers on a team might possess quite different philosophies of education. However, cooperation is a key concept to emphasize in teaming. Thus, one member must not dictate ends, means, and appraisal procedures to other members. If this is done, team endeavours are not in evidence. The ideas of each team member must be respected in planning and implementation sessions. There, perhaps, is no quicker way to defeat teaming approaches than if respect for others is not in evidence. It may be necessary to place emphasis upon basic general agreements on philosophy of teaching approaches, as well as in acceptance of involved personalities when implementing team teaching approaches. A certain amount of harmony is needed between/among team members if success in learning for pupils is to be a relevant end result.

Team members can learn from each other in planning sessions pertaining to teaching-learning strategies. Inservice education may then become an inherent part of team teaching. Each idea presented needs to be analyzed in order to ultimately provide the best in experience for pupils.

There may be a teaching team in which all members specialize in teaching a specific curriculum area, such as the language arts. An interdisciplinary team may also be involved in teaching a given set of pupils. Thus, a language arts teacher, a science teacher, and a social studies teacher may be members of one team.

Large group instruction, committee work, and individual study provide component parts in team teaching situations. Committee endeavours and individual projects and activities in clarifying that which was presented in large group sequential sessions.

Critics of team teaching state the following:

1. There are selected teachers who do a better job of teaching on an individual rather than a team basis.
2. Large group instruction methods do not provide adequately for individual differences.
3. It may be difficult for team members to agree upon a given set of objectives, learning activities, and appraisal procedures.
4. Pupils may not adjust well to several teachers as compared to an individual teacher in a self-contained room.

There, of course, are selected advantage given for advocating team approaches in teaching:

1. Members of a teaching team can learn from each other in sessions devoted to planning for teaching.

2. More than one teacher is involved in determining ends, means, and appraisal procedures in the curriculum. An improved curriculum might then result.
3. More than a single teacher is involved in planning learning activities, resulting in a variety of experiences for learners.
4. An integrated curriculum might truly be in the offering when team members represent diverse academic disciplines.

Interage Grouping

There are selected educators who emphasize pupils from several age levels working in large groups and committee endeavours. In society, younger individuals interact with older beings. The school curriculum needs to emphasize that which harmonizes with societal trends.

The Joplin (Missouri) Plan of reading instruction emphasized interage grouping. Fourth, fifth, and sixth grade pupils were regrouped to form homogeneous units.

Thus, a top group of achievers in reading might consist of selected fourth, fifth, and sixth graders being taught in a specific classroom. Pupils chosen for any level of achievement in reading needed to be as homogeneous as possible within a classroom.

One might also perceive a set of first and second grade pupils working together at diverse learning centers. Each pupil then ideally selects sequential tasks to pursue. A learner may then select easier or more complex tasks to pursue depending upon interacts, purposes, and abilities possessed. Individual as well as committee endeavours may be selected as tasks at diverse learning centers. Thus, interage grouping may well be in evidence when learning centers are utilized.

Disadvantages given for utilizing interage grouping include the following:

1. State laws are in evidence as to when pupils enter the first grade level. Once this custom has started, it becomes increasingly complex to change to other forms of grouping pupils for instruction.

2. Older pupils may have learned to frown upon working with younger children. Attitudes developed by pupils may be difficult to change.

Advantages which might be listed for interage grouping include the following:

1. It seemingly is more lifelike for individuals to interact with others of diverse age levels. Societal settings tend to encourage interage interactions.
2. Grade levels may mean very little when explaining achievement of individual pupils. Thus, a third grader, for example, may be a more proficient reader as compared to a sixth grade pupil.

The Nongraded School

The nongraded school philosophy does away with grade level designations. Thus, for example, it is inappropriate to speak about a pupil being in grade one, two, or three. Rather, toward the end of the kindergarten level of instruction, each pupil is evaluated in terms of present reading achievement levels. Teachers with principal leadership attempt to place each pupil for the next school year in terms of being in the top group, middle group, or the slowest group of achievers in reading. If a school has five roomfuls of six year olds, it is easier to group pupils homogeneously in reading achievement as compared to having two roomfuls of these learners only. The latter situation might make it very difficult to have two roomfuls of fairly homogeneous or uniform achievers in reading. With three, four, or five roomfuls of six year olds, educators in charge of grouping procedures can develop rather uniform levels of reading achievement within each classroom. Even within a classroom, further efforts can be made to emphasize homogeneous grouping by dividing learners into three reading groups, with each ultimate group being as uniform as possible in achievement.

Each group of somewhat uniform achievers with teacher guidance attempts to continually realize optimal development. Thus, a top group of readers will increasingly continue to achieve new attainable goals. Slow learners with teacher assistance will not achieve as rapidly, by any means, in reading as compared to rapid achievers. However, slower achievers in reading will also be guided to achieve as much as possible utilizing the best methods of teaching possible. Each teacher of reading needs to keep accurate records as to continuous sequential levels of achievement of each pupil. This is necessary so that a learner achieves continually and is successful in learning. The sky is the limit in terms of each pupil's attaining and accomplishing. Pupils, of course, must not be pressured to attain the unachievable.

What happens is twelve year old pupils who have completed six years of schooling beyond the kindergarten level and are reading on the ninth or tenth grade level? Most of these learners will be entering the junior high years or middle school depending upon the philosophy of the involved school, where teachers may emphasize pupils working up to grade level standards. Thus, a talented pupil may actually be reading on the ninth or tenth grade levels, but the teacher might be teaching seventh grade level in the first year of junior high school. There certainly is a problem of sequence here. Ideally, the junior high school English teacher should notice which level the entering student is reading on and provide for continual, sequential growth.

What happens to the learner who completes six years of schooling beyond the kindergarten level in a nongraded school and reads on the fourth grade level of accomplishment? Grade level designations may be somewhat arbitrary in this discussion; however, the reader needs to have certain criteria to utilize when evaluating educational ideas.

The pupil reading on the fourth grade level of accomplishment enters the seventh grade, the first year of junior high school, and may be required to read on grade seven level. There certainly is a gap in terms of where the learner is presently in achievement (fourth grade) as compared to the desired level of seventh grade, as emphasized by the involved English teacher. A traditional English teacher might have all seventh grade pupils read seventh grade literature assignments and requirements. Again, it is desirable if the seventh grade junior high school literature teacher accepts the learner where he/she is presently in reading achievement and provides for continuous optimal progress. There are high interest/low vocabulary materials which may be utilized in teaching reading to individual pupils who are reading on an achievement level lower than what is deemed desirable for average achievers.

Ragan and Shepherd list the following common features of most nongraded schools:

1. Continuous progress, vertical and horizontal movement, of pupils is provided for throughout the school year.
2. Curriculum articulation is provided by means of the identification of skills, knowledges, and appreciations to be developed within a content area or areas over a wide span of years without a specific length of time being assigned to any portion of this span.
3. The pupil is positioned in the sequence based on his ability in and achievement of these skills, knowledges, and appreciations without regard for the number of years in school.
4. Extensive reporting and record-keeping systems are developed between teachers and between teachers and parents.
5. A successful experience is provided for each pupil at his position with no failure or retention.

The Dual Progress Plan

Too frequently, pupils experience a self-contained classroom throughout the elementary school years, followed by an abrupt transition to a completely departmentalized, junior high school. Advocates of the dual progress plan of groping believe that learners on the primary grade levels need to experience a self-contained setting. On the intermediate grade levels, pupils may then experience a dual situation, a self-contained classroom for language arts and social studies. Science and mathematics are taught in a departmentalized situation.

A teacher teaching both language arts and social studies may correlate the subject matter of these two curriculum areas. Also, the teacher may become very familiar with traits of learners when teaching language arts and social studies for a longer period of time to a given set of pupils as compared to a departmentalized situation. Flexible scheduling may also be utilized. More or less time may then be given to language arts or to social studies as the need arises.

Since science and mathematics are taught in a depatmentalized setting, a teacher may specialize in teaching a specific curriculum area. Thus, a teacher having adequate background of class work in mathematics and an elementary education major may teach mathematics only, in the elementary school. The individual teacher may then specialize in teaching a specific curriculum area. Or, a teacher with a double major, science and elementary education, may then utilize his/her strengths in teaching science only, to elementary school pupils.

Too frequently, in the elementary school, a teacher cannot specialize in teaching a specific curriculum area. The dual progress plan provides opportunities for departmentalized teaching. The dual progress plan of instruction also offers opportunities to teach in a modified form of the self-contained classroom. A teacher may then teach language arts and social studies to a given set of learners.

Heterogeneous Versus Homogeneous Grouping

A long debate has been in evidence for some time pertaining to which plan of grouping pupils for instruction is better— heterogeneous or homogeneous grouping. In heterogeneous grouping of learners for instructional purposes, mixed capacity and achievement levels are present in a single classroom. Slow, average, and fast learners within a classroom might then experience learning activities cooperatively. Within each classroom, heterogeneously grouped pupils may also be separated into specific achievement level groupings for instruction in reading and other curriculum areas, as this is desirable. However, ample opportunities exist in a heterogeneously grouped classroom for learners of diverse achievement levels to interact and learn from each other in an atmosphere of respect.

Advantages given for emphasizing heterogeneous grouping of learners for instruction include the following:

1. Democracy is in evidence when pupils who possess diverse differences are not segregated from each other,

but have ample chances to learn from each other, as well as develop positive attitudes to others.

2. Society emphasizes that individuals interact with each other regardless of capacity and achievement levels. Thus, the school setting must implement strategies in which individuals learn to live together harmoniously with others regardless of capacity traits possessed.

Homogeneous grouping emphasizes that pupils similar in achievement be taught together in a single class setting. An entire classroom of pupils may be talented and gifted. Or, an entire classroom of learners may be homogeneous as to being slow learners in reading. Too frequently, it is felt that gifted/talented learners are held back in achievement by those not learning content as rapidly. Toward the other end of the centinuum, slow learners may feel frustrated when comparing themselves with high achievers in a heterogeneously grouped classroom. A homogeneous by grouped class is somewhat uniform in terms of pupil progress. Thus, in homogeneous grouping a slow learner may not compare himself/herself with others who progress at a more rapid rate in a specific class setting. Or, a fast learner does not need to be held back in accomplishing due to a teacher gearing instruction toward average achievers or slow learners.

Numerous teachers prefer to teach in homogeneously grouped classrooms. The range of pupil achievement is less in a homogeneously grouped class as compared to a heterogeneously grouped set of learners. It might be easier then to provide for optimal achievement on the part of pupils in a homogeneously grouped teaching-learning situation.

Knezevich wrote:

> After admission and enrollment, pupils must be classified for instructional purposes. Perhaps the most significant change in the classification of pupils came with the grading of the elementary schools in Boston in 1847. Such grading today represents merely a rough attempt at grouping pupils for the purposes of instruction. Further classification is necessary when there are more than enough pupils to fill one grade room or one high school class section, and considerable attention has been devoted to developing

methods of grouping that will facilitate the learning or the teaching process.

Heterogeneous grouping can be defined as class sectioning on the basis of chance factors or arbitrary standards unrelated to learning ability or past performance. Homogeneous grouping implies placement of pupils into class sections on the basis of some measure of ability. Because it is impossible to organise a section or grade in which all students have the same kind and quantity of ability or social background, "homogeneous" implies *approximately* the same kind and quality of ability as measured by some instrument. Stated another way, the range of some type of student ability is less in a homogeneous than in a heterogeneous section.

With increased mainstreaming of selected special education pupils into the regular classroom, less emphasis might be in evidence presently for advocating homogeneous grouping of pupils. Mainstreaming emphasizes placing special education pupils in the least restricted environment. No longer may all special education pupils be segregated from other pupils in the regular classroom. Thus, a blind or partially sighted pupil may receive instruction in the regular classroom setting. Individual Education Programs (IEP's) need to be written for each mainstreamed student. Parents ideally need to approve the IEP's for their child before their implementation. The IEP's consist of sequential measurably stated objectives for each pupil to achieve. Observable evidence is necessary to determine if the specific ends have been attained. There are pros and cons in administering mainstreamed programs of instruction. Advantages given include the following:

1. Special education pupils are not as separated from other learners as was true previously.
2. A democratic society does not emphasize hierarchical arrangements of individuals.

Disadvantages which might be listed for mainstreaming of pupils may include the following:

1. Teachers in a regular classroom are not educated/ trained to teach special education pupils.
2. Much paper work is involved in writing IEP's and providing evidence of learner achievement.

3. It is difficult for the teacher to provide for individual differences when the range of pupil achievement in a classroom is great.

Salzer and Drdek wrote the following:

> The placement of handicapped children in normal classes may be viewed as helpful to all concerned—the pupils with difficulties have the opportunity to learn how to function in a realistic situation, and the other children are helped to realize that classmates with special problems are more like them than they are different. For some of the same reasons it may be argued that the extremely bright and able pupil is also better off in a class of normal children, especially if the classroom program is flexibly organised so that individualized work is possible.
>
> When children who are seriously handicapped in areas of vision, hearing, speech, mental ability or mobility, are placed in regular classrooms, the demands made on the teacher undoubtedly increase. But with the help of resource people who know how to meet the difficulties that arise, the situation can be handled in ways which benefit all the pupils. Another desirable outcome is that the teacher, in working to meet the special needs of one or two pupils, may become more sensitive to the individuality of all children.

Learning Centers and Open Space Education

A flexible means of grouping learners involve the utilization of learning centers. Learning centers may be set up in a single classroom using the services of a single teacher. Learning centers may also be in evidence among diverse sets of pupils taught by a team of teachers in an open space area. Philosophical ideas to support the use of learning centers, among others, include the following:

1. Learners make decisions in terms of what to learn sequentially rather than emphasizing a teacher-determined curriculum.
2. Trust between and among teachers and pupils is necessary if the latter are to truly make choices and decisions.
3. A humane learning environment exists when pupils are involved in deciding the ends and means of learning.

4. Pupils need to accept consequences of choices made.
5. Each learner needs opportunities to fulfill personal interests rather than waiting for a future optimal adult time to enter the choice making arena.

There are numerous learning centers which the teacher might develop on his or her own. Within the flexible framework of these centers, pupils may select what to learn sequentially. Or, teacher-pupil planning might be heavily implemented to decide upon the objectives and learning activities of each center. No doubt, teacher/pupil planning is significant in choosing tasks for each center. Time factors may make it difficult to advocate involved teacher-pupil planning for each learning center. Even if the teacher determines ends and means for each learning center, the pupil must still have an open-ended curriculum to accept or reject sequential tasks to complete. To pupil ideally must always be a busy learner. There are enough tasks for each learner to continually work on, and yet perceived purposeless tasks can be omitted.

The following are examples of tasks for pupils to select and complete at one learning center:

1. Read a library book of your choosing. Draw a picture pertaining to what was read.
2. Make a relief map showing the setting of the completed library book.
3. View a filmstrip and write five main ideas of what was viewed.
4. Select a picture from the file and write a related poem.
5. Construct a model colonial village.

Any unit of study can be subdivided into various titles for learning centers. Among others, the following, for example, could provide titles for learning centers:

1. A reading center
2. Dramatization center
3. Poetry writing center

4. Speaking center
5. Art center
6. Music center
7. Creative story writing center
8. Construction center
9. Processing center
10. Interviewing center

Each learning center should possess a creative title. Instead of having the following above named titles, a reading center, dramatization center, and poetry, writing center, the teacher may creatively have as labels—"Let's Enjoy Reading," "We Dramatize Our Experiences," and "Let's Write Poetry".

Each center needs to have concrete, semi-concrete, and abstract learning activities to help each learner achieve at an optimal level. Activities encountered should stimulate pupils to develop interest, purpose, and meaning in ongoing units of study.

In Conclusion

There are diverse recommended procedures in grouping pupils for instruction. Each plan needs to be appraised in terms of assisting pupils individually to achieve optimally in intellectual, social, physical, and emotional development. Thus, each of the following plans, among others, in grouping learners for teaching-learning situations needs evaluating:

1. The self-contained classroom.
2. Departmentalization.
3. Team teaching.
4. Interage grouping.
5. The nongraded school.
6. The dual progress plan.
7. Heterogeneous versus homogeneous grouping.
8. Learning centers and open space education.

REFERENCES

1. Cunningham, LaVern. "Team Teaching and Large Group Instruction," Magnetic recording. St. Paul, Minnesota: Minnesota Mining and Manufacturing Company, no date.
2. Doll, Ronald C. *Curriculum Improvement*. Boston: Allyn and Bacon, Inc., 1986.
3. Ediger, Marlow. *The Elementary Curriculum, A Handbook*. Kirksville, Missouri: Stenographic Office, Northeast Missouri State University, 1988.
4. Flanders, Ned A. *Analyzing Teaching Behaviour*. Reading, Massachusetts: Addison-Wesley Publishing Company, 1970.
5. Hunkins, Francis P., Jan Jeter, and Phyllis Maxey. *Social Studies in Elementary Schools*. Columbus, Ohio: Charles E. Merrill Publishing Company, 1982.
6. Knezevich, Stephen J. *Administration of Public Education*. New York: Harper and Row, 1975.
7. Popham, James. *How to Prepare Teaching Performance Tests*. Filmstrip and cassette; Vimcet Associates, 1972.
8. Ragan, William B., and Gene Shepherd. *Modern Elementary Curriculum*. Fifth Edition. New York: Holt, Rinehart and Winston, 1977.
9. Roe, William H., and Thelbert L. Drake. *The Principalship,* Second Edition, New York: Macmillian Publishing Company, 1980.
10. Salzer, Richard T., and Richard E. Drdek, *"Organising for Learning". Chapter three in Curriculum for the Modern Elementary School,* Walter T. Petty (Editor), Chicago: Rand McNally College Publishing Company, 1976.
11. Wiles, Kimball, and John T. Lovell. *Supervision for Better Schools*. Fourth Edition. Englewood Cliffs: Prentice-Hall, Inc., 1975

Bibliography

Bhaskara Rao, Digumarti (199). *Animal Kingdom*. New Delhi: Discovery Publishing House. pp: 135. Rs. 200. ISBN 81-7141-274-2.

Bhaskara Rao, Digumarti (1995). *Batracology*. New Delhi: Discovery Publishing House. pp: 174. Rs. 250 ISBN 81-7141-279-3.

Bhaskara Rao, Digumarti (1994). *Scientific Aptitude*. New Delhi: Ashish Publishing House. pp: 100. Rs. 100. ISBN 81-7024-658-X.

Bhaskara Rao, Digumarti (1996). *Scientific Attitude vis-a-vis Scientific Aptitude*. New Delhi: Discovery Publishing House. pp: 143 Rs. 275. ISBN 81-7141-308-0.

Bhaskara Rao, Digumarti, ed. (1996). *Encyclopaedia of Education For All*, 5 Vols. New Delhi: APH Publishing Corporation. pp: 1460. Rs. 3000. ISBN 81-7024-759-4. (set).

Vol. I Education For All: The World Conference pp: 440. ISBN 81-7024-760-8.

Vol. II Education For All: The EPA—9 Summit. pp: 340. ISBN 81-7024-761-6.

Vol. III Education For All: Quality Education For All. pp: 250. ISBN 81-7024-762-4.

Vol. IV Education For All: Planning and Monitoring. pp: 170. ISBN 81-7024-763-2.

Vol. V Education For All: The Indian Scenario. pp: 260. ISBN 81-7024-764-0.

Bhaskara Rao, Digumarti, ed. (1996). *Global Perceptions on Peace Education*, 3 Vols. New Delhi: Discovery Publishing House. pp: 980 Rs. 1800. ISBN 81-7141-319-6.

Bhaskara Rao, Digumarti, ed. (1996). *National Policy on Education*, 2 Vols. New Delhi: Anmol Publications Pvt. Ltd. pp: 710. Rs. 1000. ISBN 81-7488-323-1.

Bhaskara Rao, Digumarti, ed. (1997). *Care the Child*, 2 Vols. New Delhi: Discovery Publishing House. pp: 616. Rs. 1000. ISBN 81-7141-394-3.

Bhaskara Rao, Digumarti, ed. (1997). *Education for the 21st Century*. New Delhi: Discovery Publishing House. pp: 288. Rs. 500. ISBN 81-7141-389-7.

Bhaskara Rao, Digumarti, ed. (1997). *Reflections on Scientific Attitude*. New Delhi: Discovery Publishing House. pp: 310. Rs. 500. ISBN 81-7141-328-5.

Bhaskara Rao, Digumarti (1997). *Scientific Attitude*. New Delhi: Discovery Publishing House. pp: 120. Rs. 225. ISBN 81-7141-381-1.

Bhaskara Rao, Digumarti, ed. (1997). *Success Story of a Primary Education Project*. New Delhi: APH Publishing Corporation. pp: 260. Rs. 400. ISBN 81-7024-850-7.

Bhaskara Rao, Digumarti, ed. (1997) *World Food Summit*. New Delhi: Discovery Publishing House. pp: 153. Rs. 300. ISBN 81-7141-386-2.

Bhaskara Rao, Digumarti, ed. (1998). *Adolescence Education*. New Delhi: Discovery Publishing House. pp: 238. Rs. 350. ISBN 81-7141-432-X.

Bhaskara Rao, Digumarti, ed. (1998). *Community and School Nutrition Education*. New Delhi: Discovery Publishing House. pp: 425. Rs. 650. ISBN 81-7141-435-4.

Bhaskara Rao, Digumarti, ed. (1998). *District Primary Education Programme*. New Delhi: Discovery Publishing House. pp: 506. Rs. 650. ISBN 81-7141-396-X.

Bhaskara Rao, Digumarti, ed. (1998). *Earth Summit*, 2 Vols. New Delhi: Discovery Publishing House. pp: 930. Rs. 1500. ISBN 81-7141-435-4.

Bhaskara Rao, Digumarti, ed. (1998). *National Policy on Education: Towards an Enlightened and Humane Society*. New Delhi: Discovery Publishing House. pp: 542. Rs. 860. ISBN 81-7141-426-5.

Bhaskara Rao, Digumarti, ed. (1998). *Reforming School Education*. New Delhi: Discovery Publishing House. pp: 575. Rs. 750. ISBN 81-7141-403-6.

Bhaskara Rao, Digumarti, ed. (1998). *Teacher Education in India*. New Delhi: Discovery Publishing House. pp: 424. Rs. 600. ISBN 81-7141-406-0.

Bhaskara Rao, Digumarti, ed. (1998). *World Summit for Social Development*. New Delhi: Discovery Publishing House. pp: 278. Rs. 450. ISBN 81-7141-420-6.

Bhaskara Rao, Digumarti, ed. (2000). *Education For All: Achieving the Goal*. 3 Vols. New Delhi: APH Publishing Corporation. pp: 830. Rs. 2000. ISBN 81-7648-152-1. (Set)

Vol. I The Global Consensus. pp: 285. ISBN 81-7648-153-X.

Vol. II Mid-Decade Review Reports of Regional Seminars. pp: 198. ISBN 81-7648-154-8.

Vol. III Issues and Trends. pp: 346. ISBN 81-7648-155-6.

Bhaskara Rao, Digumarti, ed. (2000). *International Encyclopaedia of AIDS*, 11 Vols. in 13 parts. New Delhi: Discovery Publishing House. pp: 3676. Rs. 7500. ISBN 81-7141-465-6 (set).

Vol. 1 Introduction to HIV/AIDS. pp: 246. Rs. 500. ISBN 81-7141-523-7.

Vol. 2 HIV/AIDS—Issues and Challenges, 2 parts. pp: 805. Rs. 1700. ISBN 81-7141-524-5.

Vol. 3 HIV/AIDS—Socio Economic Realities. pp: 436. Rs. 900. ISBN 81-7141-525-3.

Vol. 4 HIV/AIDS Law Ethics and Human Rights, 2 parts. pp: 859. Rs. 1800. ISBN 81-7141-526-1.

Vol. 5 AIDS and NGOs. pp: 215. Rs. 450 ISBN 81-7141-527-X.

Vol. 6 Aids and Home Care pp: 183. Rs. 400 ISBN 81-7141-528-8.

Vol. 7 STD Case Management pp: 223. Rs. 475 ISBN 81-7141-529-6.

Vol. 8 HIV Prevention and Care—Teaching Modules for Nurses and Midwives. pp: 125. Rs. 275. ISBN 81-7141-530-X.

Vol. 9 HIV/AIDS Prevention Education for Educational Institutions. pp: 75. Rs. 150. ISBN 81-7141-531-8.

Vol. 10 Instructional Modules for AIDS Education. pp: 111. Rs. 250. ISBN 81-7141-532-6.

Vol. 11 School Health Education to Prevent AIDS and STD—A package for curriculum planners. pp: 298. Rs. 600. ISBN 81-7141-533-4.

Bhaskara Rao, Digumarti, ed. (2000). *International Encyclopaedia of Science and Technology Education*. 11 Volumes. New Delhi: Discovery Publishing House. pp: 4892. Rs. 8500. ISBN 81-7141-548-2 (set).

Vol. 1 Science and Technology Education. pp: 557. Rs. 975 ISBN 81-7141-568-7.

Vol. 2 Science Education in Developing Countries. pp: 334. Rs. 600 ISBN 81-7141-570-9.

Vol. 3 Organisational Structure of Science. pp: 334. Rs. 600. ISBN 81-7141-570-9.

Vol. 4 Science Education in Asia and the Pacific. pp: 429. Rs. 750 ISBN 81-7141-571-7.

Vol. 5 Science and Technology Education For All. pp: 464. Rs. 800 ISBN 81-7141-572-5.

Vol. 6 Values, Ethics, Talent and Girls in Science and Technology Education. pp: 463. Rs. 800 ISBN 81-7141-573-3.

Vol. 7 Popularization of Science and Technology Education. pp. 334. Rs. 600. ISBN 81-7141-574-1.

Vol. 8 Scientific, Power and Society. pp: 357. Rs. 625 ISBN 81-7141-575-X.

Vol. 9 Information Technology. pp: 442. Rs. 775. ISBN 81-7141-576-8.

Vol. 10 Teacher Training in Science and Technology Education. pp: 536. Rs. 975. ISBN 81-7141-577-6.

Vol. 11 Science, Technology and Society: A Curriculum Framework. pp: 642. Rs. 1000. ISBN 81-7141-578-4.

Bhaskara Rao, Digumarti, ed. (2002). *International Studies in Education*, New Delhi: Discovery Publishing House.

Bhaskara Rao, Digumarti, ed. (2002). *Chernobyl: Never Again*, New Delhi: Discovery Publishing House.

Bhaskara Rao, Digumarti, ed. (2001). *Distance Education in Different Countries*. New Delhi: APH Publishing Corporation. pp: 574. Rs. 1500. ISBN 81-7648-229-3.

Bhaskara Rao, Digumarti, ed. (2001). *Decentralised Management of Education (Management of Education in Panchayati Raj and Municipal Bodies)*. New Delhi: Discovery Publishing House. pp: 116. Rs. 250. ISBN 81-7141-617-9.

Bhaskara Rao, Digumarti, ed. (2001). *Electrochemistry for Environmental Protection*. New Delhi: Discovery Publishing House. pp: 208. Rs. 400. ISBN 81-7141-619-5.

Bhaskara Rao, Digumarti, ed. (2001). *Global Educational Studies*. New Delhi: Discovery Publishing House. pp: 145. Rs. 300. ISBN 81-7141-616-0.

Bhaskara Rao, Digumarti, ed. (2001) *Global Synthesis of Educational Assessment*. New Delhi: Discovery Publishing House. pp: 152. Rs. 300. ISBN 81-7141-613-6.

Bhaskara Rao, Digumarti, ed. (2001). *International Encyclopaedia of Human Rights*, 7 volumes in 13 parts. New Delhi. Discovery Publishing House, pp: 6500 (Royal size). Rs. 22000. ISBN 81-7141-567-9 (set).

Vol. 1 International Instruments of Human Rights, 2 parts Rs. 3500. ISBN 81-7141-595-4.

Vol. 2 Regional Instruments of Human Rights. Rs. 1500 ISBN 81-7141-604-7.

Vol. 3 Human Rights and the United Nations, 2 parts. Rs. 2800. ISBN 81-7141-605-5.

Vol. 4 Fact Files of Human Rights, 2 parts. Rs. 3000. ISBN 81-7141-606-3.

Vol. 5 Study Stories of Human Rights, 3 parts. Rs. 5200. ISBN 81-7141-607-1.

Vol. 6 International Meetings on Human Rights, 2 parts. Rs. 3800. ISBN 81-7141-608-X.

Vol. 7 Professional Training in Human Rights. Rs. 2200. ISBN 81-7141-609-8.

Bhaskara Rao, Digumarti, ed. (2001). *Jomtein Decade of Education*. New Delhi: Discovery Publishing House. pp: 106. Rs. 225. ISBN 81-7141-618-7.

Bhaskara Rao, Digumarti, ed. (2001). *Nuclear Materials: Issues and Concerns*, 2 Vols. New Delhi: Discovery Publishing House. pp: 1100. Rs. 2200. ISBN 81-7141-611-X.

Bhaskara Rao, Digumarti, ed. (2001). *World Conference on Education for All*. New Delhi: APH Publishing Corporation. pp: 380. Rs. 995. ISBN 81-7648-274-9.

Bhaskara Rao, Digumarti, ed. (2002). *Inspiring Experiences in Teacher Education*. New Delhi: Discovery Publishing House.

Bhaskara Rao, Digumarti, ed. (2001). *World Conference on Higher Education*. New Delhi: Discovery Publishing House. pp: 306. Rs. 600. ISBN 81-7141-610-1.

Bhaskara Rao, Digumarti, ed. (2001). *World Conference on Science*. New Delhi: Discovery Publishing House. pp: 85. Rs. 200. ISBN 81-7141-612-8.

Bhaskara Rao, Digumarti, ed. (2002). *Military Conversion: Impact on Science and Technology*, New Delhi: Discovery Publishing House. Rs. 400. ISBN 81-7141-643-0.

Bhaskara Rao, Digumarti, ed. (2002). *United Nations Millennium Summit*, New Delhi: Discovery Publishing House. Rs. 225. ISBN 81-7141-632-2.

Bhaskara Rao, Digumarti, ed. (2002). *Habitat Agenda*, New Delhi: Discovery Publishing House.

Bhaskara Rao, Digumarti, ed. (2002). *Virology and Immunology*, New Delhi: Discovery Publishing House.

Bhaskara Rao, Digumarti, ed. (2002). *World Assembly on Aging*, New Delhi: Discovery Publishing House.

Bhaskara Rao, Digumarti, ed. (2002). *World Conference on Human Rights*, New Delhi: Discovery Publishing House.

Bhaskara Rao, Digumarti, ed. (2002). *World Education Forum*, New Delhi: Discovery Publishing House.

Bhaskara Rao, Digumarti, C.A.P. Swamy and B.S.V. Dutt (1997). *Self Evaluation in Student Teaching*. New Delhi: Discovery Publishing House. pp: 762. Rs. 150. ISBN 81-7141-374-9.

Bhaskara Rao, Digumarti, C. Sridevi and K. Vijaya (1995). *Achievement in Social Studies*. New Delhi: Discovery Publishing House. pp: 102. Rs. 150. ISBN 81-7141-281-5.

Bhaskara Rao, Digumarti and Digumarti Pushpa Latha (1994). *Achievement in Biology*. New Delhi: Discovery Publishing House. pp: 102. Rs. 125. ISBN 81-7141-264-5.

Bhaskara Rao, Digumarti and Digumarti Pushpa Latha (1995). *Achievement in English*. New Delhi: Discovery Publishing House. pp: 214. Rs. 275. ISBN 81-7141-283-1.

Bhaskara Rao, Digumarti and Digumarti Pushpa Latha (1995). *Achievement in Science*. New Delhi: Discovery Publishing House. pp: 159. Rs. 225. ISBN 81-7141-280-7.

Bhaskara Rao, Digumarti and Digumarti Pushpa Latha (1995). *Achievement in Mathematics*. New Delhi: Discovery Publishing House. pp: 125. Rs. 175. ISBN 81-7141-278-5.

Bhaskara Rao, Digumarti and Digumarti Pushpa Latha, eds. (1998). *International Encyclopaedia of Women*, 5 Vols. New Delhi: Discovery Publishing House. pp: 2172. Rs. 4000. ISBN 81-7141-410-9 (set).

Vol. 1 Status of World's Women pp: 427. Rs. 750. ISBN 81-7141-494-X.

Vol. 2 Women, Education and Empowerment. pp: 467. Rs. 875. ISBN 81-7141-498-2.

Vol. 3 Women Challenges and Advancement. pp: 354. Rs. 650. ISBN 81-7141-497-4.

Vol. 4 Women and Family Health. pp: 470. Rs. 875. ISBN 81-7141-497-4.

Vol. 5 Women and International Action. pp: 453. Rs. 850. ISBN 81-7141-498-2.

Bhaskara Rao, Digumarti, Digumarti Pushpa Latha and Digumarti Harshitha, eds. (2001). *Biological Warfare*. New Delhi: Discovery Publishing House. pp: 422. Rs. 800. ISBN 81-7141-597-0.

Bhaskara Rao, Digumarti, Digumarti Pushpa Latha and Digumarti Harshitha, eds. (2001). *Women as Educators*. New Delhi: Discovery Publishing House. pp: 112. Rs. 200. ISBN 81-7141-602-0.

Bhaskara Rao, Digumarti and Digumarti Harshitha (2000). *Education in India*. New Delhi: APH Publishing Corporation. pp: 280. Rs. 700. ISBN 81-7648-207-2.

Bhaskara Rao, Digumarti, and Digumarti Harshitha eds. (2001). *Assessing Learning Achievement*. New Delhi: Discovery Publishing House. pp: 128. Rs. 225. ISBN 81-7141-601-2.

Bhaskara Rao, Digumarti and Digumarti Harshita, eds. (2001). *Energy Security*. New Delhi: Discovery Publishing House. pp: 564. Rs. 1000. ISBN 81-7141-598-9.

Bhaskara Rao, Digumarti, D. Harshitha and K.R.S.S. Rao. eds. (1999). *Advanced Biotechnology*. New Delhi: Discovery Publishing House. pp: 335. Rs. 550. ISBN 81-7141-516-4.

Bhaskara Rao, Digumarti and K.R.S. Sambasiva Rao, eds. (1996). *Current Trends in Indian Education*. New Delhi: Discovery Publishing House. pp: 234. Rs. 400. ISBN 81-7141-311-0.

Bhaskara Rao, Digumarti and K. Vijaya (1995). *A Text Book Evaluation*. Ambala Cantt: The Associated Publishers. pp: 100. Rs. 160.

Bhaskara Rao, Digumarti, V.V. Rao, V.V. Lakshmi and V.V. Krishna, eds. (2000). *Status and Advancement of Women*. New Delhi: APH Publishing Corporation. pp: 570. Rs. 1100. ISBN 81-7648-169-6.

Bhaskara Rao, Digumarti and Mohan Rao (2002), *Problems of Mentally Handicapped Children*, New Delhi: Discovery Publishing House.

Bhaskara Rao, Digumarti and Sridhar (2002), *Job Satisfaction of School Teachers* New Delhi: Discovery Publishing House.

Babu, P.C. and Digumarti Bhaskara Rao, ed. (2002). *Flowers of Wisdom*, New Delhi: Discovery Publishing House.

Bhagya Lakshmi, Lingineni and Digumarti Bhaskara Rao, ed. (2000). *Reading and Comprehension*. New Delhi: Discovery Publishing House. pp: 108. Rs. 175. ISBN 81-7141-543-1.

Bhuvaneswara Lakshmi, G. and Digumarti Bhaskara Rao, ed. (2000). *Attitude Towards Science*. New Delhi: Discovery Publishing House. pp: 128. Rs. 250. ISBN 81-7141-541-6.

Devraj, T.A.S. and Digumarti Bhaskara Rao, ed. (1997). *Trace Analysis of Uranium and Thorum*. New Delhi: Discovery Publishing House. pp: 195. Rs. 350. ISBN 81-7141-375-7.

Durgani Rani, K and Digumarti Bhaskara Rao, ed. (2000). *Educational Aspirations and Scientific Attitudes*. New Delhi: Discovery Publishing House. pp: 130. Rs. 250. ISBN 81-7141-555-55.

Dutt, B.S.V. and Digumarti Bhaskara Rao (2001). *Empowering Primary Teachers*. New Delhi: Discovery Publishing House. pp. 283. Rs. 475. ISBN 81-7141-615-2.

Ediger, Marlow and Digumarti Bhaskara Rao (1996). *Science Curriculum*. New Delhi: Discovery Publishing House. pp: 309. Rs. 450. ISBN 81-7141-321-8.

Ediger, Marlow and Digumarti Bhaskara Rao (2000). *Teaching Mathematics Successfully*. New Delhi: Discovery Publishing House. pp: 279. Rs. Rs. 525. ISBN 81-7141-552-0.

Ediger, Marlow and Digumarti Bhaskara Rao (2000). *Teaching Reading Successfully*. New Delhi: Discovery Publishing House. pp: 386. Rs. 750. ISBN 81-7141-556-3.

Ediger Marlow and Digumarti Bhaskara Rao (2001). *Teaching Science Successfully*. New Delhi: Discovery Publishing House. pp: 320. Rs. 600. ISBN 81-7141-600-4.

Ediger, Marlow and Digumarti Bhaskara Rao (2001). *Teaching Social Studies Successfully*. New Delhi: Discovery Publishing House. pp: 296. Rs. 575. ISBN 81-7141-596-2.

Ediger, Marlow and Digumarti Bhaskara Rao (2002). *Improving School Administration*, New Delhi: Discovery Publishing House. Rs. 500. ISBN 81-7141-633-0.

Ediger, Marlow and Digumarti Bhaskara Rao (2002). *Philosophy and Curriculum*, New Delhi: Discovery Publishing House. Rs. 450. ISBN 81-7141-631-4.

Ediger, Marlow and Digumarti Bhaskara Rao (2002). *Elementary Curriculum*, New Delhi: Discovery Publishing House

Jayasree, Kandi and Digumarti Bhaskara Rao, ed. (1999). *Correlates of Socialisation*. New Delhi: Discovery Publishing House. pp: 160. Rs. 375. ISBN 81-7141-517-2.

John Babu, Ch., T.J.R. Prasad, G.M. Madhukar and Digumarti Bhaskara Rao, eds. (2001). *Problem Solving in Mathematics*. New Delhi: APH Publishing Corporation. pp: 125. Rs. 250. ISBN 81-7648-273-0.

Koustiouk, V.V. and Digumarti Bhaskara Rao, ed. (2002). *Refrigiration and Environment*, New Delhi: Discovery Publishing House.

Kostiouk, Valery V. and Digumarti Bhaskara Rao, ed. (2002). *A Text Book of Cryogenics*, New Delhi: Discovery Publishing House. Rs. 575. ISBN 81-7141-642-X.

Marja, Talvi and Digumarti Bhaskara Rao, eds. (1996). *Educational Leadership and Social Changes*. New Delhi: Discovery Publishing House. pp: 236. Rs. 400. ISBN 81-7141-320-X.

Prabhakaram, K.S. and Digumarti Bhaskara Rao, ed. (1998). *Concept Attainment Model in Mathematics Teaching*. New Delhi: Discovery Publishing House. pp: 122. Rs. 200. ISBN 81-7141-424-9.

Prasanth Kumar, J. and Digumarti Bhaskara Rao, ed. (1998). *Effectiveness of Distance Education System*. New Delhi: Discovery Publishing. House. pp: 152. Rs. 275. ISBN 81-7141-437-0.

Prasanth Kumar, J., and Digumarti Bhaskara Rao and G. Sundara Rao, eds. (2000). *Open University Student Support Services*. New Delhi: Discovery Publishing House. pp: 100. Rs. 200. ISBN 81-7141-550-4.

Rama Krishnaiah, D and Digumarti Bhaskara Rao, ed. (1998). *Job Satisfaction of College Teachers*. New Delhi: Discovery Publishing House. pp: 251. Rs. 400. ISBN 81-7141-438-9.

Ramesh, Ganta and Digumarti Bhaskara Rao, eds. (1998). *Environmental Education: Problems and Prospects*. New Delhi: Discovery Publishing House. pp: 324. Rs. 525. ISBN 81-7141-423-0.

Rathaiah, L. and Digumarti Bhaskara Rao, eds. (1997). *International Innovations in Education*. New Delhi: Discovery Publishing House. pp: 514. Rs. 750. ISBN 81-7141-359-5.

Rathaiah, Lavu, Digumarti Bhaskara Rao and Paturi Koteswara Rao. (1997). *Achievement Correlates*. New Delhi: Discovery Publishing House. pp: 116. Rs. 225. ISBN 81-7141-385-4.

Ratnam, M.V.R.K. and Digumarti Bhaskara Rao, ed. (2002). *Dukkha: Suffering in Early Buddhism*, New Delhi: Discovery Publishing House.

Reddy and Digumarti Bhaskara Rao, ed. (2002). *Creativity in Adolescents*, New Delhi: Discovery Publishing House.

Sanjeeva Rao, P.C. and Digumarti Bhaskara Rao, ed. (1996). *A Text Book of Geology*. New Delhi: Discovery Publishing House. pp: 320. Rs. 525 ISBN 81-7141-313-7.

Satya Narayana, V. and Digumarti Bhaskara Rao, ed. (2001). *Physical Education, Social Attitudes and Leadership Qualities*. New Delhi: Discovery Publishing House. pp: 296. Rs. 575. ISBN 81-7141-593-8.

Srinivasulu Reddy, M., K.R.S. Sambasiva Rao and Digumarti Bhaskara Rao, ed. (1999). *A Text Book of Agriculture*. New Delhi: Discovery Publishing House. pp: 296. Rs. 525. ISBN 81-7141-482-6.

Tudasamma, R. and Digumarti Bhaskara Rao, ed. (2002). *Job Satisfaction of Teacher Educators*, New Delhi: Discovery Publishing House.

Vanaja, M. and Digumarti Bhaskara Rao, ed. (1999). *Inquiry Training Model*. New Delhi: Discovery Publishing House. pp: 189. Rs. 325. ISBN 81-7141-515-6.

Veena Kumari, Balusu and Digumarti Bhaskara Rao (1996). *Operation Black Board*. New Delhi: APH Publishing Corporation. pp: 140. Rs. 200. ISBN 81-7024-711-X.

Veena Kumari, B. and Digumarti Bhaskara Rao, ed. (2000). *Psycho Social Correlates of Achievement*. New Delhi: Discovery Publishing House. pp: 136. Rs. 300. ISBN 81-7141-547-4.

Venkata Rao, P. and Digumarti Bhaskara Rao (1989). *A Text Book of Zoology—Junior Intermediate*. Guntur: Vignan Publishers. pp: 370. Rs. 57.

Venkata Rao, P. and Digumarti Bhaskara Rao (1989). *A Text Book of Zoology—Senior Intermediate*. Guntur: Vignan Publishers. pp: 480. Rs. 68.

Venugopala Rao, K. and Digumarti Bhaskara Rao, ed. (2000). *Teacher Morale in Secondary Schools*. New Delhi: Discovery Publishing House. pp: 300. Rs. 575. ISBN 81-7141-551-2.

Vidya, C. and Digumarti Bhaskara Rao, ed. (1996). *A Text Book of Nutrition*. New Delhi: Discovery Publishing House. pp: 438. Rs. 650. ISBN 81-7141-309-9.

Vijaya Bharathi, D. and Digumarti Bhaskara Rao, ed. (2000). *Educational Philosophies of Swami Vivekanand and John Dewey*. New Delhi: APH Publishing Corporation. pp: 200. Rs. 500. ISBN 81-7648-202-1.

Bhaskara Rao, Digumarti. (1986). *Dhrushya Sravana Bodhanapakaranalu* (Audio Visual Teaching Aids). Guntur: Nagarjuna Publishers.

Bhaskara Rao, Digumarti (1993). *Jeevasashtra Bodhana* (Teaching of Biology, Guntur: Nagarjuna Publishers.

Bhaskara Rao, Digumarti (1995). *Vignanasasthra Bodhana*. (Teaching of Science). Guntur: Nagarjuna Publishers.

Bhaskara Rao, Digumarti (1997). *Vidya Manovignana Sashtram*. (Educational Psychology). Guntur: Creative Press. pp. 434. Rs. 79.

Bhaskara Rao, Digumarti (1998). *DSC Study Material*. Guntur: Nagarjuna Publishers.

Bhaskara Rao, Digumarti (1998). *Upadhyayudu Vidya* (Teacher and Education). Guntur: Nagarjuna Publishers.

Bhaskara Rao, Digumarti (1998). *Vidya Dhrukpadhalu*. (Perspectives of Education). Guntur: Nagarjuna Publishers.

Bhaskara Rao, Digumarti (1999). *EdCET Teaching Aptitude*. Guntur: Nagarjuna Publishers.

Bhaskara Rao, Digumarti (2001). *Bharata Samajamulo Upadhayayudu Vidya*. (Teacher and Education in Emerging Indian Society). Guntur: Nagarjuna Publishers. pp: 256. Rs. 59.

Bhaskara Rao, Digumarti (2001). *Bhoutika Sastra Bodhana Padhatulu* (Methods of Teaching Physical Science). Guntur: Nagarjuna Publishers. pp: 324. Rs. 77.

Bhaskara Rao, Digumarti (2001). *Jeeva Sastra Bodhana Padhatulu* (Methods of Teaching Biological Science). Guntur: Nagarjuna Publishers. pp: 224. Rs. 59.

Bhaskara Rao, Digumarti (2001). *Vidya Manovignana Sastram* (Educational Psychology). Guntur: Nagarjuna Publishers. pp: 344. Rs. 77.